1965

This book may be kept

FOURTEEN DAYS

A fine of TWO CENTS will be charged for each day
the Book is kept over time.

DE 7 '66			
MAR 21 '74			

Library Bureau Cat. No. 1137.24

Yale Studies in English

Benjamin Christie Nangle, Editor

Volume 149

Prologues and Epilogues

of the Eighteenth Century

by MARY E. KNAPP

New Haven: Yale University Press, 1961

Published with aid from the foundation
established in memory of Philip Hamilton
McMillan of the class of 1894, Yale College.

PREFACE

In the eighteenth century the turning of a prologue or epilogue attracted writers differing as widely as Addison and Sheridan or Fielding and Horace Walpole. Written as acting pieces to be spoken in the theatre, the prologues and epilogues were also a popular form of literature, appearing constantly in the magazines and, after the middle of the century, in the newspapers. The pieces remain an accurate and entertaining commentary on the society that produced them. With all our records of eighteenth-century life, detailed and copious as they are, we would not wish to lose the elder Colman's description of Bagnigge Wells on summer afternoons in his prologue to *Bon Ton* or Sheridan's ridicule of the bluestocking in his epilogue to Hannah More's *The Fatal Falsehood:*

> Unfinish'd here an epigram is laid,
> And there, a mantua-maker's bill unpaid.

Moreover, the prologues and epilogues are concerned with various aspects of drama and the theatre, of taste and literary trends.

It should be emphasized at once that prologues and epilogues held an important place in the Restoration theatre and that the form had long been established before 1700. The audience, divided into pit, box, and gallery, was supposed to become attentive when the speaker of the prologue appeared, and at the end of the play they

v

welcomed the epilogue with its indecent innuendoes and lashing gibes. Although there is perhaps no eighteenth-century prologue or epilogue containing the brutality of Dryden's castigating prologue to Southerne's *The Disappointment; or, The Mother in Fashion* (1684), with its picture of an audience given over to baseness and violence, yet indecent epilogues long continued to be spoken in spite of the reformers. Against increasing opposition they appeared as late as the 1750's, but, as I shall show in the last chapter of this book, their number decreased gradually with the change that took place in the audience during the first half of the century and with the growing demand for morality in the theatre.

In many respects the eighteenth-century prologues and epilogues were continuations of those of the Restoration. Some of the special devices of presentation remained: there were armed prologues, as there had been since the time of Ben Jonson, and prologues spoken by ghosts; there were sung prologues and epilogues; there were prologues and epilogues spoken in dialogue or by a number of actors; there was the pretence that the epilogue had been lost. All these devices—along with the unceasing lament of both dramatists and actors over the popularity of foreign entertainers, denunciation of the audience for its lack of taste, and recurring metaphors, such as those comparing the critics to butchers—were retained in the eighteenth century.

Nevertheless, the prologues and epilogues of even the first decades of the eighteenth century have distinguishing characteristics that set them apart from those of the Restoration and are governed by the changing conditions of society and the drama. Presented to an audience no longer dominated by the court or the upper classes, they had to appeal to varied tastes. The fundamental difference can be seen at once by comparing the prologue and epilogue of *Venice Preserved* (1682) with Steele's prologues and epilogues or with Pope's prologue to Addison's *Cato* (1713). Even while it clung to Restoration patterns, the eighteenth century developed the moral, didactic prologue. As Joseph Wood Krutch observes in his *Comedy and Conscience after the Restoration* (Columbia University Press, 1924, p. 156): "The age of Anne was an age of reason, not only in its opposition to mysticism, but also in its reaction against the physically and politically destructive moral anarchy of the Restoration." Even if we grant that some of the moral protests may have been sops to the reformers, yet earnestness and dignity are characteristic of many of the eighteenth-century prologues. It follows that there was a sharp division made between the subject matter and tone of the prologue and the epilogue, whereas the pieces were usually undifferentiated in the Restoration. Not all eighteenth-century prologues are serious, but it early became the practice that tragedy should be introduced by a stately prologue and that the epilogue should remain frivolous. As the century advanced, the epilogues themselves showed greater variety and achieved a new quality—lightness of touch and a kind of playfulness, an excellent example of this being Garrick's epilogue to the comedy, *'Tis Well It's No Worse*. Critical and lashing as they are, and often concerned with political plots and upheavals, the prologues and epilogues of the Restoration rarely have the gaiety and sprightly ingenuity characteristic of later epilogues. Until the very end of the century, eighteenth-century prologuisers were giving happy twists to metaphors apparently worn out in the 1680's.

In assigning dates to the pieces, I have depended upon Professor Allardyce Nicoll's *A History of Early Eighteenth Century Drama* (Second Edition) and *A History of Late Eighteenth Century Drama* (Cambridge University Press,

1929; 1927), and upon the *Drury Lane Calendar* (Oxford, The Clarendon Press, 1938) and the *Catalogue of the Larpent Plays* (San Marino, Huntington Library, 1939), the latter two edited by Professor Dougald MacMillan. The dates given in parentheses after the titles of the plays refer to first performances. In a few instances I have drawn from Genest for the date of a play, and, as the footnotes show, more heavily for other information.

The passages quoted are given, in general, as they were printed with the first editions of the plays. When the play itself was not printed, I have resorted to contemporary newspapers and magazines, from which I have also taken both the date and text of occasional prologues and epilogues and of those to revivals. In many instances I have worked with prologues and epilogues that also appear in Professor Nicoll's two volumes. I have quoted from the original sources, but, like all others who are interested in eighteenth-century drama, I have been constantly aided by his knowledge.

Beyond the reward of studying the prologues and epilogues, which remain fascinating to me in their variety and humor, my greatest pleasure in preparing this book has been the friendliness of those who have helped me. I feel the deepest gratitude to Professor C. B. Tinker for his many kindnesses to me throughout the years and for his interest in my work. I am also indebted to Mr. Herman W. Liebert for his generosity in sharing his time and knowledge. Miss Marjorie Gray Wynne, the Supervisor of the Rare Book Room of the Yale University Library, has given me help in numerous ways. In my absence she has answered many questions and has verified references for me. I have also taxed the kindness of my friend, Dr. Jeannette Fellheimer.

Although the work for this book has been done chiefly at Yale, I have profited by the holdings of other libraries.

I wish to thank Dr. Louis B. Wright for permitting me to quote from the unpublished Garrick verse in the Folger Library, and Dr. William Van Lennep for introducing me to the eighteenth-century theatrical prints and the extra-illustrated books in the Harvard Theatre Collection. Quotations from *Boswell's London Journal, 1762–1763,* edited by Frederick A. Pottle (copyright 1950 by Yale University) are reprinted by permission of McGraw-Hill Book Company, Inc.

I appreciate the care with which Professor Benjamin Nangle, the Editor of the Yale Studies in English, read the book in manuscript, making suggestions for its improvement.

Finally, I wish to express my thanks for a grant in aid of publication from the Fund for Young Scholars of Yale University.

M.E.K.

Western College for Women
Oxford, Ohio
September 1960

CONTENTS

CHAPTER 1

POPULAR DEMAND FOR
PROLOGUES AND EPILOGUES

From the time of the reopening of the
theatres in the Restoration until the second decade of the
nineteenth century every full-length comedy and tragedy
was customarily introduced by a prologue and concluded
by an epilogue.[1] Although these pieces were written to be
presented on the stage, they attained wide circulation in
print, and nothing can more convincingly attest their importance than the variety of means whereby they reached
the eighteenth-century reader. The prologue and epilogue,
as they had been spoken in the theatre, were, almost without exception, printed with the play, the names of the
speakers usually being given. The dramatist frequently

1. For the prologues and epilogues of the Restoration, see Autrey Nell
Wiley, *Rare Prologues and Epilogues. 1642–1700* (New York, W. W. Norton
& Co., 1940); William Bradford Gardner, *The Prologues and Epilogues of
John Dryden. A Critical Edition* (New York, Columbia University Press,
1951); Sybil Marion Rosenfeld, *Prologues and Epilogues of the Restoration
Period, 1660–1700: Considered in Relation to the Audience, Theatrical
Conditions and the Dramatic Productivity of the Age* . . . (1925). Miss
Rosenfeld's study is among the unpublished theses of the University of
London. Mr. J. H. P. Pafford, Goldsmiths' Librarian, the University of
London, kindly supplied me with this information.

wrote his own prologue and epilogue,[2] but often the pieces
were supplied by a friend, by "a person of quality," or, as
was constantly the case with Garrick and George Colman,
the elder, by the manager of the playhouse, who was
naturally anxious for the success of the play.

Sometimes a play was graced with two prologues or
epilogues during its first run; for example, Samuel Foote
wrote and spoke two prologues to his comedy, *The
Knights,* the new prologue being spoken on February 12,
1754. On April 2 he reverted to the original prologue.[3]
Occasionally both of the prologues or epilogues were published with the play, the second usually accompanied by
an explanation for its appearance. In some cases the second
epilogue was the author's protest against the piece provided by the manager. When Dennis's tragedy, *The Invader of His Country,* was performed at Drury Lane in
1719, Cibber, who was then manager of the theatre, concluded the play with a flippant comic epilogue. Dennis
was in the audience, as he explains in his Advertisement
to the printed play, sitting at such a distance from Mrs.
Oldfield, the speaker, that he could not hear Cibber's
epilogue, but when he came to read it, he discovered it to
be "a wretched Medley of Impudence and Nonsense." He
accused Cibber of trying to influence the audience against
his play, and he forthwith published both Cibber's epilogue and one of his own.[4] Theobald and Bevil Higgons
each wrote an epilogue for Jeffreys's *Edwin* (1724). Higgons's epilogue, "being forgotten in its proper Place," was
inserted after the last leaf of the play. *Timoleon* (1730)
by Benjamin Martyn was published with two prologues

2. In this study it is assumed that, other evidence of authorship being
lacking, all unascribed prologues and epilogues were written by the
authors of the plays to which they belong.

3. *Drury Lane Calendar,* ed. Dougald MacMillan (Oxford, 1938), p. 269.

4. Cf. the spoken and revised epilogues to Young's *The Brothers* (1753).
See below, pp. 293–294.

and two epilogues, one epilogue "As it was written by the Author" and a variant, "As it was spoken by Mrs. OLD-FIELD," the implication being that the actress said more than was set down for her. Fielding published two epilogues with his comedy, *The Modern Husband* (1732). The demands of patriotism account for Home's supplying his popular tragedy, *Douglas* (1757), with two prologues— one to be spoken in Edinburgh and the other in London.[5]

The most common reason for the publication of two prologues with one play is set forth by Samuel Jackson Pratt in a prefatory note which he wrote to a prologue sent him by Anna Seward for his tragedy, *The Fair Circassian* (1781):

> The following prologue, from an honour-giving muse, of which it is truly worthy, did not arrive till after Mr. Bannister was put in possession of the excellent poetry which precedes it; and which another ingenious friend had been solicited to supply. The author of the tragedy, however, thinks Miss Seward's composition too valuable to circulate only in manuscript. Indeed, to keep such verses out of print, would not only be a private injury to the piece (which they will adorn) but an unpardonable injustice to the public.

Similar motives of gratitude induced Goldsmith to publish with his own epilogue to *She Stoops to Conquer* (1773) an abridgement of an epilogue by Joseph Cradock, "to be spoken by Tony Lumpkin." [6]

5. The prologue spoken in Edinburgh is printed in Volume I of *The Dramatic Works of John Home* (1760).

6. Prologues "design'd to be spoken" but discarded often appeared with the plays for which they were intended or found their way into print through other means. The discarded pieces sometimes have biographical or historical significance. *The Beaux' Stratagem* (1707) was printed with an epilogue "Design'd to be spoke," to inform the audience that Farquhar

During the Restoration, especially during the decade from 1678 to 1688, prologues and epilogues were frequently published separately, public interest in the pieces being due perhaps not so much to their literary or dramatic merit as to the violence of their political allusions. Separate publications of prologues and epilogues decreased after the first two decades of the eighteenth century, and many of those so published bear little reference to the public stage.[7] Occasional prologues, concerned with matters of current interest and detached by their nature from the plays which they accompanied, lent themselves most readily to separate publication. Rowe's epilogue spoken by Mrs. Barry after a performance of *Love for Love*, April 7, 1709, for Betterton's benefit, was distributed at the theatre on the night of the play.[8] Cave published the prologue which Johnson wrote for the opening of Drury Lane on September 15, 1747, with Garrick's epilogue for the same occasion, the demand for the pieces being proved by the immediate appearance of a pirated edition. Johnson's prologue spoken by Garrick on April 5, 1750, at the performance of *Comus* for the benefit of Mrs. Elizabeth Foster, Milton's granddaughter and only surviving descendant, was printed in both London and Edinburgh.[9] Christopher Smart's occasional prologue and epilogue for

---

was dying. Mr. Richard Rose wrote a farewell epilogue for Mrs. Clive, "intended to have been spoken," but the piece was supplanted by Walpole's epilogue. (Yale College Library, Folio Pamphlets, No. 10.) Samuel Ireland brazenly rejected the prologue which the poet laureate, Henry James Pye, submitted for *Vortigern* (1796) as "not being strong enough in asserting the authenticity of the Play." (*European Magazine* for February 1796, p. 76.)

7. Wiley, *Rare Prologues and Epilogues*, pp. 313–321, lists and describes prologues and epilogues in separate publication from 1642 to 1872.

8. William Oldys, *The History of the English Stage* (1741), p. 120.

9. For the publication of the two occasional prologues by Johnson, see *The Poems of Samuel Johnson*, ed. David Nichol Smith and Edward L. McAdam (Oxford, The Clarendon Press, 1941), pp. E-55.

a performance of *Othello* in Drury Lane on March 7, 1751, enjoyed two editions. Broadsides, such as those of Foote's epilogue to *The Minor,* are comparatively unusual in the eighteenth century.

From the earliest years of the century it had been the practice for the theatre notices in newspapers, as well as for the "great" bills posted throughout the city, to announce prologues and epilogues. Occasional prologues were usually described but not printed, and thus, although compared with the number spoken, few of these pieces have survived, we still have knowledge of their contents; for example, the *Daily Courant* for Monday, December 7, 1702, announced that on the following day at Drury Lane there would be performed *"The Bath, or, The Western Lass* . . . And a new Prologue, *All in Honour of the Officers of the Army and Fleet, and to Welcome them home from* Flanders *and* Vigo." As the prologues and epilogues were presented by popular actors, the names of the speakers were usually announced.[1] Virtually all revivals were accompanied by prologues and epilogues, in many cases new pieces being written for the revived plays. The great majority of the early prologues to revivals were also not printed, but the notices in newspapers indicate that their purpose was not to offer information or criticism but to entertain the audience.[2] A successful prologue to a revival sometimes reappeared after a lapse of many years. When *Every Man in His Humour* was presented at Covent Garden in 1800, William Whitehead's prologue, which Garrick had spoken in 1751, was revived with the play.[3]

1. For example, see the *Daily Courant* for the following dates: March 5, 1706; Nov. 1, Dec. 20, 26, 27, 29, 1707; Jan. 11, March 26, April 4, 1709, for epilogues spoken by Pinkethman (variously spelled), Bullock, Henry Norris, Estcourt, and Cibber.

2. See the *Daily Courant* for March 24, 1707, and the issues for the dates given above.

3. The *London Chronicle,* Dec. 16–18, 1800, records the performance of

In the second half of the century, prologues and epilogues were frequently printed in the newspapers with the names of the speakers and occasionally with comments on the reception of the pieces and on the skill of the presentation. Before a play was published, the reader could find the prologue and epilogue in such papers as *Lloyd's Evening Post,* the *London Chronicle,* the *Public Advertiser,* or the *St. James's Chronicle.* These newspapers printed many prologues and epilogues shortly after they were spoken, with an accuracy which makes them an important and reliable source for establishing texts.

Prologues and epilogues were a staple in the poetry sections of magazines throughout the century, beginning with the *Gentleman's Magazine* in 1731, continuing with the *London Magazine,* the *Scots Magazine,* the *Lady's Magazine,* the *Annual Register,* the *Universal Magazine,* and including the *European Magazine* in the last two decades of the century. Ordinarily the magazines, following the newspapers, give the names of the speakers, and provide an important supplement to the printed plays in which the pieces appeared unassigned. Not infrequently, too, a prologue which is apparently by the playwright is accurately ascribed in a newspaper or magazine. Even when the play itself remained in manuscript, the prologue and epilogue were usually published. Interest in drama was not confined to the public stage; plays presented in private theatres and in schools were provided with prologues and epilogues,

---

Every Man in His Humour at Covent Garden on Dec. 17, 1800. The critic observes: "The remark made by Garrick in his Prologue to the revival of the Comedy (in 1751) was literally verified by the representation of yesterday evening:—

'Nature was nature then—and still survives:
'The garb may alter, but the substance lives.'

The Prologue was with great propriety revived, and delivered by Mr. Cook." The prologue, originally spoken by Garrick, is correctly ascribed to William Whitehead in Chalmers's *English Poets* (1810), XVII, 272.

the latter usually being the more lively. The magazines preserve these occasional pieces which are by no means lacking in importance.[4]

Beyond the printed plays, separate publications, newspapers, and magazines, the eighteenth-century reader had still another access to prologues and epilogues in anthologies comprised entirely of such selections. Springing into sudden popularity in the 1760's, these collections increased until the end of the century. They vary in merit, but even those which are trivial and slight serve as indications of public interest and taste. The most inclusive as well as the most entertaining of the collections are *The Essence of Theatrical Wit: Being a Select Collection of the Best and Most Admired Prologues and Epilogues, That Have Been Delivered from the Stage . . .* (1768); *The Court of Thespis; Being a Collection of the Most Admired Prologues and Epilogues That Have Appeared for Many Years* (1769); *The Theatrical Bouquet: Containing an Alphabetical Arrangement of the Prologues and Epilogues, Which Have Been Published by Distinguished Wits, from the Time That Colley Cibber First Came on the Stage, to the Present Year* (1778); and *A Collection and Selection of English Prologues and Epilogues, Commencing with Shakespeare, and Concluding with Garrick* (1779)—this last being an ambitious anthology in four volumes. With these anthologies should be considered editions of the verse of Garrick, George Colman, the elder, and John Taylor—three of the most prolific prologuisers of the century.[5] The number and popularity of the collections and editions are proof of the untiring demand of readers, many of whom could recall the speakers' expression, voice, and gestures.

4. T. H. Vail Motter, *The School Drama in England* (1929), p. 102.
5. *The Poetical Works of David Garrick* (1785); George Colman, *Prose on Several Occasions; Accompanied with Some Pieces in Verse* (1787), Vol. III; John Taylor, *Poems on Various Subjects* (1827), Vol. I.

Derived though they were from the Restoration, the prologues and epilogues of the eighteenth century are characteristic of their own time, reflecting the minutiae of daily life, presenting the difficulties and triumphs of the theatre, obeying changes in taste, recording in a lively manner social and dramatic history. Rowe, Addison, Steele, Farquhar, Fielding, Goldsmith, Sheridan—every dramatist of the century wrote prologues that considered separately reveal the writer's personality and together form a commentary on various aspects of eighteenth-century drama. Culling from all sources—first editions of plays, separate publications, magazines and anthologies—an editor might have difficulty in selecting from thousands of prologues and epilogues a hundred with any claim to outstanding literary merit, but there are few which are not touched with vitality and a quickness of observation, as the following study endeavors to prove. These qualities explain the readers' demand for a form of literature meant primarily to be interplay between actor and audience.

By readers and audience alike, prologues and epilogues were considered independent performances to be judged without reference to the plays which they preceded or followed. Their success was measured by their immediate efficacy and was a matter of practice rather than of critical theory. Playwrights hoped that the prologue and epilogue would be applauded in their own right as acting pieces and thus indirectly save the play. Hopkins, the Drury Lane prompter, records in his diary that Cumberland's *The Choleric Man* (1774) was "tolerably received,—but a most excellent Epilogue was written by Mr. Garrick and spoken by Mrs. Abington, which saved the Play—prodigious Applause to the Epilogue." [6] Tate Wilkinson, discussing *The Earl of Essex* (1753) by the inspired Irish brick-

6. *Drury Lane Calendar*, p. 182.

layer, Henry Jones, gives the epilogue as one of the reasons for the success of the tragedy: "Barry's inimitable acting of Essex, Mrs. Cibber's Rutland, with an excellent Epilogue, written by Mr. Garrick, gave the said play a run of sixteen nights that season, with great relish." [7] *Lloyd's Evening Post*, November 5–8, 1784, criticizes unfavorably a current musical farce, *The Spanish Rivals*, but praises the prologue: "A Prologue, obviously written on the spur of damnation, and while the terrors of the fate of the last new comedy dwelt upon the author's mind, was spoken by Mr. Bannister, jun. It was very ably delivered, and had no inconsiderable share of merit."

The purpose of the prologue was to cajole the audience into a pleasant frame of mind so that they would be in a friendly mood before the curtain was drawn up. Thus the prologue to *Irene* by Johnson, "which was written by himself in a manly strain, soothed the audience. . . ." [8] The purpose of the epilogue was to sound their humor and to flatter or amuse them into saving the play. Occasionally the epilogue was of no avail:

> *Too late, when cast, your Favour one beseeches,*
> *And Epilogues prove Execution-Speeches.* [9]

Sometimes, too, a prologue or epilogue was directly responsible for the failure of a play. Cumberland's *The Brothers* (1769) met a hostile reception because the prologue slashed at fellow dramatists, accusing them of being literary ghouls and scavengers. [1]

7. Tate Wilkinson, *The Wandering Patentee* (1795), I, 125–126.

8. James Boswell, *Life of Johnson*, ed. Hill-Powell (Oxford, The Clarendon Press, 1934), I, 196.

9. Epilogue to Mrs. Centlivre's *The Busie Body* (1709). Unless it is otherwise stated, quotations from prologues and epilogues are from the first editions of the plays with which they appeared.

1. Stanley T. Williams, *Richard Cumberland* (New Haven, 1917), pp. 48–49, and Benjamin Victor, *The History of the Theatres of London, from the Year 1760 to the Present Time* (1771), III, 166–167.

In the "tripartite" and short-lived comedy, *Three Hours after Marriage,* Fossile makes a holocaust of his niece's papers, destroying, according to the bereft Clinket: "A Pindarick Ode! five Similes! and half an Epilogue! . . . The tag of the Acts of a new Comedy! a Prologue sent by a Person of Quality! three Copies of recommendatory Verses! and two Greek Mottos!" [2] All the necessary appendages to her play were gone and could not easily be replaced. Mrs. Pix, in the prologue to *The Different Widows: or, Intrigue All-A-Mode* (1703), complains that as a means of luring the audience to Lincoln's Inn Fields, the managers have taken to providing a "Supplemental Epilogue," which the pampered audience have now come to consider as their due. Little they know what they are asking, for rhymes are scarce. Mrs. Pix discloses the difficulties which she has encountered in finding a poet to write her prologue:

> *How have I trudg'd about, from day, to day,*
> *Barely to beg a Prologue to our* PLAY.
> *Morn, after Morn, I've sought, yet could not get*
> *(If Life had layn at Stake) one Drachm of Wit;*
> *You'd swear I'd gone a Begging in the Pit.*

She makes the rounds of the city, poets running away when they see her coming. She looks in vain for D'Urfey at the Half Moon. At last she tries Will's Coffee-house:

> *But not one* Poet *there was to be found,*
> *Except the Author of the* Country Wife,
> *But Faith, I dur'st not Wake him for my Life:*
> *Least his Plain Dealing* Muse *should let you hear*
> *Such Stinging Truths, you'd not know how to bear,*
> *And make you (in a Pet) our* House *forswear.*

2. *Three Hours after Marriage* (1717), p. 25.

Sixty-five years later, Goldsmith was experiencing similar difficulty in securing an epilogue to *The Good Natur'd Man*, Dr. Johnson having furnished him with a characteristic and somewhat solemn prologue. He was at last constrained to write his own epilogue, to which he added in the first edition of the play an explanatory note, more apologetic than the piece warrants: "The Author, in expectation of an Epilogue from a Friend at Oxford, deferred writing one himself till the very last hour. What is here offered, owes all its success to the graceful manner of the Actress who spoke it." [3] The opening lines make an allusion to the profession of which Goldsmith was a member, an allusion which Garrick later developed in his prologue to *She Stoops to Conquer:*

> AS puffing quacks some caitiff wretch procure
> To swear the pill, or drop, has wrought a cure;
> Thus on the stage, our play-wrights still depend
> For Epilogues and Prologues on some friend,
> Who knows each art of coaxing up the town,
> And make full many a bitter pill go down.
> Conscious of this, our bard has gone about,
> And teaz'd each rhyming friend to help him out.
> An Epilogue, things can't go on without it;
> It cou'd not fail, wou'd you but set about it.

His fellow-dramatists and friends all refuse to help him:

> Go, ask your manager—Who, me? your pardon;
> Those things are not our fort at Covent-Garden—

the couplet being an oblique reference to Garrick's facility in writing prologues. The difficulties thus humorously treated are not necessarily exaggerated. Securing a suitable epilogue to *She Stoops to Conquer* was not the least of the

3. The actress was Mrs. Bulkley.

vexations which Goldsmith suffered in producing that comedy.[4]

Poets, managers of playhouses, persons of sufficient prominence to be recognized by the public, friends with an aptitude for versifying were besieged by anxious authors. The following petition made by Rowe to Pope is representative of hundreds: "Dear Sr.,—If you will favour me with your prologue by this bearer, I will return it to morrow, and allways reckon it among the obligations you have been so kind as to lay upon Your most faithfull Humble servant." [5] Pope supplied Rowe with an epilogue for *Jane Shore,* designed to be spoken by Mrs. Oldfield, following the popular pattern set by the successful epilogue to *The Distrest Mother.*[6]

The prologue to *The Royal Suppliants* (1781) is an excellent and by no means uncommon example of the importance which these pieces assumed in the eyes of the playwright, the prologuiser, the audience, and, finally, the reader. Mrs. Thrale records in her diary on February 1, 1781: ". . . here comes Dr Delap begging a Prologue to the Royal Suppliants his new Tragedy, which will be acted soon:—so very soon that I must write the Prologue this very Night when I come home from the Opera. it must be something about Hercules, for the royal Suppliants are his Widow & Daughter." On February 26 she congratulates herself that the play has been successful: "I have seen his Play fairly launch'd, and it swims delightfully: the Prologue is well received too, and all goes comfortable: they made me alter the last Lines which differ a little from that spoken & printed—it is not always that second Thoughts

4. See John Forster, *The Life and Times of Oliver Goldsmith.* Sixth Edition (1877), II, 336–337, for Goldsmith's letter to Joseph Cradock, giving the history of the epilogue to *She Stoops to Conquer.*

5. *Works of Pope,* ed. Elwin and Courthope (1871–1889), X, 110.

6. Pope's epilogue is printed in *Miscellaneous Poems and Translations, by Several Hands* . . . The Third Edition . . . 1720, pp. 153–155.

are best—I like the Verses better as they stand here, than as they appear in the Front of the play." [7] She then copies down the prologue as she had originally written it. The piece was published in *Lloyd's Evening Post*, February 26–28, 1781, as "supposed to be written by a Gentleman of the highest Rank in Literature," but it appears in the *Gentleman's Magazine* for March of the same year as *"Supposed to be written by Mrs.* THR-LE." Such was Mrs. Thrale's success with prologues and epilogues that she made an attempt to turn dramatist herself.[8]

Prefaces throughout the whole course of the century testify to the importance of the prologue and epilogue. Field-Marshal Conway closed the introductory note to his comedy, *False Appearances* (1789), by thanking General John Burgoyne, himself a successful dramatist, for the epilogue: "An account of this Play cannot be closed, without some notice of the admirable Epilogue, which makes its chief ornament, to which, if the writer of this has one only reasonable objection, (that of its tarnishing the inferior merits of his own production) he thinks it fully made up to him, by so flattering and so public a testimony of its author's friendship." The success of Burgoyne's epilogue was in turn due to the skilful presentation by Miss Farren, to whom the play is dedicated.

The vogue of the prologue and epilogue was long and brilliantly sustained by Garrick in his threefold capacity of author, actor, and manager of the theatre.[9] The first

7. *Thraliana*, ed. Katharine C. Balderston (Oxford, The Clarendon Press, 1942), I, 484–485.

8. James L. Clifford, *Hester Lynch Piozzi (Mrs. Thrale)* (Oxford, The Clarendon Press, 1941), p. 333.

9. Other managers of theatres were popular prologuisers. Colley Cibber, joint-manager of Drury Lane from 1708 to 1732, and Samuel Foote, manager of the Theatre in the Haymarket from 1766 to 1777, were famous for writing and speaking prologues. George Colman, manager of Covent Garden from 1767 to 1774, and of the Haymarket from 1777 to 1789, rivaled Garrick in the skill and number of his prologues and epilogues.

printed epilogue traceable to him appeared in 1740, the
last in 1778, shortly before his death, and during the intervening years he wrote over one hundred and sixty prologues and epilogues. In the short rehearsal play, *A Peep
behind the Curtain* (1767), Garrick makes a good-natured
reference to the constant demand upon him for prologues.
Lady Fuz, the fine lady who sets herself up to be a critic
and patron of the drama, asks Glib, the author of the play
about to be rehearsed, if they are to have a prologue. "We
positively must have a prologue." The author replies,
"Most certainly; entre nous—I have desired the manager
to write me one, which has so flatter'd him, that I shall be
able to do anything with him." [1]

Samuel Crisp, author of the tragedy, *Virginia* (1754),
wrote an Advertisement to the play in which he thanked
Garrick "for his masterly performance in the representation—(that is nothing new) And for his Prologue and
Epilogue, which have met with universal applause. . . ."
Richard Tickell, the librettist, in commenting on Garrick's skill in witty, pleasing verse, says, "A couplet of
yours in the prologue to *The Invasion* saved the whole
prologue and farce." [2] From Genoa, David Mallet's daughter, Dorothea Celesia, sent Garrick a play, *Almida,* and
asked him to furnish it with a prologue, "for a prologue
wrote by you is a passport to success." [3]

Audiences had become so familiar with the playful ingenuity and liveliness of Garrick's prologues that they
immediately recognized his pieces even when they were
published anonymously; for example, Garrick contributed

The prologues of Fielding and Sheridan, although obviously the work of
dramatists and of men thoroughly conversant with the stage, were not
especially connected with their duties as manager.

1. *The Dramatic Works of David Garrick* (1798), III, 99.

2. *The Private Correspondence of David Garrick,* ed. James Boaden
(1831–1832), II, 317.

3. *Ibid.,* I, 399.

a mock prologue to *New Brooms,* a skit by Colman, with which Drury Lane opened under Sheridan's management on September 21, 1776. Colman mentions the prologue in his introductory note: "The thought proposed for the subject matter of the *Prologue,* was kindly worked up by a friend, who desired to remain concealed, but whose stile and manner are too familiar to the Stage, not to betray him to the Publick, who will doubtless be pleased to see him disposed, even in his retirement, to contribute to their amusements."

It is not only introductory notes and letters from grateful playwrights which attest the popularity of Garrick's prologues. Thomas Hull in the prologue to *The Perplexities* (1767) introduces an imaginary conversation between the manager and the speaker:

> "*Garrick* (says he) can with a Prologue tame
> "The Critic's rage—Why can't you do the same?"
> Because (quoth I) the case is diff'rent quite;
> *Garrick,* you know, can Prologues speak and write;
> If like that *Roscius* I could write, and speech it,
> I might command applause, and not beseech it.

There was no dissenting criticism—Garrick was the greatest "working Prologue-smith" [4] of the age:

> In Prologue Writing, modern Bards agree,
> The only Art, is Wit and Simile;
> But *for* that Art, we ever must complain,
> While Roscius uses it at Drury-Lane.[5]

More interesting than all other comments on Garrick's prologues are two references in Boswell. In a letter to Goldsmith, written on 29 March 1773, Boswell congratu-

4. Garrick's epilogue to Home's *The Fatal Discovery* (1769).
5. Prologue to *The Snuff Box; or, A Trip to Bath* (1775) by William Heard, presented at the Haymarket.

lates him on the success of *She Stoops to Conquer*, which,
after much indecision on the part of Colman, the manager,
and after much suffering for Goldsmith, was finally performed at Covent Garden: [6] "It gives me pleasure that our
friend Garrick has written the prologue for you. It is at
least lending you a postilion, since you have not his coach;
and I think it is a very good one, admirably adapted both
to the subject and to the authour of the comedy." [7]

One of the most brilliant passages in Boswell contains
Dr. Johnson's dictum on Garrick's prologues. Under Monday 27 March 1775, Boswell writes:

> I met him at Drury-lane play-house in the evening.
> Sir Joshua Reynolds, at Mrs. Abington's request, had
> promised to bring a body of wits to her benefit; and
> having secured forty places in the front boxes, had
> done me the honour to put me in the group. Johnson
> sat on the seat directly behind me; and as he could
> neither see nor hear at such a distance from the stage,
> he was wrapped up in grave abstraction, and seemed
> quite a cloud, amidst all the sunshine of glitter and
> gaiety. I wondered at his patience in sitting out a play
> of five acts, and a farce of two. He said very little; but
> after the prologue to 'Bon Ton' had been spoken,
> which he could hear pretty well from the more slow
> and distinct utterance, he talked of prologue-writing,
> and observed, 'Dryden has written prologues superiour
> to any that David Garrick has written; but David
> Garrick has written more good prologues than Dryden
> has done. It is wonderful that he has been able to
> write such a variety of them.' [8]

6. Forster, *Goldsmith*, ii, 330 ff.
7. *Letters of James Boswell*, ed. Chauncey Brewster Tinker (Oxford,
The Clarendon Press, 1924), i, 192–193. The comparison of the theatre and
audience to a coach and passengers was common in prologues. See, for
example, Garrick's prologue to *New Brooms*.
8. Boswell, *Life of Johnson*, ii, 324–325. The prologue, one of the most

Johnson's verdict is repeated in a short farce called *Garrick in the Shades,* published in 1779, shortly after Garrick's death. The ghost of the actor, Holland, is represented as bringing to the recently arrived shade of Garrick the unflattering comments made by Ben Jonson on his plays and verse. Garrick, always supersensitive to derogatory criticism, asks what Jonson thinks of his prologues and epilogues. The answer restores his self-esteem, for Jonson refers the question to Dryden, who pronounces Garrick the greatest of all prologue-smiths.

The judgment of commentators in general is expressed in one of the many panegyrics written at the time of Garrick's retirement from the stage:

> In no species of writing has he excelled more than in prologues and epilogues. They are universally acknowledged to be next in merit, if not equal, to Dryden's compositions in that kind. In short, they are the abstract and brief chronicles of the times; a kind of history of the various predominant passions, humours, follies, foibles, and extravagancies of this good town for more than thirty years! They are an excellent companion to Hogarth's humourous prints, and Foote's comic characters.[9]

Responsiveness to the vagaries and demands of the audience was an essential part of Garrick's genius; his prologues were devised solely to entertain them. It is true that he was occasionally annoyed by the persistence of authors who demanded his help on pain of lifelong enmity if he refused it, but there can be no doubt that his position of "pro-

successful of the century, was written by George Colman, the elder, and spoken by Thomas King. In a prefatory note to *Bon Ton,* Garrick, the author of the play, expressed his appreciation of King as actor and as friend. For the prologue and note, see below, pp. 58–59.

9. "An Eulogium on Mr. Garrick's leaving the stage." Quoted in the *Gentleman's Magazine,* July 1776, from the *St. James's Evening Post.*

logue-smith" gave him a satisfaction second only to that of his acting. As literature, his prologues are inferior not only to Dryden's but, in many instances, to those of George Colman. As acting pieces they are unsurpassed, and their success alone would be sufficient to explain the continued popularity of the prologue and epilogue on the eighteenth-century stage.

During the entire century audiences took a lively and sometimes clamorous interest in the presentation of the prologue and epilogue, and might even demand that one or the other of them be revised to suit their pleasure. They "justly disliked" the epilogue spoken by Mrs. Cibber on the first night of Thomson's *Agamemnon* (1738); where-upon Thomson altered the piece, the revision and his apologetic footnote appearing with the first edition of the play.[1] They were equally loud and persistent in their approval.

> SOME strange caprice for ever rules the stage,
> And this we call the Prologue-speaking age;
> Without a Prologue nothing can be done
> So dearly you all love a little fun!
> To tame this rage in vain we often try
> The nicest art—*Prologue* still you cry![2]

The epilogue to *Britons, Strike Home: or, The Sailor's Rehearsal* (1739) comments that contrary to former rule even farces must now be concluded with epilogues; further-more,

> *So fond of* Epilogues *our* Wits *are grown,*
> *They call for them 'fore half the* Farce *is done.*

1. See below, pp. 300–301.

2. Prologue by Arthur Murphy to *The Citizen* (1761) in *Lloyd's Evening Post*, July 3–6, 1761. "Prologue" was apparently pronounced here in three syllables.

Calling for the prologue was part of the general din and confusion which preceded the performance, and not the least important purpose of the prologue was to quell this uproar. Using a common device, Arthur Murphy, in the prologue to his comedy, *The School for Guardians* (1767), has the speaker pretend that she has no prologue because the author has refused to write one:

I told him, "You know, Sir, what a miserable plight we all
    are in,
To frown upon the performers, when pit, box, and gallery
    begin;
Whu—go the catcalls—dub-dub-dub—each dreadful crit-
    ick's stick
Prólog'—throw him over—won't ye ha some orange chips
—*Prólógué*—Cries o' London—Musick!"

Tate Wilkinson records in his *Memoirs* an extraordinary instance of the audience's insisting on the speaking of a particular prologue. Barry and Woodward, long after they had established themselves as great actors on the London stage, undertook the ownership and management of the Crow Street Theatre in Dublin. When the venture came to a disastrous end, Woodward returned to Covent Garden, thoroughly humiliated. He made his reappearance in London with a prologue called *The Prodigal's Return,* which obtained much popularity and wide circulation, being published in the newspapers and magazines. The prologue spoke disparagingly of Dublin and expressed Woodward's joy in returning to London.[3] The following December, 1763, Wilkinson, acting in Dublin, advertised in the playbills for his benefit performance that he would act *The Prodigal's Return* "in the manner of the original."[4]

3. Robert Hitchcock, *An Historical View of the Irish Stage* (1788), II, 81–106.

4. As the imitation of other actors in their popular prologues was part

Woodward saw the announcement in the *Dublin Journal* and wrote in haste to Barry, who was still managing Crow Street, that as he himself intended to return to Ireland for a short engagement, Wilkinson's caricaturing him in a prologue so offensive to a Dublin audience would be the greatest injury to him. Wilkinson, at Barry's insistence, agreed to withhold the prologue, even although it had been promised to the audience, but on the night of the performance, when Mrs. Dancer appeared as Almeria in *The Mourning Bride,* instead of being greeted with the usual applause, she was hooted from the stage with cries of, "Off! off!—Wilkinson! Wilkinson! Woodward's prologue." Wilkinson, dressed not in the traditional black of the prologue but for his part of the King, was forced to act *The Prodigal's Return.* His imitation of Woodward delighted the audience, and thereafter, let him be playing no matter how incongruous a part, he had first to present Woodward's prologue. ". . . had I played Lady Townly or Juliet, I am certain I must have spoke it." Woodward went to Ireland the following spring, but he found himself in a city hostile to him. The prologue with which Wilkinson had so thoroughly familiarized the Irish public was printed with complete directions for pelting Woodward off the stage. He did not dare to appear even on the streets, "nor did he ever visit Ireland to play again." [5]

Pit and gallery were alike tyrannically exacting about the presentation of their favorite prologues. How power-

---

of Wilkinson's repertoire, this proceeding was less egregious than it first appears. When Foote was in Dublin in 1757, he spoke for a succession of nights the prologue to *The Author,* the audience calling for the piece. Wilkinson, who was traveling with Foote, won great favor by reciting this very prologue, mimicking the older actor. Foote sat disconcerted while Wilkinson imitated "his manner, his voice, his oddities." The applause was continued until the curtain was dropped. (Tate Wilkinson, *Memoirs of His Own Life* [York, 1790], I, 174–175.)

5. Wilkinson, *Memoirs,* III, 195–209.

less an actor or even a manager was in their hands is illustrated by two entries in the diary kept by Richard Cross, Hopkins's predecessor as prompter at Drury Lane. In 1750 on the opening night of the season, Garrick spoke an occasional prologue of particular interest to the audience because of its references to current theatrical news. Cross records in his diary for September 28: "The Audience excus'd Mr. Garrick speaking ye prologue." By the next night their temper had changed: "They oblig'd him to speak it." [6] The playbills had already announced the discontinuance of the prologue, for Genest enters under September 27: "—by particular desire the occasional Prologue will be spoken by Garrick, being positively the last time of his speaking it." [7] The audience frequently called for Garrick to present his prologues. At a command performance of *Zara*, with *Lethe* as the afterpiece, at Drury Lane, on January 23, 1766: "The Prologue was called for. Mr. Garrick went on directly to speak it—as soon as he appeared, a general Clap and a loud Huzza,—and there was such a Noise, from the House being so crowded, very few heard anything of the Prologue.—" [8] The "Prologue" was that which Garrick had spoken at the command performance of *Much Ado about Nothing*, November 14, 1765, on his first appearance after his return from Europe. He did not appear in the season of 1770–71 until November 13, when he played Benedick. The audience again called for the prologue, but he made an apology for not speaking it. [9]

6. *Drury Lane Calendar*, p. 317.

7. [John Genest], *Some Account of the English Stage, from the Restoration in 1660 to 1830* (Bath, 1832), IV, 315.

8. *Drury Lane Calendar*, p. 117.

9. *Ibid.*, p. 151. When Henderson as a young actor appeared before Foote to try his ability, he chose to speak Garrick's prologue to the command performance of *Much Ado about Nothing*. (*A Genuine Narrative of the Life and Theatrical Transactions of Mr. John Henderson* . . . [1777], p. 18.)

In the prologue to Colman's *The Spleen; or, Islington Spa* (1776) Garrick refers to the popularity of Thomas King as speaker of prologues, the lines gaining point in being spoken by King himself:

> *THO' Prologues now, as blackberries are plenty,*
> *And like them maukish too, nineteen in twenty;*
> *Yet you will have them, when their date is o'er,*
> *And* Prologue, Prologue, *still your Honours roar;*
> *Till some such dismal phiz as mine comes on,*
> *Ladies and Gentlemen indeed there's none,*
> *The* Prologue, Author, Speaker, *all are dead and gone!*
> *These reasons have some weight, and stop the rout;*
> *You clap—I smirk—and thus go cringing out;*
> *"While living call me, for your pleasure use me;*
> *"Should I tip off—I hope you'll then excuse me.*
>   *So much for Prologues—.*

Sheridan's prologue to *The Miniature Picture* (1780) "is said to have been so much approved of, that the audience called for it again at the end of the play, and waited till King, who was gone home, could return to speak it." [1]

The calling for the epilogue to Ambrose Philips's *The Distrest Mother* became traditional. The piece, which has no inherent merit, owed its original popularity to Mrs. Oldfield, who spoke it at the first performance of the play at Drury Lane, March 17, 1712. The reputed author, Eustace Budgell, in the *Spectator,* No. 341, April 1, 1712, defending the epilogue, describes the acclaim with which it was greeted: "The audience would not permit Mrs. Oldfield to go off the stage the first night, till she had repeated it twice; the second night the noise of *Ancora's* was as loud as before, and she was again obliged to speak it twice; the third night it was still called for a second time; and, in short, contrary to all other epilogues, which

1. Genest, VI, 134–135. See below, pp. 59–60.

are dropt after the third representation of the play, this has already been repeated nine times." [2] Johnson in considering the expedients used to insure a favorable reception to Philips's play says: "It was concluded with the most successful Epilogue that was ever yet spoken on the English theatre. The three first nights it was recited twice, and not only continued to be demanded through the run, as it is termed, of the play, but whenever it is recalled to the stage, where by peculiar fortune, though a copy from the French, it yet keeps its place, the Epilogue is still expected, and is still spoken." [3] The epilogue descended through a long line of distinguished actresses, including Mrs. Cibber, Mrs. Bellamy, and Mrs. Siddons.

Prologues and epilogues did not hold their place without opposition. Even at the beginning of the century, authors complained that the genre had worn itself out and that only the necessity of complying with the demands of the audience kept it alive. Cibber expressed a common opinion of playwrights when he wrote:

> AN *Epilogue's a Tax on Authors laid,*
> *And full as much unwillingly is paid.*[4]

Farquhar in the prologue to David Crauford's *Courtship*

2. It should be noted that the calling for prologues and epilogues was not unusual and that they were often called for beyond the third night, as examples in this present study prove. The playbills in the newspapers show that the prologues and epilogues were frequently revived with their plays.

3. Johnson, *Lives of the English Poets*, ed. George Birkbeck Hill (Oxford, 1905), III, 315. In a footnote to Johnson's comments, Hill writes: "I have seen a marginal note by Mrs. Piozzi on this *Spectator* (*i.e.*, No. 341) where she says:—'What I cannot comprehend at all is that since my time—nay since Mrs. Siddon's [*sic*] time—the Gallery always will call for this Epilogue, which is now unreservedly given to Addison; but how the Gallery people came to know its value so well I guess not.'"

4. Epilogue to *Love Makes a Man* (1700).

A-la-mode (1700) declared that the prologue should be abolished,

> *For if the Play be good it need not crave it;*
> *If bad, no Prologue on the Earth can save it.*

Rowe, not without reason, complained that the writers of the Restoration had exhausted all the themes and that the reformers had silenced both wit and satire:

> *OF all the Taxes which the Poet pays,*
> *Those Funds of Verse, none are so hard to raise*
> *As Prologues and as Epilogues to Plays.*
> *So many mighty Wits are gone before,*
> *Th' have rifled all the Muses sacred Store;*
> *Like Conqu'ring Armies thro' the Province pass'd,*
> *Swept all, and left it ruin'd, void and waste.*
> *Yet, Conscientious you can still demand*
> *Large Contributions from the wretched Land;*
> *Expect that we should still pursue the Theam,*
> *Tho' you deny to us, what you allow'd to them.*[5]

In the prologue to *The Wife of Bath* in 1713 Gay laments that plays have become subordinate to their introductions. Eleven years later he starts the prologue to his tragedy, *The Captives,* with an attack implying that disaster would be the fate of the dramatist who defied a tradition so cherished by the public:

> *I Wish some author, careless of renown,*
> *Would without formal prologue risque the town.*

Gay himself was not the man to make the attempt, and he supplied even his unacted farce, *The Mohocks* (published in 1711), with a mock prologue "To be Spoken by the Publisher," in which he admonished his readers

5. Epilogue to *The Biter* (1704).

T' applaud our disappointed Author's Play:
Let all those Hands that would have clapp'd, combine
To take the whole Impression off from mine.

The most sustained as well as the most entertaining criticism of the prologue and epilogue was made by Fielding, who denounced the practice both in prose and rhyme, ridiculed it in numerous introductions and prefaces, and made it the subject of burlesque. He begins his epilogue to Theobald's *Orestes* (1731) with the usual complaint:

OF all the Plagues, with which a Poet's curst,
This heavy Tax of Epilogue's *the worst:*
For tho' his Muse be jaded in his Play,
Still she must speak, tho' she has Nought to say.

The epilogue to *The Author's Farce* (1730) is in the form of a playlet in which four poets are assembled for the purpose of writing the epilogue while the audience waits. They follow the customary pattern—fulsome flattery for the critics, encomiums of the play, contempt for the beaus, obscenity to please all the house. There is no need for wit, as the merit of the piece lies entirely in the acting. The prologue to *The Old Debauchees* (1732), echoing Dryden's prologue to *The Rival Ladies,* is also devoted to destructive criticism of its own species:

I Wish, with all my Heart, the Stage and Town
Would both agree to cry all Prologues down;
That we, no more oblig'd to say or sing,
Might drop this useless necessary Thing.

His chief charges are that the prologue is trite and ineffectual, accusations to which he returns in the Introduction to *Don Quixote in England* (1734), a prose conversation between the manager and the author:

Manager. No Prologue, Sir! The Audience will never bear it. They will not bate you any thing of their due.

Auth. I am the Audience's very humble Servant; but they cannot make a Man write a Prologue, whether he can or no.

Man. Why, Sir, there is nothing easier: I have known an Author bring three or four to the House with one Play, and give us our Choice which we would speak.

Auth. Yes, Sir; and I have now three in my Pocket, written by Friends, of which I choose none should be spoke.

Man. How so?

Auth. Because they have been all spoke already twenty times over.

The first of these ready-made prologues deals with the decline of the stage—the staple subject of prologues for the past ten years—and promises that the play which it precedes will raise drama from its fallen estate; the second begins with twelve lines denouncing indecency and ends with an illustration of what indecency is; the last, having been written by a poet who has not read the play, falls wide of the mark in attacking farces.

Similar criticism introduces the rehearsal play in the satire, *The Historical Register, for the Year 1736* (1737). Medley, the author, deplores the usual prologue "that will serve for every Play alike," in frightening or flattering the audience into a favorable mood. For the prologue, he substitutes an Ode, utter nonsense, a gibe at Cibber's annual Ode for the New Year, and he boasts, "Now, Sir, my Prologue will serve for no Play but my own. . . ." [6]

Pasquin (1736) provided Fielding with an excellent opportunity for sustained ridicule of the prologue and epilogue, as he furnished the mock comedy with a prologue and the tragedy with both prologue and epilogue. He supplemented the pieces with satirical comments, thus by

6. Fielding, *The Historical Register, for the Year 1736* [1737], pp. 4–5.

criticism and illustration reducing the custom to absurdity.
Trapwit's comedy, reversing the ordinary procedure, is to
be rehearsed before Fustian's tragedy, the ghost indispen-
sable to the tragedy being delayed:

> *Trap.* . . . Come, come, where's the Gentleman who
> speaks the Prologue? This Prologue, Mr. *Fustian,* was
> given me by a Friend, who does not care to own it till
> he trys whether it succeeds or no.

Here an actor enters to speak the prologue, and after
Trapwit has ordered him to make a "very low Bow to the
Audience" and to show "as much Concern as possible" in
his looks, he proceeds, parodying stock conventions. Trapwit, anxious for the success of his comedy, interrupts him:

> Oh! Dear Sir, seem a little more affected, I beseech
> you; advance to the Front of the Stage, make a low
> Bow, lay your Hand upon your Heart, fetch a deep
> Sigh, and pull out your Handkerchief.

When the actor has finished the ridiculous prologue,
Trapwit says gratefully, "Very well! Very well, Sir! You
have affected me, I am sure," his fellow playwright, Fustian,
adding with sneer, "And so he will the Audience, I'll
answer for 'em."

> *Trap.* Oh, Sir, you're too good-natur'd—but, Sir, I do
> assure you I had writ a much better Prologue of my
> own; but as this came *Gratis,* have reserv'd it for my
> next Play; a Prologue sav'd, is a Prologue got, Brother
> *Fustian.*[7]

Trapwit has no epilogue, for although he has borrowed
all the plays owned by Watts, the printer, he has been

---

7. Fielding, *Pasquin. A Dramatick Satire on the Times: Being the Rehearsal of Two Plays, viz. A Comedy call'd, the Election; And a Tragedy
call'd, The Life and Death of Common-Sense* . . . (1736), pp. 3-4.

unable to hit upon the exact amount of indecency demanded by an actress in speaking an epilogue. The mock tragedy is introduced by a prologue which Fustian modestly recommends as "writ by a Friend." It denounces current drama and flays the audience for their lack of taste. "Faith, Sir," exclaims Sneerwell, the critic, "your Friend has writ a very fine Prologue." Fustian: "Do you think so? Why then, Sir, I must assure you, that Friend is no other than my self." [8] The epilogue, spoken by the Ghost of Common-Sense, is a serious plea for the banishment of Italian opera and the return of English drama.

Fielding continued his attack on the prologue long after he had ceased writing drama. The first chapter of Book XVI, *Tom Jones,* he entitled "Of Prologues" and in it compared the similar functions of prologues and his prefatory chapters:

> To say the Truth, I believe many a hearty Curse hath been devoted on the Head of that Author, who first instituted the Method of prefixing to his Play that Portion of Matter which is called the Prologue; and which at first was Part of the Piece itself, but of latter Years hath had usually so little Connexion with the Drama before which it stands, that the Prologue to one Play might as well serve for any other. Those indeed of more modern Date, seem all to be written on the same three Topics, *viz.* an Abuse of the Taste of the Town, a Condemnation of all Cotemporary Authors, and an Elogium on the Performance just about to be represented. The Sentiments in all these are very little varied, nor is it possible they should; and indeed I have often wondered at the great Invention of Authors, who have been capable of finding such various Phrases to express the same thing.

8. *Ibid.,* pp. 35; 38–39.

> . . . it is well known, that the Prologue serves the
> Critic for an Opportunity to try his Faculty of Hissing,
> and to tune his Cat-call to the best Advantage; by
> which means, I have known those Musical Instruments
> so well prepared, that they have been able to play in
> full Concert at the first rising of the Curtain.[9]

In spite of all this adverse criticism, Fielding submitted
to the established tradition. He wrote for himself and his
fellow playwrights lively prologues and epilogues, distinguished by a rough, coarse humor. Many of them contain
pertinent criticism of the theatre, and some of them, for
example, the prologue and epilogue for the revision of
Tom Thumb, May 1, 1730, are excellently suited to their
plays.

Until the end of the century the prologue continued to
be a weapon of destructive criticism leveled against itself.
Holcroft's prologue to *The Road to Ruin* (1792) begins
with the usual pretense that the prologue is missing. The
speaker enters, *"driving a boy across the stage,"* and calling
out that he must run for the author:

> . . . We can do nothing till he appears.
> Tell him in less than five minutes we shall have the house
>   about our ears!
> [*To the audience.*]
> Oh sirs! The prompter has mislaid the prologue. . . .

The speaker gives a summary of the lost prologue, proving
that it has nothing to do with the play. The author has
been reluctant to supply one,

> For he says prologues are blots, which ought to be wiped
>   away:

9. Fielding, *The History of Tom Jones, A Foundling* (1749), Book xvi,
pp. 2–3.

A gothic practice, and, in spite of precedent, not the better
    for being old.

Protests and denunciations had no effect on the public;
the audience still considered the prologue an essential part
of their evening's entertainment. Even dramatic pieces
which were supposed to be self-sufficient, such as farces
and ballad operas, were often performed and published
with prologue, epilogue, or both. Gay writes in the Introduction to *The Beggar's Opera* (1728): ". . . as I have con-
sented to have neither Prologue nor Epilogue, it must be
allow'd an Opera in all its forms," but when his posthu-
mous opera, *Achilles,* was performed in 1733, it was introduced by a prologue.[1] William Kenrick in the prologue to
his unpublished farce, *The Spendthrift; or, A Christmas
Gambol* (1778), comments with asperity on the increasing
importance which prologues were assuming: "The Prologue is a Farce before the Play."[2] In 1796 W. T. Fitzgerald, a prolific and clever prologuiser, begins the prologue to Frederic Reynolds's *Fortune's Fool* by observing:

> To each new Play, a Prologue must appear,
> Like Poet Laureat's Ode to each New-Year.

Reynolds made the writing of a prologue the central
incident of his very amusing comedy, *The Dramatist: or,
Stop Him Who Can!* (1789). Vapid, a poet whose chief
claim to fame lies in his epilogues, knowing that "many
a dull play has been saved by a good epilogue," volunteers
to write both the prologue and the epilogue for the dramatist, "but," he says, "you needn't send me the comedy—
we never connect either with the play now—." In due time

1. The word "opera" caused a confusion in criticism, for it was applied
both to Italian opera, which obviously needed no prologue, and to native
ballad opera, which lent itself readily to humorous prologues and
epilogues.
2. The *Public Advertiser,* December 23, 1778.

he appears with the epilogue, "the very best thing I ever
wrote in my life," expecting the pleasure of hearing Ennui
read it aloud. ". . . it's all correct—all chaste! only one
half line wanting at the end to make it complete." As
Ennui is out and it is imperative that someone read it
aloud, the honor falls to Peter, the servant, who, when he
reaches the final couplet, says, *"Here's something wanting,
Sir."* The poet agonizes over the unfinished line. ". . . to
have it marr'd for want of one half line! one curst half
line! I could almost weep for disappointment." Peter
thoughtlessly advises him, "Never mind, sir, don't perplex
yourself—put in any thing," to which Vapid angrily re-
joins, "Put in any thing!—why, 'tis the last line, and the
epilogue must end with something striking, or it will be no
trap for applause—No trap for applause, after all this fine
writing! Put in any Thing!—what do you mean, Sirrah?"
The undaunted Peter, puzzled by Vapid's bombastic style,
says, "Methinks this is a strange epilogue to a comedy—."
Lewis, who played Vapid, appeared very appropriately as
the same character to present the epilogue, fortunately not
Vapid's masterpiece but one by Miles Peter Andrews, a
minor dramatist and the originator of an ingenious variety
of epilogue that paints a lively, bright picture of the noisy
theatre-goers of the late 1780's.

Popular demand for prologues continued into the early
years of the nineteenth century [3] and reached its height in
the addresses submitted for the opening of the new Drury

3. Sad evidence of the popularity of prologues in the first decade of
the nineteenth century is Lamb's letter to Wordsworth, December 11,
1806, on the failure of his farce, *Mr. H.*: "You will see the Prologue in
most of the Morning Papers. It was received with such shouts as I never
witness'd to a Prologue. It was attempted to be encored. How hard!
a thing I did merely as a task, because it was wanted—and set no great
store by;—and Mr. H—!!" (*The Letters of Charles Lamb*, ed. E. V.
Lucas, New Haven, 1935, II, 31.)

Lane Theatre, October 10, 1812. The Committee rejected all the pieces and asked Lord Byron to write the prologue, a task that he performed with seriousness and no little painstaking. At his request his occasional prologue was spoken by Elliston.[4]

But the interest in prologues waned rapidly as the century advanced. In 1823 the prologue to Mary Russell Mitford's tragedy, *Julian,* states half-heartedly that prologues are still expected:

> . . . old forms forbid us to submit
> A Play without a Prologue to the Pit.

The dramatist has supplied the piece:

> Lest this be missed by some true friend of plays,
> Like the dull colleague of his earlier days.

James Robinson Planché tells an anecdote about a play that he produced at Covent Garden on November 9, 1824, without a prologue:

> The comedy was in five acts; and, at one of the last rehearsals, Fawcett asked me if I had written a prologue. "No." "A five-act play, and no prologue!—they'll tear up the benches!" They did nothing of the sort. . . . and the custom for prologues to
> —"Precede the piece in mournful verse,
> As undertakers strut before the hearse,"[5]
> was broken through for the first time, without the slightest notice being taken of it by the public.[6]

4. For the history of Byron's prologue, see *The Works of Lord Byron, Letters and Journals,* ed. Rowland E. Prothero (1898–1901), II, 141 ff. The Drury Lane competition inspired the *Rejected Addresses* by James and Horace Smith (1812).

5. Incorrectly quoted from Garrick's prologue to Arthur Murphy's *The Apprentice* (1756). See below, p. 139.

6. James Robinson Planché, *Recollections and Reflections.* New and Revised Edition (1901), pp. 42–43. Allardyce Nicoll, *A History of Early*

Five-act plays continued to be printed with prologues and epilogues, and the pieces continued to be spoken, but they were no longer of their former importance to the audience or to readers. The magazines had all but ceased to print the pieces in their poetry sections, only a few appearing after 1810.

A number of circumstances brought about the decline of the prologues and epilogues. The greatly enlarged theatres were certainly not suited to the presentation of the pieces which depended upon the intimate relationship between actor and audience. The most obvious reason for their decrease was the predominance of musical comedies, extravaganzas, burlesques, and other entertainments traditionally unaccompanied by prologues and epilogues. Their decline can also be attributed to a change in taste. As a genre the pieces are based in reality and everyday experience and are foreign to the temper and interests of romanticism.

Nineteenth Century Drama (Cambridge, 1930), I, 30–31, in discussing the gradual disappearance of the prologue, quotes the selection from Planché. Interest in the old prologues was not entirely dead. In 1833, Douglas Jerrold brought out at Covent Garden a comedy in two acts, called *Nell Gwynne; or, The Prologue,* which ends with an actress, *"in a broad-brimmed hat and waist-belt,"* speaking Dryden's prologue to *The Conquest of Granada,* as it was originally spoken.

CHAPTER 2

SPEAKERS

Prologues and epilogues, in common with the plays to which they were attached, owed their success quite as much to their actors as to their writers. Fielding was ridiculing current epilogues as mediocre and repetitious when in the epilogue to *The Author's Farce* (1730) he made one of his poets declare that an epilogue's chief ornament is wit, and another retort:

It hath been so; but that stale Custom's broken;
Tho' dull to read, 'twill please you when 'tis spoken;

but it is nonetheless true that prologues and epilogues were written primarily to be spoken and that the best pieces were bettered in being delivered by great actors or actresses. As with the plays of another age, so it is with prologues—they can come to life for us only as we are able to recreate the voice, inflection, gestures, and byplay of their actors. Even then we may miss the essential point. In many cases the liveliness of the pieces suggested to the speaker clever and effective interpretation; such, for example, are the prologues by Farquhar, Goldsmith, Garrick, and George Colman, the elder. In other cases, justifying Fielding's censure, the success of the pieces depended entirely upon the actors' skill. Tate Wilkinson has preserved the fact that Spranger Barry received "three plaudits" for his manner of pronouncing two lines in the prologue to *Constantine* (1754):

> Their heroes seem of a superior state,
> Great in their virtues, in *their vices* GREAT.[1]

Steele, in the *Guardian,* No. 82, commenting on the death of a minor actor, William Peer, gives a convincing instance of the importance attached to the presentation of the prologue and of an actor's ability to create a subtle part out of seemingly insignificant lines.

> Mr. *William Peer* distinguished himself particularly in two Characters, which no Man ever could touch but himself, one of them was the Speaker of the Prologue to the Play, which is contrived in the Tragedy of *Hamlet. . . .* Mr. *William Peer* spoke that Preface to the Play with such an Air as represented that he was an Actor, and with such an inferior manner as only acting an Actor, as made the others on the Stage appear real great Persons, and not Representatives. This was a nicety in Acting that none but the most subtile Player cou'd so much as conceive. I remember his speaking these Words, in which there is no great matter but in the right adjustment of the Air of the Speaker, with universal Applause.

> > *For us and for our Tragedy,*
> > *Here stooping to your Clemency,*
> > *We beg your Hearing patiently.*

> *Hamlet* says very archly upon the pronouncing of it, *Is this a Prologue, or a Poesie of a Ring?* However, the speaking of it got Mr. *Peer* more Reputation, than those who speak the length of a Puritans Sermon every Night will ever attain to.[2]

1. Wilkinson, *Memoirs,* IV, 183.
2. The *Guardian,* No. 82, Monday, June 15, 1713. Steele's account of

The "Prologue" in *Hamlet,* slight as it is, continued to be considered a part of importance. Genest (II, 502) lists it among the characters played by the comedian, Estcourt.

A minor actor might make a name for himself by his skill in delivering a prologue, but in general only the great actors were allowed to speak the prologues. William Rufus Chetwood, "Twenty Years Prompter to his Majesty's Company of Comedians at the Theatre-Royal in Drury Lane," records this fact and accounts for it: ". . . as *Prologues* and *Epilogues* are the most difficult Tasks of both Sexes on the Stage, it is to be remark'd, but few, besides the capital Performers, are trusted with them; and a good Prologue and Epilogue have often help'd a bad Play out of the Mire, or, at least, sent the Audience home a little better humour'd." [3] All major actors and actresses until the beginning of the nineteenth century spoke prologues and epilogues, and, in their own age, Betterton, Wilks, Mrs. Oldfield, Mrs. Woffington, Mrs. Clive, Mrs. Cibber, Garrick, King, Mrs. Abington, Miss Younge, and Miss Farren were as celebrated for their prologues and epilogues as for their most popular characters.

Our knowledge of the actors' appearance in speaking the prologues and epilogues is not entirely dependent upon contemporary criticism and verbal accounts. There are extant many theatrical prints that with much attention to costume and gesture present the speakers as they confronted the audience. Such prints are doubly interesting when they are used as illustrations in anthologies of prologues and epilogues. A copiously illustrated set of *A Collection and Selection of English Prologues and Epilogues* is owned by the Houghton Library of Harvard University,

---

Peer's speaking the prologue in *Hamlet* is repeated, without acknowledgment of the source, in *The History of the English Stage . . .* by Mr. Thomas Betterton (1741), p. 34.

3. W. R. Chetwood, *A General History of the Stage* (1749), p. 254.

Volumes III and IV relating especially to our period. The frontispiece of Volume III shows Lee Lewes as Harlequin. The volume also includes Foote as Dr. Squintum "preaching" the sermon epilogue to *The Minor;* Parsons in the character of Paul Prig, self-consciously displaying his frills, in Colman's prologue to *The Spanish Barber;* Garrick as a Country Boy in his own prologue to Brown's *Barbarossa;* Palmer as "Christmas" in Garrick's prologue to *A Christmas Tale;* and Mrs. Barry, striking a tragic pose, in Garrick's occasional prologue commemorating her husband. The finest print in this volume is of Barry, handsome, sensitive, and elegantly dressed in the traditional black velvet,[4] as he delivered the prologue to Jones's *The Earl of Essex.* This print gives a vivid impression of the formality and restraint of the "prologue" ushering in tragedy. Volume IV contains a print of Macklin in his premature Farewell Address of 1753, and there follow Mrs. Bulkley in Goldsmith's epilogue to *She Stoops to Conquer;* Woodward in the character of a Fine Gentleman in Garrick's epilogue to *Barbarossa,* a haughty answer to the Country Boy; Mrs. Yates in the epilogue to *The Earl of Warwick;* Mrs. Abington in the epilogue to *Zingis;* and Mrs. Mattocks in the epilogue to *Know Your Own Mind.* The frontispiece to *The School of Roscius, or Theatrical Orator,* an anthology of prologues and epilogues published in 1792, is a print of Mrs. Mattocks, adorned with three great white plumes, reciting Holcroft's epilogue to *The Road to Ruin.* As a frontispiece to *The Theatrical Bouquet* (1780) there appears an engraving by Isaac Taylor of Garrick impersonating a drunken sailor, delivering the prologue to Mallet's masque, *Britannia.* He is ominously waving a playbill labelled *Zara,* Aaron Hill's translation of Voltaire's *Zaïre*

4. Cf. Holcroft's prologue to *Love's Frailties* (1794):

> Cassandra like, in black prophetic view,
> I see the massacres that may ensue!

being the main piece of the evening! The patriotism of both the prologue and the masque was intended to distract the audience from considering the origin of the tragedy. The print is of importance not only in being a likeness of Garrick in a popular character, but furthermore in picturing in detail the uniform worn by the British Navy in the mid-eighteenth century. Little can be said for the crude print of Woodward presenting the prologue to *She Stoops to Conquer*, used as a frontispiece to *The British Spouter* (1773), except that it shows the speaker dressed in black and carrying a conspicuous handkerchief—a mourner hired to lament the death of the Comic Muse. Occasionally a play was published with a print of an actor or actress delivering prologue or epilogue; for example, James Dodd's comedy *Gallic Gratitude; or, The Frenchman in India* (1779) is illustrated by an engraving of Mrs. Jackson, presenting the prologue in the character of Britannia. Over her fashionable, full-flowing gown she wears a corslet; she carries a spear and shield, and her head is covered with a forest of feathers. Prints such as these are an accurate source of information about costumes and manners of the eighteenth-century stage, and they are additional proof of the popularity of actors skilled in presenting the prologues and epilogues.

At the beginning of the century many of the great actors who had won their fame during the Restoration were still on the stage. Betterton, Mrs. Elizabeth Barry, Mrs. Bracegirdle, Mrs. Verbruggen, Verbruggen, and Cave Underhill all were assigned new prologues after 1700.[5] Their immediate followers—Mrs. Oldfield, Mrs. Porter, Wilks, Booth, Colley Cibber, Quin—learned their art and in turn passed it on. With the advent of Garrick a new order of acting

5. For a list of prologues and epilogues assigned to Restoration actors and actresses, see Autrey Nell Wiley, *Rare Prologues and Epilogues. 1642–1700*, Appendix C.

was introduced, but there is no indication that the presentation of the prologue and epilogue was essentially altered. Allowances being made for a change in the subject matter of the pieces and in the taste of the audience, an unbroken tradition of prologue speaking extends from Betterton to Kemble.

Between 1700 and 1706 there were published twelve new prologues written for Betterton. He was the first speaker of the prologue to *The Way of the World* (1700), of Nicholas Rowe's prologue to *The Gamester* by Mrs. Centlivre (1705), and of Farquhar's prologue to her next comedy, *The Platonick Lady* (1706). Cibber, who was himself both a writer and a speaker of prologues, commenting on his contemporaries and rivals in the art, gives highest praise to Betterton.

> To speak a good Prologue well is, in my Opinion, one of the hardest Parts and strongest Proofs of sound Elocution, of which, I confess, I never thought that any of the several who attempted it shew'd themselves, by far, equal Masters to *Betterton. Betterton,* in the Delivery of a good Prologue, had a natural Gravity that gave Strength to good Sense, a temper'd Spirit that gave Life to Wit, and a dry Reserve in his Smile that threw Ridicule into its brightest Colours. Of these Qualities, in the speaking of a Prologue, *Booth* only had the first, but attain'd not to the other two: *Wilks* had Spirit, but gave too loose a Rein to it, and it was seldom he could speak a grave and weighty Verse harmoniously. . . . *Wilks* had many Excellencies, but if we leave Prologue-Speaking out of the Number he will still have enough to have made him a valuable Actor.[6]

Only three prologues were assigned to Betterton after the

6. Cibber, *Apology,* ed. R. W. Lowe (1889), I, 271-272.

removal of his company from Lincoln's Inn Fields to the
newly-built theatre in the Haymarket in April 1705. Betterton was old, and the theatre was not suited to the presentation of prologues because of its size and architecture.

In the course of the passage partially quoted, Cibber remarks that Wilks looked upon all prologues as his by right.
It is obvious that Cibber was jealous of Wilks's popularity
in prologues, and he accounts for his success thus: Dryden,
shortly before his death, wrote both the prologue and epilogue to Vanbrugh's revision of Fletcher's comedy *The
Pilgrim*. Cibber was given his choice of characters in the
play, and as he chose minor parts, Vanbrugh gave him the
epilogue. "And *Dryden,* upon his hearing me repeat it
to him, made me a farther Compliment of trusting me
with the Prologue." It was, of course, unusual for an actor
to be given both the prologue and the epilogue. Wilks was
so much vexed at the attention shown Cibber that henceforth he never let an opportunity of speaking a prologue
escape him, ". . . and from this Incident, too," Cibber
concludes, "you may partly see what occasion'd so many
Prologues, after the Death of *Betterton,* to fall into the
Hands of one Speaker." [7] Whatever the reason for his popularity, Wilks was assigned over forty prologues and epilogues, some of them by the leading dramatists of the age.
He was a friend of Farquhar's, and in 1702 he spoke the
epilogue to *The Inconstant* and later the same year the
prologue to *The Twin Rivals;* in 1703 he spoke Farquhar's
prologue to a comedy, *All for the Better,* by a minor playwright, Francis Manning; in 1707 he spoke the prologue
to *The Beaux' Stratagem.* He was the original speaker of
three prologues by Steele—to *The Funeral* (1701), to Ambrose Philips's *The Distrest Mother* (1712), and to *The
Conscious Lovers* (1722)—and of three prologues by Addison—to Steele's *The Tender Husband* (1705), to Edmund

7. Cibber, *Apology,* I, 271.

Smith's *Phaedra and Hippolitus* (1707), and to *The Drummer* (1716). The last was, incidentally, an unusually long-lived piece and was adapted when the comedy was revived in 1762 during the excitement caused by the Cock Lane Ghost. Wilks was given Pope's prologue to Addison's *Cato* (1713), itself sufficient to have made the name of a lesser actor, and Gay's prologue to *The Captives* (1724). His first prologues were assigned to him before 1700; his last in 1730.

Cibber also presented prologues and epilogues throughout his entire career, his last piece being the prologue to his *Papal Tyranny in the Reign of King John* (1745). In many ways Cibber's interest in prologues resembles Garrick's. Like Garrick he was the author of prologues for his own plays and for those of other dramatists; both men as managers of the Drury Lane Theatre were called upon to provide prologues to insure the success of the plays they produced; and as actors they both conceived of prologues as acting pieces. The prologues which Cibber wrote for himself are quite as characteristic as the part of Sir Novelty Fashion, a role to which he continually reverted in speaking his prologues. Cibber's first venture in verse was an occasional prologue for the opening of Drury Lane, and his chagrin was acute when he was denied the opportunity of presenting his piece:

> You may imagine how hard I thought it, that they durst not trust my poor poetical Brat to my own Care. But since I found it was to be given into other Hands, I insisted that two Guineas should be the Price of my parting with it; which with a Sigh I received, and *Powel* spoke the Prologue: But every Line that was applauded went sorely to my Heart when I reflected that the same Praise might have been given to my own speaking; nor could the Success of the

Author compensate the Distress of the Actor. However, in the End, it serv'd in some sort to mend our
People's Opinion of me; and whatever the Criticks
might think of it, one of the Patentees (who, it is
true, knew no Difference between *Dryden* and
D'Urfey) said, upon the Success of it, that insooth! I
was an ingenious young Man.[8]

Cibber's prologues, whether written by himself or by
others, have a similarity which reveals their speaker, even
when his name is not printed with them. For example, it
is apparent that Thomas Killigrew wrote the prologue to
his comedy, *Chit-Chat* (1719), as an acting piece for Cibber,
incorporating into the fourth line Sir Novelty's affected
pronunciation.[9] On the basis of acting, the anonymous
epilogue to Farquhar's *Sir Harry Wildair* (1701) may also
be assigned to Cibber, the lines being an extension of the
part of the dishonest French refugee, which he had acted
in the play.

Comedians long established on the stage at the turn of
the century continued the coarse, boisterous, often funny
epilogue, the model for which had been created by the
Restoration actor, Joseph Haines. The epilogue of the
low comedians is characterized not only by its coarseness,
but by its spontaneity and its complete rapport with the
audience, a connection strengthened by gags and personal
references to the speaker.

Beyond all reach of rivals in the acclaim of the upper
gallery for the first twenty years of the century was the
droll, William Pinkethman.[1] Pinkethman's usual method

8. Cibber, *Apology*, I, 196.

9. *"Fops of Phaebus Strain."* The point of the familiar anecdote about
Cibber's ruining the part of Richard III by calling for a "harse" is that
he suddenly relapsed into Sir Novelty Fashion.

1. *A Comparison between the Two Stages* (1702), p. [199], describes
Pinkethman as "the Flower of . . . *Bartholomew-Fair*, and the Idol of
the Rabble. A fellow that over-does every thing, and spoils many a Part
with his own stuff." Davies, *Dramatic Miscellanies*, III, 89–90, comments

of presenting epilogues, similar to that of all other comedians, explains why a form lacking inherent merit continued to flourish during a period of great acting.[2] A popular comedian achieved his purpose by taking the audience
into his confidence, by personal reference, and by violating
Hamlet's injunction to the clown. That a speaker could
entirely alter his author's meaning without revising his
lines is shown in the epilogue spoken by Pinkethman to
Thomas Baker's *Hampstead-Heath* (1705). He can think,
he boasts, of fifty ways of improving the opening of the
epilogue, but as to the authors,

> *We with implicit Faith their Wit attest,*
> *Yet often make what they ne'er meant a Jest.*

How intimate Pinkethman's relationship was with his audience is illustrated by the lines immediately following
those just quoted:

> *I know the time when* Pinkethman *cou'd inchant ye:*
> *I'm sure you're always glad to see me,—an't ye?*
> *[To the Upper Gallery.]*
> *Each Rhyming Fop with half an Ounce o' Brains,*
> *My fair Idea in his Mind retains,*
> *And compliments me with a damn'd Side Leer:*
> *This Part will fit your Humour to a Hair.*

This is exactly the method used in the latter part of the
century by Foote and King and, *mutatis mutandis,* by
Mrs. Abington. Pinkethman maintained the same close

on Pinkethman's improvising to please the upper gallery. See also Leo
Hughes, *A Century of English Farce* (Princeton University Press, 1956),
pp. 182–183.

2. In addition to his fame in legitimate acting, Pinkethman achieved
lasting notoriety by speaking an epilogue while mounted on an ass. The
feat was first performed by the Restoration comedian, Dogget, and was
repeated by his successor, Haines. After Pinkethman's death, the epilogue
was inherited by a long line of comedians and was spoken as late as
1818 by Liston in Covent Garden. (See Wiley, *Rare Prologues,* pp. 199–
203, and Genest, VIII, 661.)

relationship with the audience in the prologue to Mrs.
Centlivre's *The Basset-Table* (1706) and in the epilogue
to Betterton's *The Sequel of Henry the Fourth* (1707).
Leonard Welsted in the prologue to Steele's *The Conscious
Lovers* (1722), spoken by Wilks, describes various strata-
gems used by current writers to win over the audience:

> *Some fix all Wit and Humour in Grimace,*
> *And make a Livelyhood of* Pinkey's *Face.*

Prologues frequently coupled the names of Pinkethman
and Henry Norris, the comedian who earned an im-
mortality by his brilliant interpretation of the part of
Dicky in Farquhar's *The Constant Couple or a Trip to the
Jubilee* (1699). In Cibber's *Love Makes a Man* (1700),
Norris played Sancho, the servant, and Pinkethman the
whimsical but kind old man, Don Lewis. The prologue
assures the audience that the play will contain enough
mistakes to please the critics, fashions for the beaux, tears
for the ladies, and

> *For the Galleries, we've* Dicky *and* Penkethman.

Gay, in the mock prologue to the unacted farce, *The
Mohocks,* published in 1712, refers to both comedians,
but with some reservations in his praise. The lines are "To
be Spoken by the Publisher":

> *THIS Farce, if the kind Players had thought fit,*
> *With Action had supply'd its want of Wit.*
> *Oh Readers! had you seen the* Mohocks *rage,*
> *And frighted Watchmen tremble on the Stage;*
> *Had you but seen our Mighty* Emperor *stalk;*
> *And heard in* Cloudy *honest* Dicky *talk,*
> *Seen* Pinkethman *in strutting* Prig *appear,*
> *And 'midst of Danger wisely lead the Rear,*
> *It might have pleas'd; for now-a-days the Joke*
> *Rises or falls as with* Grimace *'tis spoke.*

The inclusion of personal references to the speaker remained a favorite device for low comedians and flourished with such actors as Foote and Shuter,[3] but was by no means confined to them. The audience was always avid for information about actors and amused by gossip concerning their affairs, private and professional. Sometimes the author referred to the entire company; for example, in the prologue to *The Rivals*, spoken on the tenth night, following the current disavowal of the *comédie larmoyante*, Sheridan describes all the leading actors of Covent Garden as done to death by the Sentimental Muse. Murphy, in the prologue to *No One's Enemy but His Own* (1764), a comedy in which Woodward and Shuter played the leading characters, reveals the difficulties the author encounters in confronting the critics and adds:

> These are known dangers; and, still full as certain,
> The bard meets other ills behind the curtain.
> Little you think, ere yet you fix his fate,
> What previous mischiefs there in ambush wait;
> What plagues arise from all the mimic throng:
> "My part's too short;—and, Sir, my part's too long."
> This calls for incident; that repartee.
> "Down the back-stairs pen an escape for me.
> "Give me a ladder, Mr. Bayes, or rope;
> "I love to wear the breeches, and elope.
> "Something for me the groundlings ears to split.
> "Write a dark closet, or a fainting-fit.
> "Fix Woodward in some whimsical disgrace:
> "Or be facetious with Ned Shuter's face."

The personal reference could also be of a more serious nature and could be used with finesse. In the opening lines

3. See, for example, Foote's egregious, but very entertaining piece, *The Trip to Paris*, spoken by Shuter at a benefit performance and printed in *A Collection and Selection of English Prologues and Epilogues*, III, 172–174.

of the epilogue to *The Brothers* (1769), Cumberland paid
Garrick a graceful compliment:

> WHO but has seen the celebrated strife,
> Where *Reynolds* calls the Canvass into Life;
> And, 'twixt the Tragic, and the comic Muse,
> Courted of both, and dubious where to chuse,
> Th' immortal Actor stands?—[4]

Garrick was in the audience and was pleased with so flattering a description.[5] The lines lost nothing by being spoken
by Mrs. Yates and in the rival theatre.

Throughout his prologues Garrick made frequent references to his theatrical career, and such was his fame that
an indirect and somewhat subtle allusion to his acting
would be understood even in a provincial theatre; for example, he obviously intended the comparison in the
prologue for the opening of the Bristol Theatre in 1766
to recall to the audience his interpretation of Abel Drugger
in *The Alchemist*. The stage-manager in his new venture
is seeking the philosopher's stone:

> But in projection comes the dreadful stroke,
> The glasses burst, and all is bounce and smoke!
> Tho' doubtful still our fate—I bite my thumbs,
> And my heart fails me,—when projection comes.

The lines supplement the vivid description by Georg
Christoph Lichtenberg, a German traveller and an enthusiastic theatre-goer, who visited England in 1775 and
was astonished at witnessing Garrick's complete transformation of his highly sensitive features into the blankness of the slow-witted tobacconist.[6]

4. Sir Joshua Reynolds's famous portrait of Garrick between Tragedy
and Comedy was painted in 1762.

5. Genest, v, 282.

6. Georg Christoph Lichtenberg, *Lichtenberg's Visits to England as
Described in His Letters and Diaries*, ed. Margaret L. Mare and W. H.

The personal reference was often used as a rhetorical device to introduce impersonation. Mrs. Yates, speaking Garrick's epilogue to Murphy's *The Orphan of China* (1759), pretends that a member of the audience has asked her about the social customs of the Chinese:

> *I long to know it—Do the creatures visit?*
> *Dear Mrs. Yates, do, tell us—Well, how is it?*

A comment made by Lichtenberg explains the popularity of the epilogue to *The Orphan of China*. In describing Mrs. Yates, he says: "She is so skilled in the management of her arms that from this woman alone could be made an abstract of the art of gesticulation." [7] The epilogue, with its personal reference to the actress, was written for the sole purpose of giving the audience the pleasure of seeing Mrs. Yates flirt with her fan. Mrs. Yates was one of the greatest tragic actresses of the English stage, statuesque and capable of expressing the deepest pathos by her elocution and gestures. Her versatility is proved by her success in such impersonation in the frivolous epilogue.

This particular kind of personal reference, introduced as an imaginary conversation between the actor and audience, was common at the close of the century. The opening lines of Jerningham's epilogue to *The Siege of Berwick* (1793) show how closely subsequent writers followed Garrick's method:

> *Methinks I hear you say, Dear Mrs. POPE,[8]*
> *Amidst what mould'ring Annals did you grope,*

Quarrell (Oxford, The Clarendon Press, 1938), pp. 3–4. The prologue, epilogue, and playbill for the opening night are printed in Richard Jenkins, *Memoirs of the Bristol Stage* (Bristol, 1826), pp. 77–80.

7. Lichtenberg, *Visits*, p. 14.

8. Mrs. Pope was Elizabeth Younge until her marriage in 1785 to the actor, Alexander Pope. Although she made her first appearance in 1768, no epilogue seems to have been assigned to her before 1772, when she

> *And dig, from out the mine of tragic ore,*
> *A tale unfashion'd from the days of yore.*

Reference of somewhat the same kind was used by Matthew Gregory Lewis in the prologue to *The East Indian* (1799) in an ecstatic allusion to the popular actress, Mrs. Jordan, for whose benefit the play was performed:

> Thalia bids his play to-night appear,
> Thalia call'd in heaven, but Jordan here.

There is a personal quality about all the epilogues written for Mrs. Jordan which proves how certain she was of the response of her audiences. In the epilogue to *The Greek Slave* (1791) she comments on her most successful characters, a device commonly used to win the audience by pleasant reminiscences, declaring that critics will certainly condemn the manager who has turned their Hoyden and Romp into a tragic princess.[9]

The personal reference could be extended into a sort of dramatized biography, a fact rather painfully illustrated by the address spoken by Mrs. Siddons on May 21, 1782, upon her leaving the Bath Theatre for Drury Lane.[1] For this occasion, after appearing as Andromache in *The Distrest Mother,* she delivered an epilogue in the course of which she introduced to the audience her "three reasons" for leaving Bath, *i.e.* her three children, whom she had kept out of sight in the dressing room until they were needed on the stage. The quality of Mrs. Siddons's address may be judged by the following couplet, spoken as she pointed to her children:

---

appeared in Garrick's epilogue to Murphy's *The Grecian Daughter.* She distinguished herself in epilogues by Cumberland and Holcroft.

9. The *European Magazine*, April 1791, p. 307.

1. See Genest, VI, 236.

These are the moles that heave me from your side,
Where I was rooted, where I could have died.[2]

Authors vied in prologues in paying tribute to Mrs. Siddons. Arthur Murphy, commemorating Mrs. Cibber and Garrick, describes Melpomene discovering their great successor:

> She mourn'd their loss, then fled to western skies,
> And saw at *Bath* another Genius rise.
> Old *Drury's* scene the goddess bade her chuse—
> The actress heard, and spake herself a muse.[3]

Colman's prologue to a performance of *Tancred and Sigismunda* in 1784 contains a fine compliment to Mrs. Siddons in the part of the heroine.[4] But Mrs. Siddons herself, unlike Mrs. Cibber and Mrs. Yates, was entirely unfitted to deliver comic epilogues. Such appeals as that which she makes in the epilogue to Mrs. Cowley's *The Fate of Sparta* (1788),

COUNSELLOR SIDDONS—do you know the name!

are leaden, and while the words purported to be frivolous, the actress remained the Tragic Muse.

Obviously it was not through personal or biographical reference but through the prologues as acting pieces that the speakers were revealed. In general the author of a prologue kept in mind the temperament and special ability, the "prologue character," of the speaker for whom he was writing, and around these he built his piece. Woodward, great comedian though he was, could not have spoken prologues written for Foote, dependent upon a

---

2. James Boaden, *Memoirs of Mrs. Siddons* (1827), I, 285.
3. "Occasional Prologue to Introduce Miss Brunton," the *European Magazine*, October 1785, p. 308.
4. The *London Magazine*, July 1784, pp. 75–76.

particularly insinuating grimace; much less could Foote
have spoken Woodward's prologues, sedate and refined
even when they are playful. Mrs. Clive could not have
spoken Mrs. Abington's or Miss Farren's epilogues, which
imitate the airs of the fine ladies in the boxes; Mrs. Abington and Miss Farren would have disdained attempting
Mrs. Clive's boisterous epilogues, addressed to the pit and
galleries. There is a similarity between the epilogues written for Mrs. Barry and Mrs. Mattocks in that they are directed to an audience entirely different from that of the
opening years of the century. Their pieces are commonplace in subject and lack subtlety in humour, but even
within these limits, Mrs. Mattocks developed a style, in
speaking an epilogue, peculiar to herself.

In Garrick the prologue as acting piece reached its
height. Throughout his entire career, 1741 to 1776, he was
in constant demand as a speaker of both prologues and
epilogues, at least twenty of which he wrote in order to
give full play to his power of rapid impersonation. During
these years Garrick appeared in over thirty new prologues
and epilogues, almost half of which fall between 1750 and
1760. His pieces are invariably lively and are further characterized by frequent references to theatrical news, topical
allusions, and parodies of famous lines from Shakespeare.
Above all else they were parts to be acted, as will be illustrated in the following chapter. His most popular prologues and epilogues established themselves as independent
pieces in his repertoire.[5]

Thomas Davies, commenting on the prologue which
Garrick spoke at the command performance of *Much Ado
about Nothing* (1765), makes an observation applicable
to all Garrick's prologues and epilogues: "Whatever de-

5. See *Drury Lane Calendar*, passim, for the enthusiasm which greeted
Garrick in his prologues.

fects the critical eye may discover in reading this composition, they were all amply supplied by the speaker. The
archness of his look, the propriety of his action, and the
general touch of humour and pleasantry which accompanied every line he spoke, drew from the audience loud
and involuntary mirth, with the greatest applause which
had ever been known in a theatre." [6]

The same defense is urged by Dr. John Brown regarding
Garrick's prologue and epilogue to the tragedy, *Barbarossa* (1754). Garrick allowed Brown to have both pieces
printed simply because it was customary for them to appear
with the play. "He is very sensible that they can have little
or no Merit in the Reading, their Effect wholly depending
upon the Characters which speak them, and the Novelty of
introducing them." [7]

These and similar caveats to the reader find ample justification in many of Garrick's prologues. An excellent example occurs in the prologue to Delap's *Hecuba* (1761),
a piece written for Garrick by his friend, Robert Lloyd,
author of *The Actor*. In themselves the lines are crude
and the personal reference gross, but they provided Garrick
an opportunity for brilliant acting by rapid change of
facial expression from eager alertness into the most passive
blankness. Lloyd pretends to wish that the devices of the
Greek stage could be revived. Garrick, lacking in stature,
would then strut a giant, while he was safely hidden behind
his mask:

> *No features then the poet's mind would trace,*
> *But one blank vizor blot out all the face.*
> *O! glorious times, when actors thus could strike*
> *Expressive, inexpressive, all alike!*

6. Thomas Davies, *Memoirs of the Life of David Garrick, Esq.* . . .
Third Edition (1781), II, 100–101.

7. See Brown's note in the first edition of *Barbarossa*, 1755.

Parts like Lloyd's prologue to *Hecuba* led Johnson to observe of Garrick that "no man's face has had more wear and tear." [8]

For the complete understanding of any prologue, the reader must reconstruct with his imagination the entire presentation—the interplay between the audience and the actor and the actor's voice, gestures, and facial expression. Genest, after recording that Garrick spoke the prologue to *The Male Coquet* (1757) at a performance on March 27, 1759, makes the comment: "—this Prologue has but little merit, yet Garrick seems to have been particularly fond of speaking it." [9] Genest failed to consider in the prologue the series of impersonations on which it is built. Garrick wrote it to delight the audience in seeing him assume the "gaping Bumpkin," the gamester, the fickle fine lady, and finally the great actor, David Garrick, as the Macbeth of the banquet scene.

Almost as popular as Garrick himself in prologues was the comic actor, Thomas King, to whom after 1760 Garrick entrusted prologues which otherwise would have fallen to his own lot. King spoke the prologue to *Polly Honeycombe* on December 5, 1760, and from then until the end of the century, he remained without a rival and in constant demand. The article on King in *Theatrical Biography*, written before he reached the height of his success, concludes:

> As a prologue-speaker in the comic style, he is undoubtedly unapproachable (but by Mr. Garrick.) There is a happy distinction in his ease, manner, familiarity, and acting those dramatic exordiums, so as to render them, in his possession, entertainments of the first kind; indeed, the audience are so sensible of this, that they never omit calling for them on those

8. Boswell, *Life*, II, 410.
9. Genest, IV, 548.

nights the pieces are represented, with an avidity and
impatience that strongly indicate their pleasure.[1]

There was a general agreement that a play introduced by
King would meet with favor:

> —says the Bard, Master King,
> My Diligence here is a slight little thing;
> But slight as it is, perchance it may thrive,
> Could I get such a Coachman as you are to drive.[2]

An anonymous tribute to King's acting was printed in
the *Public Advertiser* for October 31, 1764, at the time
when Garrick was travelling on the continent. The verses
refer to Ranger, the hero of Hoadly's *The Suspicious Husband*, a part originally written for Garrick and one of
his most distinguished characters, but the author thinks
King quite his equal. The comparison is implied in the
title: *On Seeing Mr. King in the Character of Ranger.*

> Ah me! cry'd Nature—*Garrick* gone!
>   Thalia then adieu.
> My fav'rite Son from Drury flown,
>   No Joy I find with you.
>
> The Muse their mutual Loss confess'd,
>   But begg'd her lovely Friend

---

1. *Theatrical Biography: or, Memoirs of the Principal Performers of
the Three Theatres Royal* (Two vols., 1772), I, 120–121.

2. Epilogue to the anonymous and unpublished farce, *Jehu* (Drury
Lane, February 19, 1779), printed in *Lloyd's Evening Post*, Feb. 24–26,
1779. All that is known about the piece is that it failed because of its
satirical nature (*Biographia Dramatica*, II, 343) and that "The Whip
Epilogue, written by the Author of the Piece, and spoken by Mr. King,
was humourous, and very well." *Lloyd's Evening Post*, Feb. 22–24, 1779.
The main piece of the evening was Jephson's *The Law of Lombardy*, "The
Prologue to be spoken by Mr. Farren, and the Epilogue by Miss Younge."
Public Advertiser, Feb. 20, 1779. Hence King's epilogue was the second
spoken during the evening.

(To calm the Grief that swell'd her Breast)
Next Evening to attend.

In Drury's Pit the Couple met,
    When *King* in *Ranger* shone;
Soon Nature cry'd, with Heart elate,
    I still have left a Son.

In the character of Ranger, King delivered the famous epilogue, *Bucks, Have at Ye All,* which he first spoke after a
benefit performance of *The Suspicious Husband* in Dublin
in 1754. The authorship of the piece is uncertain. It has
been attributed to Thomas Mozeen, a minor playwright,[3]
to Garrick,[4] and to King himself.[5] *Lloyd's Evening Post,*
March 4–6, 1771, printed the epilogue as it had appeared
annexed to "*an Heroic Poem, entitled* CRICKET, *by Mr.
Love.*" *Theatrical Biography,* published the following
year, also attributes the piece to James Love (*i.e.* James
Dance), who after a few years on the English stage had gone
to Ireland, and ". . . at this period wrote his much admired prologue of '*Bucks have at ye All,*' for Mr. King,
the speaking of which acquired that admirable comedian
so much applause." [6] The epilogue, which will be discussed
in reference to the audience of the eighteenth century,[7] is a
noisy, intimate piece, fitted equally to Ranger and to King,
and still alive with the clamor and excitement of the playhouse:

3. John O'Keeffe, *Recollections* (1826), I, 215.
4. "Bucks, Have at Ye All; or, The Picture of a Play-House." By David
Garrick, Esq., *Supplement to Bell's British Theatre* (1784), IV, 391–392.
5. *Catalogue of the Larpent Plays in the Huntington Library.* Compiled
by Dougald MacMillan (1939), Item 175, p. 30. Lacy and Garrick applied
to have the piece licensed on March 26, 1760, to be spoken at King's
benefit, under the title, *The Picture of a Play House; or, Bucks Have
at Ye All.* To the licenser's entry J. P. Collier added a note: "King's
writing and authorship."
6. *Theatrical Biography,* I, 138.
7. See below, p. 154.

>   Ye *Bucks* assembled at your *Ranger's* call,
>   By Heav'n I know ye, and *have at ye all!*

The upper-gallery, who have most eagerly called for the epilogue, "out-talk the players," and, engaged in their own conversation, give no heed to the "chatt'ring" of Tom King:

>   . . . *entre nous,* behind the Scenes he 'as swore,
>   And bad me say't—he'll answer you no more.[8]

The most amusing of the many personal references to King's prologues is in Garrick's rehearsal play, *A Peep behind the Curtain.* King, who is acting the part of the hopeful author, Glib, says to Patent, the manager: "I depend upon *you* for a prologue—your genius.—" Patent, *i.e.* Garrick, replies: "You are too polite, Mr. Glib—have you an Epilogue?" The conversation proceeds to the amusement of an audience quite aware of the incessant demands for Garrick's prologues and of King's mannerisms and eccentricities which made him the first of prologue speakers. Glib admits: "I have a kind of Address here, by way of Epilogue, to the town—I suppose it to be spoken by myself, as the Author—who have you can represent me?— no easy task, let me tell you,—he must be a little smart, degageè, and not want assurance." Patent considers, "Smart, degageè, and not want assurance—*King* is the very man." Glib replies, ". . . Thank, thank you, dear Mr. Patent,—the very man—is he in the house! I wou'd read it to him." Patent thinks that Mr. King is not in the house,

---

8. Other actors adopted King's epilogue. Tate Wilkinson added it to his repertoire. (*Memoirs,* III, 64, 69, 86.) Lewis was so popular in *Bucks Have at Ye All* that the epilogue became a bugbear to him. He finally stipulated one evening, when the audience called for it, to recite it a given number of times and then no more. O'Keefe's *Recollections,* II, 293–294.

for since his success in Garrick's musical sketch, *Linco's Travels,* he has been at home practicing on his fiddle, whenever he is not needed at Drury Lane. Glib says sadly, "Conceit, conceit, Mr. Patent, is the ruin of 'em all," and King imitates his own presentation of epilogues: "I could wish, when he speaks this Address, that he wou'd be more easy in his carriage, and not have that damn'd jerk in his bow, that he generally treats us with." When Patent answers, "I'll hint as much to him," the author demonstrates how an actor should comport himself in presenting the epilogue. It would be difficult to find a scene which illustrates more vividly the interest of the audience in the delivery of epilogues in general and of King's in particular. Here Garrick, who, as author and manager in good earnest, is relying on the applause which he knows will greet King's presentation of his epilogue, has King ridicule his own acting in order to show how a skilful actor would perform the piece!

King was a man whom everyone liked; his prologues, written for the most part by Garrick and Colman, are all genial and reflect his friendliness and good-nature. In the opening lines of Bickerstaffe's prologue to *The Absent Man* (1768)—a farce bearing a very happy dedication to "Mr. King"—King admonishes the audience:

> ERE the curtain draws up, list a little to me:
> Are you all in a very good humour? Let's see.

Authors made constant use of the goodwill of the audience for King as a man. Garrick's prologue to *A Peep behind the Curtain,* as well as the epilogue that I have just discussed, was spoken by King. Introducing the plot of the play and the character that King is to act, Garrick has him declare:

I, Thomas King, *of* King-street, *am the poet,*

and surely no audience would damn a play written by
King!—a clever stroke by Garrick to insure favor for his
play.

The murder's out—the murderer detected;
May in one night, be try'd, condemn'd, dissected.
'Tis said, for Scandal's tongue will never cease;
That mischief's meant against our little piece:
Let me look round, I'll tell you how the case is—
There's not one frown a single brow disgraces;
I never saw a sweeter set of faces!
Suppose Old Nick, *before you righteous folk,*
Produce a farce, brimful of mirth and joke;
Tho' he, at other times, wou'd fire your blood;
You'd clap his piece, and swear, 'twas devilish *good!*
Malice prepense! 'tis false!—it cannot be—
Light is my heart, from apprehension free—
If you wou'd save Old Nick, *you'd never damn poor me.*

Garrick is looking askance at an audience given to uncritical acceptance of farce, but at the same time he is
making success sure by relying on King's popularity.

   Garrick wrote prologues for King to offset the mood of
sentimental comedy; for example, Hugh Kelly intended to
have a serious prologue to *False Delicacy* (1768), ". . . but
as Mr. King was to speak it, Mr Garrick, with great propriety, thought a piece of humour would be best suited to
the talents of that excellent actor," and he therefore completely revised Kelly's prologue.[9] When he found it expedient to sponsor what Goldsmith called the "laughing
comedy," he wrote literally "laughing" prologues for King.
Like Samuel Foote, King could win an audience by simple

   9. Kelly's note to *False Delicacy* (1768).

58 PROLOGUES AND EPILOGUES

grimace and leer, but his insinuations, unlike Foote's, were never used for selfish or satirical purposes. Garrick ends his prologue to *Albumazar* (1773) with an allusion to King's purchase of a part of Sadler's Wells, a place where laughter is still secure. The stage directions following the prologue read, *"Exit huzzaing and laughing."* For over fifty years King afforded his audience this kind of merriment.

Colman's brilliant prologue to Garrick's *Bon Ton* (1775) [1] provided King an opportunity for varied and most entertaining impersonation. The piece is still amusing, and it has through the lapse of time acquired the additional merit of being instructive, as it is a lively description of London in the latter years of the eighteenth century. It was this prologue which Johnson at Mrs. Abington's benefit "could hear pretty well from the more slow and distinct utterance." [2] In the comedy King acted the part of the earnest old knight, Sir John Trotley, who is shocked at the frivolity and dissoluteness of London society. The character is foreshadowed in the prologue, which is a commentary on current fashions and pastimes. King impersonates, in turn, the "roaring boy" of 1775; the citizen's wife, complacent and prosperous; and the belle, whose life consists of routs and loo. The prologue, as it was printed, contains a criticism of the Earl of Chesterfield, the *Letters* having appeared in 1774, the year after the Earl's death.

1. *Bon Ton* was published by Garrick's friend, Thomas Becket, in 1775, with the following note:

THIS little Drama, which had been thrown aside for many years, was brought out last season, with some alterations, for the benefit of Mr. KING, as a token of regard for one, who, during a long engagement, was never known, unless confined by real illness, to disappoint the Public, or distress the Managers—The Author is sincerely apprehensive that the excellence of the performance upon the stage, will greatly lessen its credit with the readers in the closet.

2. See above, p. 16.

The passage is an absurdly distorted summary of Chester-field's advice and, according to a footnote in the first edition of the play, it was "omitted at the Theatre"; but the lines were written for King to act and are an excellent illustration of the kind of impersonation in which he most excelled. Colman has just described and given specific examples of the triviality and irresponsibility of the aristocracy. *"This is* Bon Ton, *and this we call* the world!"

True, says my Lord; and thou my only son,
Whate'er you're faults, ne'er sin against Bon Ton!
Who toils for learning at a publick school,
And digs for Greek and Latin is a fool.
French, French, my boy's the thing! jasez! *prate, chatter!*
Trim be the mode, whipt-syllabub the matter!
Walk like a Frenchman! for on English pegs
Moves native aukwardness with two left legs.

.   .   .   .

.   .   .   .

But never laugh, *whatever jest prevails!*
Nothing but nonsense e'er gave laughter birth,
That vulgar way the vulgar shew their mirth.
Laughter's a rude convulsion, sense that justles,
Disturbs the cockles, and distorts the muscles.
Hearts may be black, but all should wear clean faces;
The Graces, boy! the Graces, Graces, Graces!

Even after these lines, so admirably adapted to King, had been forfeited, the piece was received with great applause. Genest records: "—the Prologue by Colman was so good and so well delivered, that King always spoke it till he left the stage," [3]—a period of twenty-seven years.

In 1780 Sheridan wrote King an acting prologue to Lady Craven's *The Miniature Picture,* some lines of which refer to the importation of French actors into Drury Lane The-

3. Genest, v, 450.

atre and to the offer of a friend to teach the regular company to speak French:

> Told us 'twas time to study what was good,
> Polish, and leave off being understood;
> That crouded audiences we thus might bring
> To Monsieur Parsons and Chevalier King.

Sheridan used the first thirty lines of this inordinately long
piece as the prologue to *Pizarro* (1799), and again after
this lapse of nineteen years the prologue was "spoken by
Mr. King." [4] The lines which are suitable to *The Miniature Picture* are an entirely unfitting introduction to the
overwrought emotions and the odd mixture of romanticism
and violence of *Pizarro*. As it was extraordinary even in
the last years of the century to have so frivolous a prologue
to a tragedy, the inference is that the lines were revived
as a separate acting piece by which King could once more
delight the audience.

The most famous of all King's prologues is that by
Garrick to *The School for Scandal* (1777). King, who that
night reached the acme of his career as Sir Peter Teazle,
impersonated alternately the disreputable Lady Worm-
wood, given to malicious gossip, and her servant, Lisp,
ready to divert her by reading scandal from the newspaper.
The imaginary conversation is carried over directly into
the opening speeches of the play.

King's acting inspired his authors. One of the best of his
epilogues was written by Harriet Lee for her sister Sophia's
tragedy, *Almeyda* (1796).[5] The piece is so characteristic of
King that I shall quote it at length. He enters "in a Crier's
Gown, and with a Bell," making the usual pretense that
the epilogue has been lost and that he must supply one:

4. See above, p. 22. The thirty lines constitute the entire prologue to
Pizarro, except for the final couplet.
5. King's name does not appear with the epilogue printed with the
play. For the ascription, see the *European Magazine*, May 1796, p. 347.

—*Rare work, there, my friends! rare storming and fury.*
No Epilogue's coming to-night, I assure you!—
Sure never poor author like ours has been crost:
When meant to be spoken, she found it was lost.
Lost, *Ma'am, says the Prompter, all pale at the sound!*
Lost, Ma'am, do you say? was re-echoed around.—
Lost—stol'n, *she replied; 'tis in vain to deny it;*
So, dear Mr. KING, *be so good as to cry it.*
The thought was an odd one, you'll say—so did I:
But when ladies intreat, we are bound to comply.
Oyez! Oyez! Oyez! [Rings the Bell again.
    Be it known,
To all it concerns, Wit, Critick, or Town,
That whoe'er brings it back shall receive, besides praise,
A handsome reward of a crown, too—of bays;
Whereas, if detain'd, heavy law-suits will follow,
And damage be sued for, in court of Apollo.
Rare menaces these! you see how it stands—
She'll indite you all round; so up with your hands.
I'll examine each face, too—In truth, a fine show.—
Whom first shall I try? Oh! my friends here below.
The Box claim precedence: but there I've my fears;
Perhaps they'll demand to be tried by their peers.
Yet methinks, when I view the fair circle around,
I'm in hopes they'll not ask for what cannot be found.
An Epilogue stol'n, cries Old Crusty, out yonder!
                    [Pointing to the Pit.
A fine prize, indeed! who should steal it, I wonder?
He, surely, must be a strange dolt, who contested
A bill on Parnassus, so often protested.—
Nay, Sirs, 'tis a loss; so, pray ye, don't flout it.—
Good or bad, custom's all, *and we can't do without it.*
Yet, in search of our stray, I'll e'en now look elsewhere.
There's no wit in't, I'm sure, so it cannot be there.
—*Higher up, then—Hey—what—Nay, come, I'll not*
    wrong ye.

[To the Galleries.
Not one roguish face can I spy out among ye.
But sound hearts and sound heads, with too great a store
Of mirth in yourselves, to steal from the poor.
All good men and true. So I give up the cause.
And since, then, our Bard can't bring you to the laws,
E'en let her be the Culprit, and steal—your applause.
         God save the King!
                              [Rings the bell, and exit.

The devices used in this epilogue had been used in hundreds of others, but King gave them new life. Even the pun
in the last line is eloquent of his popularity.

   Although in the latter half of the century no actor surpassed Garrick and King as speakers of prologues, yet they
had distinguished rivals. Foote, entirely lacking in King's
geniality, had his own method of making the audience
laugh, partly through facial expression and partly through
admonition:

You all have a right your sweet muscles to curl,
From the old smirking prude, to the titt'ring young girl;
And ever with pleasure my brains I cou'd spin,
To make you all giggle, and you, ye gods, grin.[6]

Foote's special "humour" in his prologues was an extension
of that in his plays—the illustration by specific examples
of his Aristophanic theory of satire.

   A comedian of a very different stamp from either King
or Foote was Henry Woodward, celebrated in his prologues for grace and dignity, coupled with a kind of elfish
fantasy. One of his first prologues is a prototype of all those
that followed it until his death in 1777. He played Tom
Thumb at Goodman's Fields on May 5, 1731. Genest
quotes a notice of the performance: "Tom Thumb—Mas-

   6. Prologue by Garrick to Bickerstaffe's *Dr. Last in His Chariot* (1769).

ter Woodward, with a new Prologue written by Master
Woodward and spoken by the author in the character of
Tom Thumb." [7] The following year a pantomime, *Harlequin's Contrivance,* was performed, in which Harlequin
was "to be attempted by Young Woodward." [8] As a member of Rich's Lilliputian Troupe at Lincoln's Inn Fields,
Woodward had been instructed by John Rich, and, excepting his teacher, he became at once the greatest Harlequin of the English stage. He revived famous pantomimes
such as *Harlequin Dr. Faustus* and *Harlequin Sorcerer* and
devised new ones of his own.[9] His pantomime, *Queen Mab,*
first acted in Dublin in 1748, was two years later trans-
ferred to Drury Lane. Murphy says that Garrick used the
piece in opposing the rival company under Rich at Covent
Garden, "and through the rest of the season the success
was so great, that Rich began to tremble on his throne." [1]
Mrs. Cibber, in the prologue to her one-act fantasy, *The
Oracle* (1752), pays Woodward a compliment on the popularity of the pantomime:

> *But then we have some Pantomime to shew,*
> *Machines in shape of men that come and go;*
> *A Fairy too—Odso!—I should not blab—*
> *Well—but—I know you hugely lik'd* Queen Mab.

But Woodward's greatness also lay in his interpretation of
characters other than Harlequin. Murphy describes the
rival productions of *Romeo and Juliet* in 1750: "Woodward, in *Mercutio,* was a tower of strength; a character so
highly finished, so whimsical, yet natural, so eccentric, yet
sensible, and altogether so entertaining, cannot be found

7. Genest, III, 320.
8. Genest, III, 357.
9. For Woodward's pantomimes, see Allardyce Nicoll, *A History of Late
Eighteenth Century Drama 1750–1800,* pp. 209; 317; and below, Chapter 5,
p. 196, n. 8.
1. Arthur Murphy, *The Life of David Garrick, Esq.,* (1801), I, 199.

in any play whatever, and no actor ever reached the
vivacity of Woodward." [2] Woodward's success as Harlequin
and Mercutio suggested to Garrick his trivial social satire,
Lilliput. A Dramatic Entertainment (1756). The prologue,
spoken by Woodward, introduces scraps of Mercutio's description of Queen Mab, fragments of poetry ill-suited with
Garrick's own prosaic observations on the nature of fairies,
but both the comedy and the prologue met with favor.

Although there is a delicacy of humor and a general liveliness in all the pieces written for Woodward, they lack in
the reading the strongly marked features of prologues for
Garrick or King; nonetheless he had characteristics and
mannerisms which could be imitated. Mrs. Abington
deeply offended him when they were both in Ireland in
1762 by speaking an epilogue after a performance of *Rule
a Wife and Have a Wife* in Woodward's manner, ridiculing
him.[3] His prologues in general seem an expression of his
personality rather than acting pieces.

Woodward died on April 17, 1777. James Boaden in the
Memoirs of Mrs. Siddons, recording the date, mentions his
genius for pantomime and his triumph in the part of
Marplot, the hero of Mrs. Centlivre's long-lived comedy,
The Busie Body: "Lee Lewes, in default of a better, had
destined himself some way to succeed Woodward, and
Sheridan, to whom everybody now turned as the rising
muse, honoured his benefit with a few lines, which he
spoke in the character of Harlequin, to the memory of
Woodward." [4] Boaden then quotes Sheridan's lines in
which the names of Rich and Woodward are joined:

"But hence with tragic strains, unless to mourn
That LUN and MARPLOT here shall ne'er return;
The comic muse, who still with anxious pride

2. *Ibid.,* I, 193.
3. Wilkinson, *Memoirs,* III, 90.
4. Boaden, *Memoirs of Mrs. Siddons,* I, 107.

The claim of motley Pantomime denied,
Now humbly hangs o'er Woodward's recent bier,
Sees the fantastic mimic mourner there,
Yet deigns to join in grief, and sheds a kindred tear."

I have been unable to discover where this prologue was printed. It was spoken at the revival of *The Royal Chace; or, Harlequin Skeleton,* a pantomime which had been performed at Covent Garden as early as 1738 and revived for Lewes's benefit on April 23, 1777.[5] Sheridan might well mourn the death of Woodward for there was no other actor on either stage who could achieve his quality of mingled playfulness, dignity, and difficult humor which characterize his prologues.

In the closing years of the century the most popular speakers of prologues were John Palmer [6] and a younger actor, John Bannister, usually mentioned as "Mr. Bannister, jun." to distinguish him from his father, Charles Bannister, also an actor. The number of prologues assigned to Palmer, many of them by Colman, the elder, is sufficient proof of his success, although his pieces in general lack liveliness and apparently offered more opportunity for elocution than for acting. The epilogue to *Ways and Means* (1788) by George Colman, the younger, spoken by Palmer, is an excellent acting piece, but this is the exception rather than the rule. The speaker is a critic who has high praise for the actors and is certain that the comedy will soon rise to fame:

"*Young Bannister* bustled, in hopes of it's rising,
"And *Palmer's* exertions were really surprising."

5. The *Public Advertiser* for April 23, 1777, announces the pantomime to be performed that day, "With a Prologue, in the Character of Harlequin, by Mr. Lee Lewes." Lewes played Harlequin Jupiter. The pantomime and prologue were repeated on April 24 and May 1.
6. He is not to be confused with the other John Palmer, Mrs. Pritchard's son-in-law. See *Drury Lane Calendar,* p. xxiii.

The prologues written for Bannister are acting pieces, full of the noise and gaiety of the crowded theatre. Bannister's biographer, John Adolphus, says that the actor owed his favorable reception on the London stage to his skill in speaking Garrick's prologue to Murphy's *The Apprentice*. The prologue, originally spoken by Murphy himself in 1756, became the recognized property of Woodward, who spoke it in the character of Dick, the apprentice. When Bannister appeared in the comedy at the Haymarket in 1778, he "did not shrink from the comparison; and his success in delivering these prefatory verses assured his favourable reception throughout the performance. In fact, the part appeared to be made for him." Adolphus ends his account of Bannister as Dick by saying that the play was never announced in the bills without "the original prologue." [7] Among Bannister's most amusing pieces are the prologues to *A Turk and No Turk* (1785) by Colman, the younger; to *The Projects* by James Cobb (1786); and Holcroft's prologue to Mrs. Inchbald's *The Widow's Vow* (1786)—all excellent in their sprightliness. Bannister was the last actor of the century to be famous as a speaker of prologues.

The epilogue was of even more strategic importance than the prologue, for if it gained applause in its own right, it thereby "saved" the play. The prologue was usually assigned to an actor, the epilogue to an actress, the chief exception being, as the previous discussion has shown, epilogues spoken in character by comic actors, such as Weston, King, and Shuter. Great actresses were not all equally successful in presenting epilogues; furthermore, the epilogue during the course of the century underwent a transformation, so that the special skill demanded of

7. John Adolphus, *Memoirs of John Bannister, Comedian* (1839), I, 26–27.

Mrs. Oldfield in speaking the epilogue to *The Distrest Mother* (1712) was different from that demanded of Mrs. Abington in speaking the epilogue to *The Maid of the Oaks* (1774).

Mrs. Oldfield was by far the most popular speaker of epilogues in the first three decades of the century. Cibber, Addison, Rowe, Vanbrugh, Pope, Prior, and Gay wrote epilogues for her. She inherited from the Restoration a definite kind of comic epilogue that had become stereotyped when the success of the epilogue to *The Distrest Mother* [8] gave it renewed and long life. The epilogue to Benjamin Martyn's tragedy, *Timoleon*,[9] which she spoke in 1730, the year of her untimely death, is a good example of the method, subject-matter, and tone of these pieces. In the last act of the play, a servant reports that the heroine, "the lovely, the fair Cleone," has plunged a dagger into her breast rather than submit to the villain, Timophanes: "In yond Apartment lies the bleeding victim." A few minutes later the play ended, and Mrs. Oldfield "came forward" to banter with the audience:

> *Well, poor* Cleone *had a rav'nous Lover,*
> *A piteous Conflict; thank her Stars—'tis over.*
> *Nay, frown not, Ladies; make the Case your own,*
> *What cou'd she do?—Eh!—What wou'd you have done?*
> *Not have consented, sure!—Ye Pow'rs forbid it!*
> *No,———*
> *As* Mackbeth *says*—You cannot say she did it.
> *Yet, when from Friends remov'd, all Ears at Distance,*
> *A strong Gallant, much Love, and no Assistance,*
> *Who cou'd have blam'd the Doctrine then of* Non-
> Resistance?

8. See above, pp. 22–23, and below, pp. 295–297, for Mrs. Oldfield's success in this epilogue and for its long-lived popularity.

9. See above, pp. 2–3.

Well, 'twas a sprightly Age, that same of Greece! ⎤
'Twere hard, if copying thence, shou'd fail to please; ⎬
A Ravisher, determin'd, makes a fine Distress. ⎦
Your jolly Greeks *(as old Historians tell us)*
Were ever held a Race of charming Fellows.
Their manly Passions knew t' enhance the Joy,
And sav'd Coquette's the Pain of being coy.

.   .   .   .

But our tame Breed of Lovers does so dwindle, ⎤
Our Sparks with Shapes so small, and Legs so spindle, ⎬
Are forc'd to use all Helps to make their Passions kindle. ⎦
Poor callow Youths, just sent abroad from Weaning,
Are always blundring round about the Meaning.

.   .   .   .

Poor modish Ideots, to lose their Time in Chat,
When each well knows what t' other would be at.

.   .   .   .

Mrs. Oldfield's indecent banter delighted the audience who had sat through five acts of *Timoleon*. In such pieces she was no longer the tragic heroine, nor Mrs. Oldfield, but "the epilogue."

An actress frequently assumed and kept a distinguishing role in epilogues, creating a character quite as definite as those which she represented in the play itself, and authors wrote their epilogues to suit the speaker. The most amusing as well as the most consistent of all speakers of such epilogues was the great comic actress, Mrs. Catherine Clive. The first epilogue printed with her name, spoken while she was still Miss Raftor, was written by Fielding for his comedy, *The Lottery*, performed at Drury Lane, January 1, 1732; the last was her Farewell Address by Horace Walpole, which she spoke at Drury Lane on the night of her final appearance, April 24, 1769. During the intervening thirty-seven years, she delighted audiences with her forthright, noisy epilogues, full of references to her tumultuous personality and to her acting.

One of Mrs. Clive's most admirable traits, and she had many, was her loyalty to the Drury Lane Company, especially in times of stress. In 1733 when the theatre was suffering from the incompetent management of Highmore, many of the actors "deserted" and established themselves in the Little Theatre in the Haymarket, but Mrs. Clive remained at Drury Lane. Fielding made the evil fortunes of the theatre the subject of the prologue and epilogue to a revival of his satire, *The Author's Farce* (1734).[1] The prologue is one of the few of Mrs. Clive's pieces marked by seriousness and dignity. The speaker was in entire sympathy with the author in lamenting the fallen estate of Drury Lane and in attempting to aid the distressed actors. In former years the theatre had prospered,

> *But now, alas! how alter'd is our Case!*
> *I view with Tears this poor deserted Place,*
> *None to our Boxes now in Pity stray,*
> *But Poets free o' th' House, and Beaux who never pay.*

The critics have all abandoned the pit, and the drama reflects the lack of discriminating censure.

Fielding dedicated *The Author's Farce* to Mrs. Clive in an Epistle in which he pays the highest tribute to her genius and congratulates himself that the town owes something to him for having been the first to discover her and justly appreciate her merit. He extols her not only as an actress but as "acting in real Life the Part of the best Wife, the best Daughter, the best Sister, and the best

1. The prologue and epilogue appear with the third edition of *The Intriguing Chambermaid,* published in 1750. Genest, III, 411, under Jan. 15, 1734, records: "Author's Farce—in which will be introduced an Operatical Puppet Show, called the Pleasures of the Town—with great additions and a new Prologue and Epilogue . . . Mrs. Clive acted Harriet in *The Author's Farce* and Mrs. Novel in *The Pleasures of the Town. . . .*"

Friend." He ends his Epistle by describing her staunch support of the Drury Lane Company and its ill-fated manager.[2] The epilogue, also by Fielding, is in Mrs. Clive's usual blustering manner and afforded her means of emphasizing her very genuine hatred of Italian opera.

Writers following Fielding soon learned to hit Mrs. Clive's special vein. Aaron Hill, author of many prologues and epilogues and of few good ones, wrote a clever acting piece for Mrs. Clive in the epilogue to *Zara* (1736). The tragedy has ended with the violent deaths of Zara and Osman, when suddenly appears Mrs. Clive rampant, with a warning to the audience, wrought to a high pitch of excitement:

> HERE, *take a Surfeit, Sirs, of being* Jealous;
> *And* shun *the* Pains, *that plague those* Turkish *Fellows.*

Making a somewhat strained reference to the tragedy, she laments the desolate life of a Turkish lady, who if she plays at cards at all must play with a menial. Worse yet, if she should by fortune find a better partner, "Poignard's the Word!"

> *'Slife! shou'd the* bloody Whim *get Ground, in* Britain,
> *Where* Woman's FREEDOM *has such* Heights, *to sit on;*
> Daggers, PROVOK'D, *wou'd bring on* DESOLATION:
> *And,* murder'd Belles un-people *half the Nation!*—
> *Fain wou'd I help this Play, to move* Compassion;
> *And live, to* hunt SUSPICION *out of Fashion.*—

She enumerates the reasons why a husband should never be jealous:

2. Fielding's *Epistle to Mrs. Clive* was written in 1734 and, like the prologue and epilogue to *The Author's Farce,* published with the third edition (1750) of *The Intriguing Chambermaid.* For the condition of Drury Lane in 1734, see the *London Magazine,* January 1734; Doran, *"Their Majesties' Servants"* (1865), I, 301–308; Wilbur L. Cross, *The History of Henry Fielding* (New Haven, 1918), I, 154 ff.

> *First then—A Woman* WILL, *or* WON'T—*depend on't:*
> *If she* will *do't, she* WILL:—*and,* there's *an* End *on't.*

The epilogue continues in a noisy, straightforward fashion
and ends in really serious advice that men learn to regard
their wives without suspicion if they wish them to be
faithful. In relation to the tragedy which it concludes the
epilogue is grossly inartistic; as an acting piece for Mrs.
Clive it is excellent.

A temperament and manner so pronounced as Mrs.
Clive's, while resulting in a striking and distinct kind of
epilogue, placed little demand upon the originality of a
writer. James Miller's epilogue to *The Universal Passion*
(1737), an adaptation of *Much Ado about Nothing,* in
which Mrs. Clive played Liberia, *i.e.* Beatrice, suggests
both how her acting complied with and how it deviated
from the usual presentation of the comic epilogue in the
third decade of the century. Mrs. Clive informs her audience:

> *I wanted to be wanton, pert, and witty,*
> *Sneer at the Beaux, and Joke upon the City;*
> *To you, Gallants, a meaning Leer impart,*
> *And smile a Hint to glad the Fair One's Heart;*
> *With artful Shrugs Satirick Strokes convey,*
> *And wink a Reputation clean away;*
> *Then with this Standard boldly thus advance,*
> *And rout the squeaking, skipping Troops of* Italy *and*
>   France,
> *Till the whole House should roar—*That's fine, that's fine!
> *And clap me thundringly at every Line.*

The first six lines very clearly describe the ribald comic
epilogue; the last four lines were written for Mrs. Clive.
Miller wrote an even more characteristic piece for Mrs.
Clive in the epilogue to *Art and Nature* (1738), in which,

after considering two epilogues, "Suited as you should *Damn* or *Save* this Play," she "goes forward" and confides to the pit:

> *But, Gentlemen and Ladies, as I was assur'd this Play was certainly to be Damn'd, I have only studied one of the Epilogues; however if, contrary to all Expectation, it should chance to succeed, I'll have the other ready by the Author's Night. But now hear what a furious Taking the poor Mortal's in; he supposes his Play is damn'd you must remember.*

To act "a furious Taking" was what Mrs. Clive most enjoyed.

Occasionally a boisterous epilogue of this sort overreached itself or at least failed of its purpose; for example, in the epilogue to *The Fatal Retirement* (1739), Mrs. Clive shoves off the stage the actor who is to announce the play for the following night, derides the tragedy which has just been acted, and admonishes the audience to damn the play—advice which was immediately taken.

Of all Mrs. Clive's epilogues none preserves more vividly her mixture of good nature, quick temper, and innocent egotism, which was with her a kind of self-respect, than that written especially for her by Christopher Smart to conclude Murphy's *The Apprentice,* a farce in which she had no part. She enters in her usual agitation, "reading the Play-Bill."

> *A very pretty Bill,—as I'm alive!*
> *The Part of—Nobody—by Mrs.* Clive!
> *A paltry, scribbling Fool—to leave me out—*
> *He'll say perhaps—he thought I could not spout.*

She proves her competence at "spouting"—the harmless attempt of the apprentices at amateur theatricals, a pastime for which they had the precedent of the company managed

by Peter Quince. Since Mrs. Clive can "spout" with the
best London apprentice, she ascribes the omission to
Murphy's envy of her burlesque, *The Rehearsal: or, Bays
in Petticoats* (1750).[3]

> *Malice and envy to the last Degree!*
> *And why?—I wrote a Farce as well as He.*
> *And fairly ventur'd it—without the Aid*
> *Of Prologue dress'd in black, and Face in Masquerade;*
> *O Pit—have Pity—see how I'm dismay'd!*

The "Prologue dress'd in black" is Smart's gibe at Murphy
for presenting his own prologue to the play in the livery
of an undertaker. The epilogue ends with a playful address
to the young women apprentices in the audience, who
imagine themselves potential Ophelias, Zaras, and Lady
Townlys, and to the young men who neglect their work to
attend Spouting Clubs:

> *O, Little do those silly People know,*
> *What dreadful Trials—Actors undergo.*
> *Myself—who most in Harmony delight,*
> *Am scolding here from Morning until Night.*
> *Then take Advice from me, ye giddy Things,*
> *Ye Royal Milliners, ye apron'd Kings;*

3. Dodsley published this short and amusing rehearsal play in 1753,
with the title page reading: *The Rehearsal: or, Bays in Petticoats. A
Comedy in Two Acts. As it is performed at the Theatre Royal in Drury-
Lane. Written by Mrs. Clive. The Music composed by Dr. Boyce.* The
burlesque was performed at Drury Lane, March 15, 1750, with a distinguished cast—Woodward, Beard, and Mrs. Clive herself as the heroine.
The scene moves between the heroine's dressing room and the stage of
the Drury Lane Theatre. The entire piece is interesting in revealing how
inseparable Mrs. Clive's life and thoughts were from Drury Lane and its
affairs. She delighted in flouting Garrick and in ridiculing her own
difficult temper and conceit. She managed a particularly scathing observation about Covent Garden: "Ay, the Actors can't play there above
three Days a Week. They have more need of a Physician, than a Poet,
at that House."

> *Young Men beware and shun our slipp'ry Ways,*
> *Study Arithmetic, and burn your Plays;*
> *And you, ye Girls, let not our Tinsel train*
> *Enchant your Eyes, and turn your madd'ning Brain;*
> *Be timely wise, for oh! be sure of this;—*
> *A Shop with Virtue, is the Height of Bliss.*

Murphy was fortunate in both the author and the speaker of the epilogue to *The Apprentice.*

The blustering, busy epilogue to Mrs. Elizabeth Griffith's *The Platonic Wife* (1765) contains a song for Mrs. Clive, urging the audience to be kind to the author because she is a woman. After singing the stanza, Mrs. Clive declares that she herself will write a song:

> . . . then you'll roar
> Bravo! bravissimo! divine! encore!

But checking her own aspirations, she suddenly remembers the purpose of an epilogue, looks into the pit, and observes:

> What's this to th' play? . . . our author, there she sits!
> As I'm alive, she's going into fits!

Mrs. Clive's last epilogue, barring her Farewell Address, was written by Garrick for Mrs. Griffith's *The School for Rakes* (1769). It accurately describes the kind of character in which she had delighted her audiences for almost forty years:

> . . . I told the scrib'ling dame,
> This part of *Winifred,* is much too tame;
> Ask but the town, said I, they'll all agree,
> That a *tame* character, will not suit *me.*

Mrs. Clive's epilogues all retain something of her comic genius and vivacity. Davies, bookseller, actor, and dramatic

SPEAKERS   75

critic, said, "I shall as soon expect to see another Butler, Rabelais, or Swift, as a Clive." [4]

The special talent of a speaker, such as Mrs. Clive, determined the manner of the epilogue, but the mental and moral level of the audience influenced its matter. As it will be shown in a later chapter, the epilogue, though remaining "comic," adapted itself to the change occurring in the audience. Thus during the last decade of Garrick's management of Drury Lane, pit and gallery alike were pleased with commonplace, sentimental, and usually "moral" epilogues. Ann Spranger Barry was the last of the great actresses famed for "pathetic" characters, who could successfully adapt their talent to the comic epilogue. Mrs. Siddons regarded Mrs. Barry as a dangerous rival because of her success in such parts as Desdemona, and Lady Randolph,[5] and Lichtenberg considered her as possibly the greatest actress on the English stage in 1775, especially extolling her Cordelia.[6] It is a tribute to her adaptability that she could descend from tragic parts to act Garrick's comic epilogues.

The epilogue to Home's *Alonzo* is a case in point. *Alonzo* (1773) is a ghastly but not convincing tragedy in which a jealous king causes his innocent bride to stab herself. Mrs. Barry, for whom Home wrote the part of the queen, Ormisinda, exceeded herself in the character, and to her Home attributed the success of the play, "vouched, not only by the loudest applause that ever shook the stage, but by the greatest effusion of tears. . . ." [7] Immediately after the closing lines, Mrs. Barry appears to speak Garrick's extremely silly epilogue:

4. Thomas Davies, *Dramatic Miscellanies*, III, 345.
5. See Joseph Knight's article on Ann Spranger Barry in the *Dictionary of National Biography*.
6. Lichtenberg, *Visits*, pp. 31–33.
7. Home's Advertisement to *Alonzo*.

THO' *lately dead, a Princess, and of Spain,*
I am no Ghost, but Flesh and Blood again!
No time to change this Dress, it is expedient,
I pass for British, and your most obedient.

The epilogue, virtually an afterpiece in monologue, continues some fifty lines further, Mrs. Barry impersonating
the jealous husband as he is found in various European
countries. There is no indication that the unusual length
of the piece was a tax on the actress, even after her ex-
hausting part in the tragedy.

During the last two decades of the century the particular
variety of comic epilogue made popular by Garrick fell to
Mrs. Isabella Mattocks. Mrs. Mattocks began her career as
a speaker of epilogues as early as 1767 with the epilogue to
Hull's *The Perplexities,* and thereafter spoke epilogues by
Garrick, Colman, and Sheridan, but it was not until 1789
that she found her proper medium in the epilogues written
for her by Miles Peter Andrews. These pieces deal realisti-
cally with the domestic concerns of the upper gallery. Yet
dull as they are now in print, they came to life when they
were acted by Mrs. Mattocks; indeed they were her best
parts. The author of *The Children of Thespis,* an appraisal of the stage, modelled after *The Rosciad,* considers
Mrs. Mattocks slovenly and incompetent, although he
grants that her low comedy parts are good,

And her *epilogue speaking* can gladden and warm me,
In that Envy's minions *must* own when they mind her,
She leaves Competition—a furlong behind her.[8]

The epilogue to Robert Merry's *Lorenzo* (1791) is typical
of Andrews's acting pieces for Mrs. Mattocks. She imper-

8. Anthony Pasquin (*i.e.,* John Williams), *The Children of Thespis,*
Thirteenth Edition (1792), p. 227. For this reference, see also Joseph
Knight's article on Mrs. Mattocks in the *Dictionary of National Biography.*

sonates a clown at a fair, an ill-bred mother and daughter, a young beau strutting in Fops' Alley in the Pantheon, an Italian singer, and a French danseuse. The characters are absurdly drawn but the acting was lively. That Mrs. Mattocks was assigned thirty-two new prologues and epilogues is sufficient proof that her impersonations pleased the audience.

Of a very different nature are the epilogues written for Mrs. Abington, the "fine lady" of the stage from 1765 to 1790. She was famous for her Beatrice, Millamant, Mrs. Sullen, and Lady Teazle,[9] but equally famous for the rôle which she sustained in her epilogues. In her professional dealings she was dishonest, selfish, undependable, and a continual vexation to Garrick as manager of Drury Lane. He agreed with King, who declared, "Sure there never was such an infernal woman as Mrs. Abington," [1] and he left an accurate appraisal of her character in the lines spoken by her in the epilogue to *Albumazar:*

> *To heav'nly bodies we have no relation,*
> *The* Star *that rules us is our* inclination!
> *Govern'd by that, our* earthly *bodies move,*
> *Quite unconnected with the things above.*

At the same time Garrick appreciated Mrs. Abington's skill and for her he wrote eleven of his most sprightly and ingenious epilogues. The part of fine lady in the epilogue demanded elaborate dress of the most recent fashion so that the actress became a model for the ladies in the boxes. In Garrick's epilogue to Hugh Kelly's *The School for Wives* (1773) [2] she asks:

9. For Mrs. Abington's characters, see Genest, VII, 446–449.
1. Garrick, *Private Correspondence*, II, 121.
2. For Garrick's authorship of the epilogue to Kelly's *The School for Wives* (1773), see the Preface to the play.

> *Are not* we *qualify'd to take degrees?*
> *We've* caps, *and* gowns, *nay* bands *too, if you please,*
> Cornelly's, *and* Almack's, *our Universities!* [3]

Kelly finished his Preface to the play with an enthusiastic tribute to Mrs. Abington's acting, which he describes as elegant and vivacious: "Her Epilogue was delivered with an animation not to be conceived, and manifested the strict propriety, with which she is called the first priestess of the Comic Muse in this country."

Occasionally Garrick wrote Mrs. Abington's epilogues in the form of a conversation for two speakers—for example, the epilogue to *The English Merchant* (1767) in which both King and Mrs. Abington appear, the lady in a well-bred tempest—but more often the pieces are imaginary dialogues, she speaking both parts. The best example of Mrs. Abington's skill in impersonation is the epilogue to *The West Indian* (1771). Here she is alternately the shallow fine lady and the pert young daughter, posing and answering questions. The epilogue is provided with stage directions: "The lines in Italics are to be spoken in a catechise tone."

The playfulness and charm which Garrick achieved in all his pieces for Mrs. Abington is at its highest in the epilogue to Burgoyne's comic opera, *The Maid of the Oaks* (1774). The theatre is Parliament, before which Mrs. Abington appears to move the question:

> Is it your pleasure that this Bill should pass—
>
> .   .   .   .
>
> You that would pass this play, say *Aye* and save it;
> You that say *No* would damn it—the *Ayes* have it.

3. Compare the opening lines of the epilogue for Mrs. Abington to Miles Peter Andrews's *Dissipation* (1781):

> FASHION'S the word—again at her command
> To mark her sovereign sway I take my stand.

A first-hand description of Mrs. Abington in this epilogue has come down to us in Lichtenberg's diary. Lichtenberg saw her in *The Maid of the Oaks* and was delighted with her acting: ". . . she speaks the epilogue in a masterly fashion. In it she compares the boxes with the Upper House, and the pit and gallery with the Lower, gesticulating, murmuring, and whispering, so that it was a pure joy to see her." [4] In a long analysis of Mrs. Abington's acting, Lichtenberg says that she was best in attacking the follies of the great and if she chose to parody absurdities, "they must be only such as can be tolerated by propriety and expressed with grace. . . ." [5]

This requisite Garrick kept in mind in all his epilogues written for Mrs. Abington. He was aware that she was as popular in her epilogues as he was in his prologues. She spoke the first lines of the epilogue to Murphy's *Zenobia* (1768) peeping at the audience from behind the curtain and calling to them, "Beat but your hands, that instant I will come." The stage directions read: *"She enters upon their clapping."* Most of her entries for her epilogues were made with a similar show of coyness and a great deal of affected pleasure in her ability to meet the demands of the audience. They are also accompanied by a self-complacency which separated from the charm of the speaker is not pleasant:

> Two Epilogues are past, and yet, absurd!
> They urge, nay push me forth, to speak a third. [6]

How far Mrs. Abington could depend upon the audience to sympathize with her overweening comments on her abil-

4. Lichtenberg, *Visits*, p. 69.
5. Lichtenberg, p. 34.
6. The epilogue was printed in *Lloyd's Evening Post*, December 8–11, 1775, under the title: "The new Epilogue spoken after the Dramatic Entertainment of *The Maid of the Oaks*, by Mrs. Abington." For the date, see the *Drury Lane Calendar*, p. 191.

ity is illustrated by the *Occasional Address* on her first appearance in Covent Garden in 1782. She comes before the audience without fear, though she is to undergo "a noviciate now at Covent Garden"; she imitates her own acting of well-known parts, and she coyly trusts that the critics in the pit, deep-read in Aristotle, will not accuse her of violating the unity of place in deserting Drury Lane.[7] Her popularity was again attested when, seven years after she had retired, she returned to Covent Garden and before beginning "a favourite epilogue" was greeted with "such repeated plaudits that it was a considerable time before she could speak." [8]

Mrs. Abington's rival and successor in the part of "fine lady" was Elizabeth Farren, a member of the Drury Lane Company from 1778 until she left the stage in 1797 to marry the Earl of Derby. When Mrs. Abington joined the Covent Garden Company in 1782, Miss Farren inherited her characters, and during the decade of 1780–1790, she was by far the most popular speaker of the kind of epilogue designed for a frivolous audience. The importance which authors attached to Miss Farren's presentation of their epilogues may be judged from Burgoyne's Preface to his comedy, *The Heiress* (1786), in which, while thanking the actors in general for their diligence, he singled out Miss Farren as deserving special thanks for her "inimitable manner of delivering the Epilogue." The minor dramatist, Edward Topham, wrote an exceptionally clever epilogue for Cumberland's *The Natural Son* (1784), parodying a "puff" such as he hopes may appear in the newspapers the next day. Miss Farren as speaker extols the comedy, "The dresses, scenery,—and situation," and above all the acting, especially "Miss Farren's widow." [9]

7. *Lloyd's Evening Post,* December 9–11, 1782.
8. Mary Julia Young, *Memoirs of Mrs. Crouch* (1806), II, 262. Colman, the younger, wrote a laudatory prologue for her return to Covent Garden, Oct. 6, 1797. (The *European Magazine,* October 1797, p. [262].)
9. Other appraisals and panegyrics of Miss Farren's acting appear in

The tributes to Miss Farren make it clear that her epilogues demanded as much skill as her performance in the preceding play. This is characteristic of the prologues and epilogues throughout the century; they were roles of an exceptionally difficult nature, for on the one hand they were governed by tradition, but on the other they had to suit the genius of the speaker and the varying taste of the audience. Some of the pieces, such as many of the occasional prologues and the solemn prologues ushering in tragedy, required declamation, but these, too, were essentially dramatic, and they convey even to the twentieth-century reader a lively impression of the speaker and of the audience to be swayed by his voice. It should be noted that declamation could be accompanied by acting; for example, Garrick's prologue for the benefit of the Drury Lane Theatrical Fund,[1] the piece with which he closed his acting career on June 10, 1776, is as much a role as his Abel Drugger, Ranger, or Don Felix. From Barton Booth to Bannister, jun. and from Mrs. Oldfield to Miss Farren, the prologues and epilogues were cherished roles and as such they should be mentioned in theatrical history and biography.

Tate Wilkinson, *The Wandering Patentee* (1795), II, 30–31; III, 42–43, 85–87; the *European Magazine*, April 1797, p. 261; Boaden, *Memoirs of Mrs. Siddons*, II, 318. For Fanny Burney's detailed, first-hand description of Miss Farren as she presented Miles Peter Andrews's epilogue to *Seduction* (1787), see *Diary and Letters of Madame D'Arblay (1778–1840) As edited by Her Niece Charlotte Barrett. With Preface and Notes by Austin Dobson* (1904–05), III, 238–239.

1. The prologue, an appeal for indigent actors, was printed in the *Public Advertiser*, June 17, 1776, and in *The Poetical Works of David Garrick* (1785), II, 325–327. The original version of the prologue, in Garrick's hand, is in the Folger Library, with three variants for the conclusion, annotated:

> 1765 Every Man
> 1767 Susp' Husbd
> 1768 Hamlet

The *Drury Lane Calendar* (p. 199) refers to the prologue as the "Usual Address."

CHAPTER 3

PRESENTATION

To give individuality and life to prologues and epilogues was a constant challenge to both
authors and actors. Decade after decade ingenious writers
hit upon new applications of old theatrical devices and
gave new turns to long-established prologue comparisons
by adapting them to current plays, current conditions of
drama and the theatre, passing whims and interests of the
audience, and, above all, to the speaker.

Customs connected with the presentation of the pieces
remained very little altered during the century. Robert
Lloyd included a lively description of the theatre in his
verses, *To George Colman, Esq. A Familiar Epistle. Written January 1, 1761.* There is the deafening uproar of
sticks, catcalls, orange girls with their, "Cha' some
oranges"; there is the poor, trembling playwright,

> Peeping the curtain's eyelet through;

and there is the orchestra playing in the midst of the din:

> 'Till, decent sables on his back,
> (Your prologuisers all wear black)
> The prologue comes; and, if it's mine,
> It's very good, and very fine:

> If not, I take a pinch of snuff,
> And wonder where you got such stuff.

The play about to be performed is Colman's comedy, *The
Jealous Wife*, with the prologue written by Lloyd himself
and spoken by Garrick. The statement that *all* speakers of
prologues wore black needs qualification, for there were
many exceptions, such as pieces spoken in character. Lloyd
gives the order of events at the conclusion of the prologue:

> That done, a-gape the critics sit,
> Expectant of the coming wit.
> The fiddlers play again pell-mell:
> —But hist!—the prompter rings his bell.
> "—Down there! hats off!"—the curtain draws!
> What follows is—the just applause.[1]

The orchestra played during three separate intervals before the performance of the play. At the end of the "second
music," the prologue was presented; then followed the
"third music" and the ringing of the prompter's bell. The
prologue to Farquhar's *The Inconstant* (1702) bids the
orchestra: ". . . *up let the Musick strike*," and Charles
Johnson in the prologue to *The Successful Pyrate* (1712)
refers to the *"landskip"* which will be disclosed *"When
our Musick bids the Curtain rise."* [2]

1. Chalmers, *English Poets*, xv, 92–93.
2. Charles Johnson, *The Successful Pyrate*. The Third Edition, 1713.
For the orchestra and the first, second, and third music, see Montague
Summers, *The Restoration Theatre* (New York, Macmillan, 1934), pp. 108–
109. Summers quotes a note from Peter Whalley's edition of Ben Jonson
(1756) upon *After the second sounding* at the commencement of *Every
Man out of his Humour*: "These several *Soundings* are in the modern
theatre, termed first, second, and third music." But opposed to this explanation is W. J. Lawrence, *The Elizabethan Playhouse and Other Studies*
(Stratford-Upon-Avon, 1913), p. 155, where the simile from *Cynthia's Revels*,
III, iv, "like an unperfect prologue at third music," is taken as a reference
to "the third trumpet blast which invariably heralded the Prologue's coming." Stage conventions are notoriously long-lived, but I know no allusion
in eighteenth-century prologues to the heralding trumpet.

That the prologue was usually given before the curtain was drawn is also proved by references in the prologues themselves. Gay ends his prologue to *The Captives* (1724) with a rather bitter condemnation of the prejudice of the critics in the pit, who will not give new plays a fair hearing:

> . . . *Plays are like paintings try'd,*
> *You first enquire the hand, and then decide:*
> *Yet judge him not before the curtain draws,*
> *Lest a fair hearing should reverse the cause.*

In the prologue to a performance of an unpublished play, *The Contrast* (1789), the speaker describes the author's anxiety:

> . . . The poor Bard, whose Play's about t' appear,
> Shrinks ere he soars, perplex'd 'tween hope and fear;
> And tho' your smile bespeaks indulgence certain,
> Still, still he fears the drawing up the curtain.[3]

To speak the prologue to Garrick's Christmas entertainment, *Lilliput* (1756), Woodward was dressed as a conjurer,

> BEHOLD *a Conjurer—that's something new,—*
> *For as Times go—my Brethren are but few.*
> *I'm come with magic Ring, and taper Wand,*
> *To waft you far from this your Native Land.*

The stage directions printed with the last line of the prologue indicate that Woodward was raised and lowered through a trap placed before the curtain:

> England *is vanish'd*—(waves his Wand) *Enter* Lilliput.
>   (Strikes the Curtain and sinks.)

An unexpected use made of the curtain during the presentation of the prologue to *Alonzo* (1773) is recorded in the

3. The *European Magazine*, August 1790, p. 152. The comedy, by a Mr. Wilton, was written and performed in Calcutta.

stage directions printed with the play in *The Dramatic Works of John Home* (1798). The curtain rising discovers "Witches and Ghosts"; then shortly

> The Prompter gives the Sign, and down they go;
> > [*The Curtain falls.*
> Alive descending to the Shades below.

Rules regarding the presentation of the epilogue were less firmly fixed. There are instances in which the epilogue was delivered after the curtain fell; for example, the epilogue to Samuel Madden's *Themistocles* (1729) gives the specific directions: "The Curtain being down." The occasional epilogue to *The Indiscreet Lover,* performed at the Haymarket in 1768, is printed with the instructions: "Spoken in the Character of a *Soldier* and a *Sailor,* who, after the Curtain is let down, come from each Side, and shake Hands in the Middle of the Stage." Garrick's epilogue to Murphy's *Zenobia* (1768) is printed with the stage directions for Mrs. Abington: "She peeps thro' the Curtain," and the first eight lines are said off-stage. But the usual procedure was for the speaker to walk forward on the apron to be as near to the house as possible and, before the curtain fell, to deliver the epilogue while the other actors who had appeared in the last scene were still on the stage. Frequently the playwright arranged an exit toward the end of the last act to give the speaker time to change the costume she had worn during the play, but whether or not in costume, she addressed the audience in her part of speaker of the epilogue rather than in the character she had assumed for the play. For the epilogue to *Philip of Macedon* (1727), the entire cast having left the stage, the speaker, Mrs. Younger, who has played the heroine, Olympias, reappears and addresses the audience:

> '*TIS mighty well!—that anxious Pomp is o'er,*
> *That stiff uneasy Grandeur of an Hour!*

> *Nor Queen nor Princess (thank my Stars!) am I;*
> *Were you, O Ladys, were you but to try*
> *What Pleasure 'tis—the laying Greatness by!*

Of the many examples of this inartistic metamorphosis the most explicit is Cibber's epilogue to Charles Johnson's *The Victim* (1714), an adaptation of *Iphigenia in Aulis*. Mrs. Oldfield, having just died as the heroine, Eriphile, comes forward as the epilogue and comments on her appearance and costume:

> *For Form, I could have meal'd my Face, and chose*
> *In Peals of Thunder through the Stage t' have rose.*
> *But troth! I had rather spoil the Jest, than dawb*
>   *my Cloaths.*
> *A Hole but two Foot wide! Sure Bays must doat!*
> *I'm ribb'd with nine wide Whale-bone Yards of Petticoat.*
> *Beside, my own way (take my Word's) as good,*
> *I full as well shall please in Flesh and Blood.*

Peg Woffington, who played Volumnia in Thomson's revision of *Coriolanus* (1749), had time to return to her own features and dress before she appeared in the epilogue, a piece perfectly suited to her manner, as it would also have been to Mrs. Oldfield's or Nell Gwyn's. Her sudden transformation as well as the pertness of the lines resulted in a complete severance of dramatic illusion:

> *If an old Mother had such pow'rful Charms,—*
> *To stop a stubborn* Roman's *conquering Arms,—*
> *Soldiers and Statesmen of these Days, with you*
> *What think you wou'd a fair young Mistress do?*
> *If with my grave Discourse, and wrinkled Face,*
> *I thus could bring a Hero to Disgrace,*
> *How absolutely may I hope to reign*
> *Now I am turn'd to my own Shape again!*

Mrs. Mattocks, speaking the epilogue to Holcroft's *The Road to Ruin* (1792), makes a matter-of-fact statement regarding her reappearance:

> MY scenic faults and follies laid aside,
> No widow now, nor disappointed bride,
> My own plain self I once again resume;
> Sent by the author here, to know his doom.

Even when a disguise was assumed for the epilogue, the actress established with her audience a rapport impossible in the play itself. Elizabeth Younge, the Miss Archer of Mrs. Cowley's *More Ways than One* (1783), reappears as Venus and emphasizes the personal nature of the epilogue in describing the three ways, not always clearly defined, in which it could be presented. She asks: "Am I Miss Archer, Venus, or Miss Younge?"

It was an almost invariable rule that actresses should not appear in prologues, but even this convention could be broken. Colman's clever prologue to *The Sister* (1769) by Charlotte Lennox, spoken by Mrs. Mattocks, begins with a protest against actresses being restricted to the epilogue:

> *THE law of custom is the law of fools—*
> *And yet the wise are govern'd by her rules.*
> *Why should* Men *only prologue all our plays,*
> *Gentlemen-Ushers to each modern Bayes?*
> *Why are the Fair to Epilogues confin'd,*
> *Whose tongues are loud, and gen'ral as the wind?*
> *Mark how in real life each sex is class'd!*
> *Woman has* there *the* first *word and the* last.

The closing lines, built up on a playful but exact comparison, also contain important information about the presentation of prologues and epilogues in general.

> *Plac'd at the threshold of the weather-house,*
> *There stands a pasteboard husband and his spouse,*

Each doom'd to mark the changes of the weather,
But still—true man and wife!—ne'er seen together.
When low'ring clouds the face of heav'n deform,
The muffled husband stands and braves the storm;
But when the fury of the tempest's done,
Break out at once the Lady and the Sun.
Thus oft has man, in custom's beaten track,
Come forth, as doleful Prologue, all in black!
Gloomy prognostick of the bard's disgrace,
With omens of foul weather in his face.
Trick'd out in silk and smiles let me appear,
And fix, as sign of peace, the rainbow here;
Raise your compassion and your mirth together,
And prove to-day an emblem of fair weather!

The prologue or epilogue was frequently introduced and sometimes even accompanied by stage business to attract or hold the attention of the audience. The stage directions for the epilogue to Gildon's tragedy, *The Patriot* (1703), represent one of the most common of these devices and at the same time give the audience the name of the author: "*Mr.* Mills *comes forward and makes an Apology for want of an Epilogue; and then Mr.* Penkethman *enters dress'd like a Beaux, and says he has one by a Friend, Mr.* Farquhar." Pinkethman in the character of a stage beau then speaks Farquhar's epilogue. A similar device was used by Holcroft in 1798 in his epilogue to *He's Much to Blame.* As Pope prepares to speak the epilogue, Quick interrupts him and takes his place; Quick, in turn, "*begins a grave and stately bow,*" but Mrs. Mattocks "*eagerly advancing*" declares, "All Epilogues of right to me belong." Quick is driven off and Mrs. Mattocks completes the rather stupid epilogue.

Occasionally the prologue entered while the musicians

were playing. Garrick spoke his own prologue to *The Fairies* (1755)—thus giving countenance to an absurd medley based on *A Midsummer Night's Dream*—for which he entered interrupting the musicians with the command: *"A Moment stop your tuneful Fingers, pray."* The stage directions for the prologue to the one-act farce, *The Trip to Portsmouth* (1773), are more detailed: "Bell rings for the music to stop. A short silence ensues; then a man, with a book in his hand, supposed to be the Prompter, runs upon the stage, after Mr. *Weston* has been called upon two or three times behind the scenes." Weston refuses to speak the prologue and orders the prompter to be gone with it to Foote, who will do it justice. He then delivers an extempore prologue in which he bewails his popularity with playwrights:

> *Thus they come o'er me:* Weston, you're a Soul!
> Do speak my Prologue—you're so dry and droll.

Not infrequently prologues were introduced by a noisy encounter of actors at the stage door; for example, the prologue for the opening of Covent Garden in 1774 begins with an argument between Woodward, *"without the Stage-door,"* and the doorkeeper, who insists he is not to go on.[4] The conversation is sometimes between the actor and author but more often between two actors. When Quick chose to appear as Richard III for his benefit performance in 1790, Robert Merry supplied him with a prologue for Ryder, who enters speaking:

WELL, get back to the Green-room, retire do, with speed,
'Tis too late to repent of your own act and deed.
                                              [*Coming forward.*
Quite pale with ambition—of tragedy sick,
In plight the most doleful, I have left my friend QUICK.

4. *Lloyd's Evening Post*, September 21–23, 1774.

The prologue describes the actor as so overcome with terror at the ordeal before him that he can hardly find courage to appear:

"I'm so overcome, and already so spent,
"That I'm sure I shall faint with my fright in the tent:
"Or, if I should longer have power to encroach,
"When I call for my horse, let 'em call me a coach.
"Then take me home quietly, and put me to-bed,
"And say I've a fever, or swear that I'm dead!"

This at first glance seems an unpromising introduction to the hero of the evening, but the audience needed some preparation, for Quick since the death of Woodward had been the chief comedian of Covent Garden. He had "created" Tony Lumpkin and Bob Acres and was famous in Shakespeare's clowns. "His Dogberry may be said to have been as perfect a personation as any ever represented, even by Garrick. His affected pity at the ignorance of Vergis, while he glaringly exposes his own, made the audience always regret that the scene was not longer." [5] The prologue ends by asking the audience to forget his merits as a comedian and try him as if he were a new actor.

An epilogue written for a performance of Cumberland's *The Brothers* at Covent Garden, February 10, 1770,[6] was spoken by Woodward in the character of Ironsides, the captain in the comedy. *"The curtain draws up, and young Belfield enters, as if to give out a Play."* As he begins to address the audience, *"Ironsides enters from the door":*

5. John Taylor, *Records of My Life* (1832), II, 148–149. The prologue was printed in the *London Chronicle*, April 6–8, 1790. The *European Magazine*, April 1790, p. 307, ascribes it to Merry.
6. The *Public Advertiser*, February 10, 1770, announces *The Brothers* as the play for the day at Covent Garden, "With a new Epilogue by the Author of this Comedy to be spoken by Mr. WOODWARD, in the Character of Ironsides."

. . . Avast! you Rogue,
Sheer off, and let me speak the Epilogue.
                              (*Exit young Belfield.*)
Up with the main sail, boys!
              (*The curtain is drawn up quick.*)
                              and clear the stage;
The signal's hoisted, and we must engage.[7]

It should be noted that here the curtain was lowered at the end of the play and raised again for the epilogue.

The prologue and epilogue admitted considerable variation even in their basic structure and there were many deviations from the usual declamatory introduction and the *vos plaudite* conclusion. D'Urfey's comic opera, *Wonders in the Sun* (1706), was ushered to the stage by a "satyr" who spoke an Introduction emphasizing the fact that ordinarily operas had no prologues. After announcing that the play is to be satirical, the speaker concludes:

This, Stealing out, I thought was fit to say,
For you'll have no set Speech before the Play.
That were to do the Rules of Opera *wrong,*
So, in new Mode, the Prologue's *to be Sung;*
An Act in length, I hope 'twon't be too long.
This Novel Whim, he hopes will please the Town,
So I sneak off, the Machine's *coming down.*

The piece thus introduced as a prologue is a masque with the various parts sung by Apollo, "Caliope," a satyr, Orpheus and Eurydice. The opera has an acting epilogue spoken by two actresses.

Epilogues in song were not uncommon. Garrick concluded his epilogue to Murphy's *All in the Wrong* (1761) with a clever song based on the title of the play, the stage directions reading: "Enter two BALLAD SINGERS, who sing

7. *Lloyd's Evening Post*, February 12–14, 1770.

the following Song." The song concluding Garrick's *The Irish Widow* (1772) is also a true epilogue, sung by Mrs. Barry as an extension of the character she had acted in the play. It is addressed to the various levels of the house and, like all epilogues, is a plea for the favor of the audience.

To vary the prologue or epilogue, writers not infrequently wrote the pieces as skits involving two or more actors. One of the most elaborate of these is the prologue to Elkanah Settle's *The City-Ramble* (1711), an adaptation of *The Knight of the Burning Pestle*, "Spoken by a Person representing an Alderman in a Gold Chain, etc." Following Fletcher, Settle has part of the actors form an audience: "In the Middle Gallery Side-Box are seated the Common Council-man, his Wife, and *Jenny* their Daughter, as Spectators. The Common Council-man calls to the Speaker of the Prologue." Thereupon follows a controversy between the imaginary audience and the speaker regarding the immorality of the theatre, after which the councilman and his wife appear on the stage, and the speaker hands them into "the Stage-Box below."

The epilogue to James Miller's *The Mother-in-Law* (1734), which may be ascribed to Cibber on the basis of its queer egotism, was presented by three actors. Fielding's epilogue to *The Author's Farce; and The Pleasures of the Town* (1730) is an acting piece for six characters. Garrick's long epilogue to *The Clandestine Marriage* (1766) is an afterpiece for the members of the company who had not appeared in the play. At the end of the last act the curtain was drawn to discover an assembly room with the actors engaged in playing cards. When the game is done, they rise and advance to the front of the stage, where they conclude the epilogue with a chorus.[8]

8. Garrick wrote a similar piece for the benefit of the Actors' Fund to be presented by the aged and infirm members of the company in 1777— eleven years after the first performance of *The Clandestine Marriage*—

A dialogue between an actor and actress was often used as a device to catch the interest of the audience and to introduce a formal epilogue. Garrick's epilogue to Colman's *The English Merchant* (1767) opens with a dialogue as an extension of the play, the speakers, Mrs. Abington and King, retaining their parts of Lady Alton, a disreputable fine lady, and Spatter, the scandalmonger. The dialogue begins with the directions: "Enter *Lady Alton* in a Passion; *Spatter* following," and ends with the lady's commission to Spatter to slander her enemies. King leaves the stage, and Mrs. Abington comes forward to speak the epilogue.

The epilogue to Murphy's farce, *The Citizen* (1761), is also an extension of the plot and consists of a dialogue between Old Philpot, played by Shuter, and his son, George, played by Woodward. The father has, when the occasion demanded hypocrisy, larded his conversation with wise saws and clichés that the son imitates. Says Old Philpot, who is a grasping, unscrupulous merchant:

May Britain's thunder on her foes be hurl'd;

upon which George improves:

And London prove the market of the world! [9]

For the epilogue to *The Heir at Law* [1] by George Colman, the younger, the entire cast remained on the stage. Fawcett, acting the part of Dr. Pangloss, a ridiculous pedant who flaunts his learning by quoting scraps of verse, attributing them to their authors with a conceited "Hem," comes forward in character for the epilogue, offering his services to the audience:

some of the actors of the epilogue then reappearing on the stage. See the *Public Advertiser* for April 30, 1777.

9. *The Works of Arthur Murphy, Esq.* (1786), II, 297-300.

1. The first licensed edition of *The Heir at Law* was published in 1808, although the play was performed in 1797.

If any body wants a tutor here,
My terms are just three hundred pounds a year.
On their own merits modest men are dumb:
"Plaudite, et valete!"—Terence.—Hum!

The prologue could be used as a means of introducing a
character of the play and thus lead directly to the first
scene. Pinkethman spoke the prologue to Mrs. Centlivre's
The Basset-Table (1705) in the character of Buckle, the
witty footman. As this prologue is important in picturing
the audience of the first decade of the century, it will be
quoted at length below.[2] The dissimilar but equally clever
epilogue to Mrs. Inchbald's *Lovers' Vows* (1798) was
spoken by Munden as Verdun, the butler, the part chosen
by Tom Bertram in *Mansfield Park*. Throughout the play
the butler has on all occasions burst into rhyme, and the
epilogue is a purposely lengthy piece in anapests whereby
he continues to prove his skill in verse. Garrick wrote and
presented an epilogue to *The Lying Valet* (1741) as an
extension of Sharp, the quick-witted valet whom he had
acted in the play.[3]

One of Garrick's most entertaining epilogues, and the
last that he wrote as an acting piece for himself, is *Sir
Anthony Branville's Address to the Ladies,* Sir Anthony
being the elderly and ridiculous beau in Mrs. Sheridan's
comedy, *The Discovery*. Garrick had acted the part when
The Discovery was first performed in 1763, but he wrote
and presented the epilogue for a revival of the play on
January 22, 1776,[4] just before he made the public an-

2. See below, pp. 161–162 for the prologue to *The Basset-Table*.
3. The epilogue was printed in the second (1743) edition of *The Lying
Valet*. It may have been first spoken when the play was performed at
Drury Lane on March 3, 1743.
4. The *Public Advertiser* for January 22, 1776, after announcing *The
Discovery*, adds: "With an Address to the Ladies, by Sir Anthony Branville."

nouncement of his retirement. Both the letter and the
spirit of the play are continued in the *Address*, Garrick
delighting the audience with the formal graces and self-
centered gallantries of Sir Anthony. The piece is an excellent example of the artistic merit of the epilogue designed as an extension of character and thus as part of the
play. Here the dramatic illusion is not only unbroken but
intensified:

LADIES, before I go, will you allow,
A most devoted slave to make his bow?
Brought to your bar, ye most angelic Jury!
'Tis you shall try me for my am'rous fury.
Have I been guilty, pray, of indecorum?
My Ardors were so fierce I cou'd not lower 'em;
Such raging passions, I confess an evil,
In flesh and blood like mine, they play the devil!
Bound on the rack of love poor I was laid,
Between two fires, a *Widow*, and a *Maid*!
My heart, poor scorched Dove, now pants for rest,
Where, Ladies, shall the flutt'rer find a nest?
Take pity, fair ones, on the tortur'd thing,
Heal it, and let it once more chirp, and sing:
Yet to approach you were infatuation; ⎫
If souls like mine so prone to inflammation, ⎪
Shou'd meet your tinder hearts—there wou'd be ⎬
    conflagration! ⎭
Indeed so prudent are most men of fashion,
They run no danger, for they feel no passion:
Tho' fairest faces smile, they can defy 'em, ⎫
Tho' softest tongues shou'd plead, they can deny 'em, ⎬
Mankind wou'd cease, but for such loving Fools as I am; ⎭
When I amongst them with my Ardors glow,
I'm Mount Vesuvius in the midst of snow!
Had I the power, and of each sex were ruler,

I'd *warm* the one, and make the *other* cooler.
When I address the fair, no art can smother
The mutual flame, we kindle in each other;
I'm now electrify'd!—therefore expedient,
To fly combustibles!—Ladies your obedient.[5]

The correspondent who submitted *Sir Anthony Branville's
Address* to *Lloyd's Evening Post* added a note that ". . . it
is impossible for the Reader, who has not seen the late
revived Comedy of *The Discovery,* to conceive the particular Humour of Sir Anthony Branville's Character, and
consequently of the following Lines. . . ." In the epilogue
Garrick presented his own conception of Sir Anthony—
which, according to Davies, differed from Mrs. Sheridan's [6]
—this being his last original character.

Colman wrote a similar and equally successful acting
piece for Woodward in the prologue to *The Oxonian in
Town* (1767) to be spoken "in the Character of a Gentle-
man-Commoner," the part which he was to continue in the
play itself. The prologue is an example of Colman's particular humor at its best, a sort of mock earnestness, perfectly fitted to Woodward's manner. The gentleman-
commoner surveys himself with satisfaction and points out
the charm which attends a tassel, well-starched bands, and
surplice. As to learning, he thinks it not quite fashionable:

*You think perhaps we read—perhaps we may,
The News, a Pamphlet, or the last new Play:
But for the Scribblers of th' Augustan age,
Horace, and such queer Mortals, not a Page.
His brilliant sterling Wit we justly hold
More brilliant far transform'd to sterling Gold.*

5. *Lloyd's Evening Post,* February 23–26, 1776. Garrick's "Address" had
been anticipated by Charles Coffey's prologue to *The Female Parson*
(1730), unassigned but "Spoken by Modely. (*i.e.* A Beau extremely Fop-
pish.)"
6. Davies, *Life of David Garrick,* I, 310–311.

Tough Euclid we digest without much Pain,
And solve his Problems into brisk Champagne.
Fir'd with this Juice—why let the Proctor come—.

Prologues of this kind, functionally inherent parts of the
plays they introduce, may be considered independent acting pieces written quite as carefully for their speakers as
Ranger was for Garrick or Lord Ogleby for King.

Epilogues in character became increasingly popular in
the last decades of the century and were often substituted
for the original epilogues. Miles Peter Andrews wrote a
new epilogue to *The Road to Ruin* (1792) to be spoken by
Lewis in the character of Goldfinch after a benefit performance on March 23, 1793.[7] The piece is directly connected with the plot of the play and presents unchanged
the character of Goldfinch, even to his favorite slang,
"Here's your sort." Andrews's pieces, which incidentally
exhibit considerable facility in rhyme, often begin with
entertaining comment on the characters; for example, his
epilogue to Frederic Reynolds's *How to Grow Rich* (1793),
spoken by Lewis in the character of Pavè:

BEHOLD the hero, who with motives sinister,
Thought he had got the daughter of the minister.

The epilogue in character occasionally assumed the importance of an afterpiece. George Colman, the younger,
who in some degree inherited his father's ability as dramatist and prologuiser, supplied such an epilogue to Reynolds's comedy, *Management* (1799). The piece was spoken
by Fawcett "in the character of Mist," the good-natured,
garrulous manager of a country theatre, with ambitions of

7. Yale Library, Folio Pamphlets, No. 10, p. 157. Genest, VII, 103, under
March 23, 1793, records: "For bt. of Lewis. Road to Ruin—(52d time) . . .
with a new occasional address by Lewis, in the character of Goldfinch—."
See below, p. 310.

becoming manager of one of the great London companies.
He has dubbed himself "M.P." (Manager of Playhouse),

> A London Manager of high degree,
> I, Peter Mist, now enter here O.P.[8]

He is in desperate straits, for his country playhouse with
all its properties has been sold at public auction—"What
was a barn will be a barn again." His clouds, thunder,
wigs, and daggers are all gone. Mist—and it may be observed that in this he resembles Garrick—the model of a
successful manager, lays violent hands on Shakespeare for
the pleasure of his audience:

> Thus all my country stock, as Shakespeare says,
> "My cloud-capt towers, my gorgeous palaces,
> "Yea, my great globe," (the barn,) so much involv'd,
> And "all it did inherit, have dissolv'd."
> But if some future Manager should take
> My "solemn temple," which I now forsake;
> My "fabric of a vision," he will find
> That I have left a cursed "wreck behind."

His first task as a London manager will be to write an
account of the evening's performance to be inserted in
the newspapers the next day:

> "A five act play last night was represented,
> "By an amazing *Dramatist* [9] invented!
> "Author's and Actors' merits were immense,
> "And Fawcett e'en surpass'd his usual excellence!
> "Great care 'tis plain was taken in rehearsal;
> "And"—may I add with truth?—"applause was universal."

8. "O.P." The Epilogue entered the stage from the "opposite prompt"
door.
9. *The Dramatist* was a successful comedy by Reynolds.

The epilogue even while it compliments the playwright and actor and glances at the usual newspaper notice does not depart from the smug but laughable Mist.

As a variation of the prologue in character the speaker might appear in a guise in which he had achieved popularity. Thus Moody, who was famous in Irish comic characters, spoke Garrick's prologue to Bickerstaffe's *'Tis Well It's No Worse* (1770) as Captain O'Cutter, a part which he had originated in Colman's *The Jealous Wife*. The appropriateness of the character lies in the fact that Bickerstaffe was, like Moody, Irish:

> Oho! there ye are!—Before one word I utter,
> I must tell you, my dears—that I, *Captain O Cutter,*
> With silent respect, will a thing or two say
> About my relation who wrote this new play.

In the same meter is Colman's prologue, *Scrub's Trip to the Jubilee* (September 16, 1769),[1] an enthusiastic account of Garrick's Shakespeare Jubilee, which had been held at Stratford earlier in the month. The piece was written for Weston, who surpassed all contemporary actors as Scrub in *The Beaux' Stratagem*.

> FROM Stratford arriv'd—piping hot—gentle folks,
> From the rarest fine shows and most wonderful jokes,
> Your simple acquaintance, Scrub, comes to declare
> 'Twas fuller by far than our Litchfield great fair.

As Weston played Scrub to Garrick's Archer, the piece is an extended compliment to Garrick, "my brother Mar-

1. *Scrub's Trip to the Jubilee,* "a new occasional prologue by Mr. Weston," was presented at the Haymarket on September 16, and was published on September 26, 1769. See the *Public Advertiser* for the respective dates. It is quoted here from Francis Gentleman's *The Stratford Jubilee* (1769). The prologue is ascribed to Colman in *A Collection and Selection of English Prologues and Epilogues,* III, 198–200.

tin." [2] Garrick continued both the meter and lively banter of *Scrub's Trip* in the prologue to his farce, *The Jubilee*, which opened at Drury Lane, October 14, 1769.

Colman, who was second not even to Garrick himself in the ingenuity of his prologues, wrote the prologue to *The Spanish Barber* (1777) to be spoken by Parsons as the smart London tailor, Paul Prig, from Foote's comedy, *The Cozeners:*

> ONCE more from Ludgate-Hill behold Paul Prig!
> The same spruce air you see! same coat! same wig! [3]

The prints of Garrick and Parsons, to which I have already referred, prove their popularity in these roles.

Such transference of a character was the highest compliment in being an indisputable testimony of success. One of the latest eighteenth-century actors to receive this particular mark of approval was John Bannister, who spoke the prologue to Cumberland's *The Last of the Family* (1797) in the character of Sheva, the part that he had played in *The Jew.*

An unusual deviation in presentation occurs in the prologue to Foote's comedy, *Taste* (1752)—the prologue which Garrick is composing in Hogarth's portrait, *Garrick and His Wife*. In the play the part of an auctioneer, Peter Puff, was acted by Yates, but the prologue was spoken by Garrick "in the Character of an Auctioneer":

> *Before this Court I* PETER PUFF *appear,*
> *A* Briton *born, and bred an* Auctioneer. [4]

2. For Garrick as Archer and Weston as Scrub, see Lichtenberg, *Visits*, pp. 25–27. For the prologue to *The Jubilee*, see below, Chapter 9, p. 291, n. 5.

3. From the *London Magazine*, September 1777, p. 480.

4. During one of Garrick's frolics with the Burney family, he auctioned off Dr. Burney's library to the delighted children: ". . . a rare bargain, gemmen and ladies! a rare bargain! down with your copper!" Madame D'Arblay, *Memoirs of Doctor Burney* (1832), I, 349.

The prologue or epilogue presented as an extension of character was most successful artistically in being an inherent part of the play, but only a comparatively few of the total number of pieces fall into this class. Quite as frequently they were designed to be spoken by actors in costume, representing characters not connected with the play. The speaker might appear as a "university man" (prologue to *The Lady's Choice,* 1759), or a native of Otaheite (Colman's epilogue to Hull's *Henry the Second; or, the Fall of Rosamond,* 1773)—

> *Stretch to the Southern Ocean your Idea,*
> *And view, in me, the* Princess Oberea—

or a fortune-teller (Garrick's epilogue to Dow's *Sethona,* 1774). Usually such pieces center around the character assumed by the speaker and often are a commentary on the play; for example, Holcroft's bustling prologue to *The School for Arrogance* (1791) has stage directions for the speaker in the character of a newshawker: *After sounding and calling "Great news!" without, enter with a postman's horn, newspapers, cap, and livery.* The prologue is noisy and full of current excitement—disasters, crimes, "the grand specific for the gout," notices regarding bankrupts, money-lenders, suicides:

> Here! Here's the fifty thousand, sold at ev'ry shop!
> And here's the Newgate calendar—and drop.
> Rare news! Strange news! Extraordinary news!

The most remarkable news of all is, of course, the new play at Covent Garden.

Garrick had a number of low comedy characters which he enjoyed playing, and he often wrote prologues to provide himself with these favorite impersonations. One of these parts was the drunken sailor, "fuddled and talking to himself," presenting the prologue to Mallet's *Britannia.*

He enters singing, "How pleasant a sailor's life passes."
The most flagrant of patriotic prologues, the acting as
well as the theme assured it immediate success. Arthur
Murphy comments on the enthusiasm of the audience for
the sailor and his noisy prologue: "It was delivered with
the greatest humour, and from the nature of the subject
was so popular, that it was called for many nights after the
Masque itself was laid aside, and Garrick was obliged,
though he did not act in the play, to be in readiness to
answer the public demand." [5] The ample stage directions
with which the piece was published and the print by Taylor, showing Garrick dressed as the sailor, create a clear
impression of how this prologue was presented on the
Drury Lane stage in 1755.[6]

Prologues were as frequently addressed to the pit as to
the upper gallery, the speaker appearing as a printer, bookseller, critic, shabby poet, or printer's devil:

I am a devil, so please you—and must hoof
Up to the poet yonder with this proof—[7]

Garrick wrote the prologue to Murphy's *The Desert Island*
(1760) [8] as an acting piece for himself in the character of
a drunken poet whose play has been rejected by the manager. He knew to his sorrow all the arguments a determined author could advance for the acceptance of his play
and for its reconsideration and all the contumely he could
pour upon the offending manager. With drunken persistence, the poet will not be deflected from his grievance:

5. Murphy, *The Life of David Garrick, Esq.*, I, 270.
6. See above, pp. 37–38, for reference to the print of Garrick in the
prologue to *Britannia*. The prologue is printed in *The Works of David
Mallet* (1759), I, [185]–187.
7. Cumberland's prologue to *The Fashionable Lover* (1772).
8. Prologue to *The Desert Island* published in Murphy's *Works*, III,
[387]–389.

I've try'd all ways to bring my Phoenix on—

If the play could be submitted to the audience, their decision would be different. He finally "staggers off," quoting from Cibber's adaptation of *Richard III:*

"A little Flattery sometimes does well,"

a line which reminded the audience of one of Garrick's best-known characters—an additional means of "saving" the evening's performance. In creating the drunken poet, Garrick simply extended the part of Lord Chalkstone, his famous character from the afterpiece, *Lethe.* The prologue was itself sufficient to have insured the acceptance of any play for which Garrick chose to perform it.

Colman, following Garrick, wrote an amusing prologue to *The Man of Business* (1774), spoken by Woodward, who entered *"as an Author with a Manuscript."*

> SEE here, good folks, how genius is abus'd!
> A play of mine! the manager refus'd!

This is the best of the prologues for embittered playwrights, but the character persisted; for example, Thomas Vaughan's prologue to Delap's *The Captives* (1786), an excellent acting piece for Bannister, is printed with the stage directions: "The Speaker Mr. Bannister, jun. in the Character of a distressed and disappointed Poet, peeping in at the door, looks round the house."

During the first half of the century, and especially during the first three decades, comic epilogues were frequently spoken by actresses dressed as men. These pieces were in general indecent; hence their popularity and longevity. Hester Santlow (Mrs. Barton Booth) was celebrated for her success in speaking epilogues in boy's clothing; in 1710, for example, she appeared as a boy for the epilogue to Mrs.

Centlivre's *The Gamester,* D'Urfey's *Don Quixote,* and to
revivals of *Hamlet* and *Valentinian.*[9] She was followed by
Miss Robinson, the leader of a Lilliputian company. As
typical of her style may be taken Aaron Hill's epilogue to
Mallet's pseudo-classical tragedy, *Eurydice* (1731). Whatever may be the intrinsic merit of this pert epilogue, the
vivacity of Miss Robinson's acting was obviously a relief to
an audience after Mallet's fustian.[1] Peg Woffington, unsurpassed as Sir Harry Wildair, was the last great actress to
appear frequently in "breeches" epilogues. In the spring
of 1746 she was highly applauded for an epilogue, attributed to Fielding, spoken in the character of a volun-
teer.[2] Chetwood, writing in 1749, concludes his sketch of
Mrs. Woffington by observing: "I shall leave this Lady to
proceed in her Path of Merit where she still leads, with an
Epilogue wrote purely for her Manner of Speaking . . ."
He then gives the epilogue entire.[3] As the century advanced, there was far less demand for actresses to appear as
men, an indication of the change in the audience. Mrs.
Barry as Sir Harry Wildair spoke a new epilogue by Arthur
Murphy after a performance of *The Constant Couple* in
1772, an acting piece, decent but dull.[4] Colman's epilogue
to *The Spleen; or, Islington Spa* (1776) was spoken by
Mrs. King in the character of Dr. Anodyne, *i.e.,* Laetitia,
the heroine of the play, in disguise. For an actress who has
played Sir Harry Wildair or Dr. Anodyne to continue the

9. See Genest, II, 435, for entries regarding these epilogues. *A Collection
and Selection of English Prologues and Epilogues,* II, 59–61, contains the
epilogues to *Valentinian* and *Don Quixote.*

1. For Miss Robinson's epilogues, see Nicoll, *Early Eighteenth Century
Drama,* p. 49, and under "Breval," pp. 299–300.

2. Cross, *The History of Henry Fielding,* III, 338, records this epilogue
as "Probably by Fielding." It was printed with variant readings in the
True Patriot, February 18–25, 1746.

3. W. R. Chetwood, *A General History of the Stage* (1749), p. 254.

4. See Murphy, *Works,* VII, 48–50, for the epilogue and *Drury Lane
Calendar,* p. 161, for the date.

part in the epilogue is a very different matter from Miss Santlow's appearing in boy's clothes in an epilogue to *Hamlet*. Garrick wrote only one epilogue for an actress disguised as a man—that to Colman's *The Suicide* (1778), spoken in character by Miss Farren.[5]

A certain kind of prologue popular in the eighteenth century, as it had been in the Restoration and Elizabethan theatre, was presented by a speaker who impersonated an abstraction or assumed the guise of some great personage from national or literary history. The enduring popularity of these prologues is due to their being spectacular and patriotic. Dennis provided his tragedy, *Iphigenia* (1700), with a prologue printed with the stage directions: "The Genius of *England* rises to a Warlike Symphony." The Genius appears from the trap door and begins with a burst of patriotic enthusiasm:

> *SEE,* Brittons, *see, before your ravish'd eyes,*
> *See* England's *lofty Guardian Genius rise.*
> *Admiring see that formidable mien,*
> *That is by Gods with veneration seen;*
> *That from great* Neptune *due Respect can draw,*
> *And keep the watry trembling world in awe.*

It is difficult to maintain this kind of address on a sublime level, and Dennis is guilty of much amusing bathos, while he admonishes the audience to extend their manliness and patriotism to include the drama. At the conclusion of the speech the Genius of England *"sinks to the same Symphony that he rose."* In 1756 Holland spoke the prologue to Brown's *Athelstan* in the character of the Genius of England.[6] Henry Mackenzie's prologue to his tragedy, *The Prince of Tunis* (1773), was spoken in Edinburgh by Mrs.

5. The epilogue to *The Suicide* was printed in the *London Magazine*, July 1778, p. 331. The play was not published.
6. *Drury Lane Calendar*, p. 209.

Yates "in the character of the Genius of Scotland. Amidst a wild, romantic scene, the GENIUS advances to the sound of music." The prologue starts in an exalted strain, describing the Genius of Scotland as dwelling in desolate mountains and torrents, but turns prosaically to recounting the material blessings of commerce and peace. In 1779 Mrs. Jackson spoke the prologue to *Gallic Gratitude; or, The Frenchman in India* in the character of Britannia. Reference has already been made to the print showing her spear, shield, and helmet with plumes. The prologue is a vigorous denunciation of French treachery "in this unhappy broil," to wit, the American Revolution. Garrick wrote a patriotic epilogue to Brooke's *The Earl of Essex* (1761) for Mrs. Pritchard in the character of Queen Elizabeth, who appears as a judge to pronounce sentence on the decadent morals and manners of the audience. Matthew Gregory Lewis parodied this bombast in his epilogue to *The East Indian* (1799), spoken by Bannister—"*Thunder and Lightning. The Ghost of* Queen Elizabeth *rises in a Flash of Fire.*" The burlesque over-reached itself and was too gross to be successful.

The epilogue to Thomson's *Tancred and Sigismunda* (1745) begins with the usual banter of the comic epilogue, but the actress suddenly breaks off:

But bless me!—hold—What Sounds are these I hear!—
I see the TRAGIC MUSE *herself appear.*

Thereupon "the Back-Scene opens, and discovers a romantic Silvan Landskip," from which there emerges Mrs. Cibber in the character of the Tragic Muse. She advances slowly to music and, banishing the flippant epilogue, proceeds with another which is a patriotic plea for the revival of English tragedy.[7]

7. The original epilogue to *Tancred and Sigismunda* was again spoken by Mrs. Cibber in the character of the Tragic Muse when the play was

Ghosts in the prologue were made popular by Betterton, who had appeared in 1679 in the Dorset Garden Theatre as the Ghost of Shakespeare to present Dryden's prologue to *Troilus and Cressida:*

> SEE, *my lov'd* Britons, *see your* Shakespeare *rise,*
> *An awfull ghost confess'd to human eyes!*

In the epilogue to Gildon's revision of *Measure for Measure* (1700) the Ghost of Shakespeare, acted by Verbruggen, laments the barbarous treatment his plays have received at the hands of adapters and imitators who have left him mangled and murdered:

> ENOUGH *your Cruelty Alive I knew;*
> *And must I Dead be Persecuted too?*
> *Injur'd so much of late upon the* Stage,
> *My* Ghost *can bear no more; but comes to Rage.*

Bevil Higgons's prologue to Granville's *The Jew of Venice* (1701) is a dialogue between the ghosts of Shakespeare and Dryden, who "arise Crown'd with Lawrel." Not forgetting Granville, they bandy compliments. The prologue, like the play it introduces, is ridiculous, but it is not without historical significance.[8] Dennis wrote a stirring patriotic prologue for the subscription performance of *Julius Caesar* in 1707, in which "*The Ghost of Shakespeare rises to trumpets and flutes, playing alternately.*"[9] The "ghost" prologue suffered little change and persisted until the end of the century. The prologue to Bate's *The Magic Picture* (1783), an alteration of Massinger's *The Picture,* was spoken "in the Character of the Ghost of Massinger," who rises at the

---

revived at Drury Lane, March 7, 1749. (Genest, IV, 268; *Drury Lane Calendar,* p. 330.)

8. See below, p. 254.

9. For the "Subscription," see Cibber, *Apology,* ed. Lowe, II, 4–5. The prologue is printed in *A Collection and Selection of English Prologues and Epilogues,* III, 1–3.

tolling of a bell. This, like almost all similar prologues, laments the depraved taste of the audience.

Beyond such scenic and rhetorical devices used to attract the attention of the audience, the most pervasive characteristic of the eighteenth-century prologue is the protean nature of the comparisons whereby the speaker, author, playhouse, stage, and even the pieces were metamorphosed. The most obvious of these comparisons, as old as the prologue itself, presented the speaker as an advocate, the author as the culprit being tried, and the audience as the jury. Terence made an unadorned explanation of the device in the prologue to *Heautontimoroumenos,* in which the speaker says of the author:

> oratorem esse voluit me, non prologum.[1]

The comparison was so frequent that Garrick ridiculed it in the opening lines of his prologue to Hoadly's *The Suspicious Husband* (1747), but at the same time was sufficiently confident of its success to base his prologue upon it.

> WHILE *other Culprits brave it to the last;*
> *Nor beg for Mercy till the Judgment's past;*
> *Poets alone, as conscious of their Crimes,*
> *Open their Trials with imploring Rhymes.*
> *Thus cram'd with Flatt'ry and low Submission,*
> *Each trite dull Prologue is the Bard's Petition.*
> *A stale Device to calm the Critick's Fury,*
> *And bribe at once the Judges and the Jury.*

Goldsmith turned the convention into a pun in the closing lines of the epilogue to *She Stoops to Conquer* (1773), spoken by Mrs. Bulkley, who played Miss Hardcastle:

1. *Terence with an English Translation* by John Sargeaunt (Loeb Classical Library, 1912), I, 118.

The Bar-maid now for your protection prays,
Turns Female Barrister, and pleads for Bayes.

The comparison itself allowed for various applications. In Charles Johnson's epilogue to *The Successful Pyrate* (1712), the writer is the culprit and the audience the jury who will try him by the rules of Aristotle and Horace. The ladies in the boxes are—as they long had been and would continue to be—the court of final appeal. James Miller's prologue to *The Humours of Oxford* (1730) describes the different methods used to persuade the "jury":

As *crafty Lawyers, to acquire Applause,*
Try ev'ry Art to gain a doubtful Cause,
Pervert the Use of Words, and wrest the Sense of Laws:
So Authors try as many diff'rent Ways,
With artful Prologues, *to secure your Praise.*
One, with a soothing, supplicating Speech,
Humbly submits—and won't presume to teach;
By powerful Fees of Flattery hopes to gain ye,
And thinks with smooth-tongu'd Brib'ry to retain ye.
Another, bravely bids you bold Defiance,
And strives, by Storm, to force you to Compliance.

The speaker might try to instruct the critics in rendering their decision, and many of the pleas end by reminding the audience that a fair trial is the acknowledged right of Englishmen:

For this best British *privilege we call:*
Then—as he merits, let him stand, or fall.[2]

The most exhaustive treatment of the client-court comparison is Sheridan's prologue to *The Rivals* (1775) for the third performance of the play, an acting piece spoken as a dialogue between Woodward, the serjeant-at-law, and

2. Thomson's prologue to *Mustapha* (1739).

Quick, the attorney. The opening lines refer to the failure
of *The Rivals* when it was first performed on January 17,
1775:

> *Serj.* WHAT's here!—a vile cramp hand! I cannot see
> Without my spectacles. *Att.* He means his fee.
> Nay, Mr. Serjeant, good Sir, try again. [*Gives money.*
>   *Serj.* The scrawl improves [*more*] O come, 'tis pretty
>   plain.
> How's this! The Poet's Brief *again!* O ho!
> Cast, I suppose? *Att.* O pardon me—No—No—
> We found the Court, o'erlooking stricter laws,
> *Indulgent* to the *merits* of the Cause;
> By *Judges* mild, unus'd to harsh denial,
> A Rule was granted for *another trial.*

The original prologue to *The Rivals* was apparently not
printed and has never been discovered in manuscript. The
prologue published with the first edition was printed in the
Town and Country Magazine for February, 1775. Sheridan's editor, R. Crompton Rhodes, observes: "On the First
Night, according to *The Town and Country Magazine* for
January, 1775, the Prologue was spoken by Mr. Lee in the
character of a Serjeant-at-Law and Mr. Quick as an Attorney. The original Prologue, unless it was reverted to on
the Third Night, is lost." [3] That it was not reverted to is
proved by the prologue itself in which the comparison, as
it develops, presents facts concerning not only the play but
its prologues:

> *Serj.* Then heark'ee, *Dibble,* did you *mend* your *Plead-
>   ings,*
> *Errors,* no few, we've *found* in our *Proceedings.*

3. *The Plays & Poems of Richard Brinsley Sheridan*, ed. R. Crompton
Rhodes (Oxford, B. Blackwell, 1928), I, 25. See also Walter Sichel, *Sheridan*
(London, Constable & Co., 1909), I, 542–546.

Att. Come, courage, Sir, we did *amend* our *Plea,*
Hence your *new Brief,* and our *refreshing Fee.*

Lloyd's Evening Post for January 16–18, 1775, harshly criticizes *The Rivals* and ridicules the prologue: "By the Prologue, our curiosity respecting the Author of this Piece is happily satisfied; for we are told 'that he is a Student, who, finding Coke, Littleton, Plowden, Blackstone, and other Law Writers, afford but dull amusement, hath commenced Poet, to grace his brow with a sprig of bay from Mount Parnassus.' " This is not a summary of the prologue as we now have it, although the serjeant gives a sharp answer to the young attorney's remark that a "legal waste of wig" is adorned by a "decent sprig of bays":

> *Serj.* Full-bottom'd Heroes thus, on signs, unfurl
> A leaf of laurel—in a grove of curl!
> Yet tell your Client, that, in adverse days,
> This Wig is warmer than a bush of Bays.

The attorney then goes, leaving directions which very accurately describe Woodward's manner in prologues:

> *Att.* Do you then, sir, my Client's place supply,
> Profuse of robe, and prodigal of tye—
> Do you, with all those blushing pow'rs of face,⎤
> And wonted bashful hesitating grace,   ⎬
> Rise in the Court, and flourish on the Case. ⎦

Woodward then completes the plea to the jury of critics:

> *Serj.* For practice then suppose—this Brief will shew it,—
> Me, Serjeant *Woodward,*—Council for the Poet.
> Us'd to the ground—I know 'tis hard to deal
> With this dread *Court,* from whence there's *no appeal;*
> No *Tricking* here, to blunt the edge of *Law,*
> Or, damn'd in *Equity*—escape by *Flaw:*
> But *Judgment* given—*your Sentence* must remain;

—No *Writ of Error* lies—to *Drury-lane!*
Yet when so kind you seem—'tis past dispute
We gain some favour, if not *Costs of Suit.*
No spleen is here! I see no hoarded fury;
—I think I never fac'd a milder Jury!
Sad else our plight!—where frowns are transportation,
A hiss the gallows,—and a groan, damnation!
But such the public candour, without fear
My Client waves all *right of challenge* here.

The new prologue spoken on the tenth night by Mrs.
Bulkley announces the success of the play:

>   GRANTED our Cause, our suit and trial o'er,
>   The worthy Serjeant need appear no more.

Writers of prologues, in general, proceeded on the
principle that a play was damned until it was saved. As a
natural conclusion, the court-client comparison sometimes
ended with the "jury" sentencing the "culprit" to be
hanged.

>   *Quacks* set out Bills, *Jack-Pudding* makes Harangues,
>   And Thief, at *Tyburn,* speaks before he hangs:
>   I pray you then give Ear to what I say,
>   For this to me is Execution-day.
>   *Tyburn* the Stage is, Boxes, Galleries, Pit,
>   Where You, our Judges, and our Hangmen sit.[4]

The epilogue to Mrs. Centlivre's *The Gamester* (1705) begins rather shockingly with a comparison of the prologue
to the execution speech:

>   *AS one Condemn'd, and ready to become*
>   *For his Offences past, a Pendulum;*

4. *A Prologue sent to Mr.* Row, *to his new Play, call'd,* The Fair
Penitent. *Design'd to be spoken by Mr.* Betterton, *but refus'd.* From *Poems*

> *Does, e'er he Dies, bespeak the Learned Throng,*
> *Then, like the Swan, Expires in a Song.*

The comparison persisted throughout the century. In the prologue to Hugh Kelly's *The School for Wives* (1774), Garrick inserts an account of ballad-hawkers crying *"a faithful true relation"* of the unhappy career and violent death,

> *"Of the birth, parentage, and education,*
> *"Last dying speech, confession, character*

of the author

> *"Who suffer'd* Monday *last at Drury Lane;*
> *"All for the price of half-penny a piece."*

Closely allied to the court-client epilogue is the comparison whereby the theatre becomes Parliament and the pit the members casting their votes for or against the "motion" which has just been presented. Garrick's epilogue to Burgoyne's *The Maid of the Oaks* (1774), an excellent acting piece for Mrs. Abington to which I have already referred, is the best example of the sustained use of this comparison:

IN Parliament, whene'er a question comes,
Which makes the Chief *look grave, and bite his thumbs,*
A knowing-one is sent, sly as a mouse,
To peep into the humour of the house:
I am that mouse; peeping at friends and foes,
To find which carry it—the Ayes *or* Noes:
With more than pow'r of parliament you sit,
Despotic representatives of wit!
For in a moment, and without much pother,
You can dissolve *this piece, and* call *another!*

---

on *Affairs of State* (1704), III, 417. The prologue is a violent attack on Rowe and was not designed to be spoken by anyone.

After an elaboration of the comparison, the epilogue ends:

> You that would pass this play, say *Aye* and save it;
> You that say *No* would damn it—the *Ayes* have it.

For the prologue to Lady Craven's *The Miniature Picture* (May 24, 1780), Sheridan seized upon the excitement caused by the Dunning Resolution of the preceding April 6, "that the influence of the Crown has encreased, is encreasing, and ought to be diminished." He turned the Resolution into a fine compliment to the ladies in the boxes:

> But if the men presume your pow'r to awe,
> Retort their churlish Senatorial law:
> This is your House—and move—the gentlemen withdraw:
> Then they may vote, with envy never ceasing,
> *Your Influence has encreas'd and is encreasing.*
> But there, I trust, the resolution's finish'd;
> Sure none will say—*It ought to be diminish'd.*

This and the epilogue to Samuel Jackson Pratt's *The Fair Circassian* (1781) are closely connected with Sheridan's career. *The Fair Circassian* was produced at Drury Lane on November 27, 1781, seven days after Sheridan made his first speech in Parliament. Miss Farren, appearing for the epilogue, informs the audience, "Pit—Box—and Gallery —Peers and faithful Commons":

> OF late at Westminster, in order due,
> A gracious speech first made, debates ensue.

She continues with a reference to "packing the house," a custom which lent itself very readily to the comparison:

> Ere yet you opposition-criticks rise
> To move for censures, and refuse supplies;
> Or partial friends pour down corrupt applause,

By *orders* pension'd in the author's cause,
From either party—none will sure impeach
My sovereign title to pronounce the speech.

The epilogue seeks to arouse the "constituents" to resist the dangers threatening the "dramatic state," and ends in the most amusing of all summary dismissals of foreign entertainers, this current theatrical news being introduced in the development of the simile.[5]

Lacking classical precedent, but even more frequently used than the court-client simile, was the comparison of the author to a sailor tempting the dramatic seas in his frail bark of a play. He must brave the critic shoals, the whirlpool of hisses, the rattling hail from the upper gallery, and the lightning from the ladies' eyes. The divisions of the playhouse, pit, gallery, and boxes, lent themselves perfectly to the comparison. The epilogue to Mrs. Centlivre's *The Basset-Table* (1705), a lively and instructive delineation of the theatre in the first decade of the century, illustrates the adaptability of the comparison and its inherent and apparently indestructible vigor:

THis goodly Fabrick to a gazing Tarr,
Seems Fore and Aft, a Three Deckt-man of War.
Abaft, the Hold's the Pit, from thence look up,
Aloft! that Swabber's Nest, that's the Main-Top.
Side-boxes mann'd with Beau, and modish Rake,
Are like the Fore-castle, and Quarter-Deck.

In the middle gallery there were the vizard masks—"*Those dark disguised, advent'rous, black-nos'd few*"—; there

5. For the correct attribution of this epilogue to Sheridan, see Rhodes's edition of Sheridan, III, 282–283. The identification of Sheridan as the author was made by Mr. Iolo A. Williams in an article published in the *London Mercury*, August 1924. In a postscript to a letter to Sheridan, Pratt writes that he has a copy of the epilogue and asks if he may print the author's name, "or only say in my printed Tragedy, by a friend." Apparently Sheridan did not give Pratt permission to print his name.

were the orange women, *"Powder-Monkies running up and down."*

> *The Poet's Captain, but half dead with fright,*
> *She leaves her Officers to maintain the Fight.*

The middle gallery pelt the stage-deck with "eighteen pounders," *i.e.* oranges and apples; the upper gallery fire their hail of peas, and the pit their chain-shot of wit. Yet the helpless mariner can sail only by the help of her pole star, the audience.

This scheme, with the adaptations made necessary by the gradual change in the audience, remained the basis of many eighteenth-century prologues. Nahum Tate's epilogue to *Injur'd Love,* published in 1707, boasts:

> *And if our Scout-boat Prologue fails to take ye,*
> *We have our Epilogue Chase-guns to rake ye.*

The author declares that he could easily have created a *"slight New-fashion'd Play,"* built to founder,

> *But chose a Vessel that would bear the shock*
> *Of Censure; Yes, old Built, but Heart of Oak.*

The play is laid in Rome; deriving from Webster, it has its dukes and cardinals, its poisonings and violent deaths, its ghost and "pan of Lilly Flowers with a Scull in 't" but the epilogue is as indigenous as the play is foreign.

Arthur Murphy made an extended application of the author-mariner comparison in the opening lines of the prologue to *No One's Enemy but His Own* (1764), in which he frankly acknowledged a foreign source. This highly-polished but lively and entertaining prologue is addressed to the pit, as the reference to Horace proves.

> Bold was the man, and fenc'd in ev'ry part
> With oak, and ten-fold brass about the heart,

To build a play who tortur'd first his brain,
And then dar'd launch it on this stormy main.
What tho', at first, he spreads his little sails
To Heav'n's indulgent and propitious gales,
As the land gradual lessens to his eye
He finds a troubled sea, and low'ring sky:
Envy, detraction, calumny, and spite,
Raise a worse storm than when the winds unite.
Around his bark, in many a dang'rous shoal,
Those monsters of the deep, the critics, prowl.
"She's a weak vessel, for these seas unfit,
"And has on board her not a spice of wit:
"She's French-built too; of foreign make," they cry;
Like geese still cackling that the Gauls are nigh.
If thrown on rocks by the hoarse dashing wave,
Th' unhappy crew no hand is stretch'd to save;
But round the wreck, like Moors, with furious joy,
The witlings crowd—to murder and destroy.

Garrick, in the prologue to *'Tis Well It's No Worse*
(1770), informs the audience that Bickerstaffe has rebuilt
a Spanish play—"An old crazy vessel, ill built, rigg'd, and
plann'd." James Cobb's prologue to *The Female Captain*
(1780) begins with allusion to "shipwreck" attended by
catcalls:

By critic storms, how many vessels tost,
Have on the drama's dangerous seas been lost!
Though mann'd with heroes of old Greece and Rome,
The boatswain's *whistle* has pronounced their doom.

He makes an ingenious acknowledgment of his source; the
privateer playwright has come upon an enemy boat com-
manded by "one *Monsieur Mariveaux.*"

At once she struck, resistance was in vain,
She was sent into port at Drury-Lane,

Her cargo all to Sheridan and Co.
Was *then* consign'd—but *now* is here on shew.[6]

In Garrick's prologue written for the opening of the new
theatre on Richmond Green, June 15, 1765, the theatre
itself, rather than the play, is to be launched. "Rigg'd,
mann'd, well built, and a rich Freight on board," she has
been made a "Royal Sloop" by commission.

May Heav'n from Tempests, Rocks, and Privateers,
Preserve *The* RICHMOND!—Give her, Boys, three Cheers!
          [*Three Huzzas behind.*[7]

Cumberland's prologue to his tragedy, *The Carmelite*
(1784), linked the metaphor to the plot of the play. The
opening lines give the setting and the name and history of
the hero who, after twenty years in the Holy Land, fighting the pagans, is at last home but in desperate plight—
shipwrecked on the coast. The author is just such a shipwrecked wanderer, struggling to make the shore,

> *Now here, now there, as fashion's current veers:*
> *Rouse, rouse for his protection! you, you, who sit*
> *Rang'd in deep phalanx, arbiters of wit!*
> *And you aloft there, keep your beacon bright,*
> *Oh, make your Eddy-stone shew forth it's light;*
> *So shall our Bard steer to its friendly blaze,*
> *And anchor in the haven of your praise.*

It was the "Dire critic shoals, and actor-marring rocks!" [8]
which were deprecated. As late as 1794 the prologue,
"Cloak'd up in metaphor," still foretold that "critic bat-
teries" would rake the newly launched play.[9] Occasionally

6. *Lloyd's Evening Post*, September 18–20, 1780. *The Female Captain*
is an adaptation of Marivaux's *La Fausse Suivante*.
7. *Lloyd's Evening Post*, June 19–21, 1765.
8. Occasional prologue to *Tancred and Sigismunda* by George Colman,
the elder. *London Magazine*, July 1784, pp. 75–76.
9. Prologue to James Boaden's *Fontainville Forest* (1794).

the venturous author had put forth other barks which
"gain'd a fav'ring breeze" and reached the harbor,[1] but in
general the mariners looked for nothing but shipwreck,
Holcroft's prologue to *The Man of Ten Thousand* (1796)
expressing the usual fear:

Should one more hurricane o'ertake him, here,
Should bursting yells and howls, from yonder skies,
Bid the wild billows of damnation rise,
Courage and skill in vain the storm oppose,
He founders in the gulph, and down he goes!

Of all the prologues based on the author-mariner comparison, the best sustained is Goldsmith's sprightly prologue to Joseph Cradock's *Zobeide* (1771), spoken by
Quick. In June 1771 Captain Cook had returned from his
first voyage to the South Pacific, and hence the timeliness
of Goldsmith's allusions.

IN these bold times, when Learning's sons explore
The distant climate and the savage shore;
When wise Astronomers to India steer,
And quit for Venus, many a brighter here;
While Botanists, all cold to smiles and dimpling,
Forsake the fair, and patiently—go simpling;
When every bosom swells with wond'rous scenes,
Priests, cannibals, and hoity-toity queens:
Our bard into the general spirit enters,
And fits his little frigate for adventures:
With Scythian stores, and trinkets deeply laden,
He this way steers his course, in hopes of trading—
Yet ere he lands he 'as ordered me before,
To make an observation on the shore.
Where are we driven? Our reck'ning sure is lost!
This seems a barren and a dangerous coast.
Lord what a sultry climate am I under!
Yon ill-foreboding cloud seems big with thunder.

1. Prologue to Charles Morris's *False Colours* (1793).

(Upper Gallery.)

There Mangroves spread, and larger than I've seen 'em—

(Pit.)

Here trees of stately size—and turtles in 'em—

(Balconies.)

Here ill-condition'd oranges abound—

(Stage.)

And apples (takes up one and tastes it) bitter *apples*
strew the ground.
The place is uninhabited I fear;
I hear a hissing—there are serpents here!
O there the natives are—a dreadful race!
The men have tails, and women paint the face!
No doubt they're all barbarians—Yes, 'tis so,
I'll try to make palaver with them though; (making signs)
'Tis best however keeping at a distance.
Good Savages, our Captain craves assistance;
Our ship's well stor'd;—in yonder creek we've laid her,
His honour is no mercenary trader;
This is his first adventure, lend him aid,
Or you may chance to spoil a thriving trade.
His goods he hopes are prime, and brought from far,
Equally fit for gallantry and war.
What no reply to promises so ample?
I'd best step back—and order up a sample.

Goldsmith gave a characteristic twist to an outworn comparison. By the ingenuity of his application of one comparison, he avoided the profusion of metaphors, a common
defect of the eighteenth-century prologue. The piece is, of
course, in no sense an introduction to the tragedy, *Zobeide,*
except that it informs the audience that the play is a first
venture and has a foreign source and that the author is not
a professional playwright. It was an acting piece whereby
Quick won the favor of the audience by presenting to them
the author-mariner comparison in new garb.

The comparison in the prologue could be presented from the point of view of the theatre itself, the manager, the author, the prologue, or the speaker, but it was always inseparable from the audience. In Colman's prologue for the opening of the Haymarket on May 15, 1777, the manager is a journeyman selling his master's wares to the audience. The two "great warehouses, for winter use"— Drury Lane and Covent Garden—produce huge bales of merchandise eight months of the year, but

> Out with the swallow comes our summer Bayes,
> To shew his taffata and lutestring plays;
> A choice assortment of slight goods prepares,
> The smallest haberdasher of small wares.

Colman changes the comparison in the concluding lines to pay Foote a nicely turned compliment based on a pun— their "good old hay-maker" will not forsake the fields which he has long mowed but will help the present manager make hay while the sun shines.[2] The prologue by Richard Tickell to Griffith's *Variety* (1782) is based on the merchant comparison and, playing on the title, describes the great "variety" of goods offered by the two powerful companies—"new furbish'd remnants," native "home-spun stuff," imported fabrics, oriental luxuries, and all these at *"Nothing but full price"*; that is, all presented as new pieces for which full admission prices could be charged.

Garrick's success as a writer of prologues lay partly in his skill in hitting upon apt similes. Very few of these were original, but he gave them a personal application which seldom failed to excite the attention of the audience. In

2. The *London Magazine*, July 1777, pp. 376–377. Colman bought the patent of the theatre in the Haymarket from Foote on January 16, 1777. (Cooke, *Memoirs of Samuel Foote, Esq.*, I, 233; 238.) The Haymarket by terms of the patent was a summer theatre. Foote did not live to fulfil Colman's hopes. He died on October 21, 1777.

his prologue to Colman's skit, *New Brooms!*, performed on September 21, 1776, for the opening of Drury Lane under Sheridan's management, he announces:

> Another simile we mean to broach—
> A new one too!—The Stage is a Stage-Coach.—

The manager is the coachman, the audience the passengers in the crowded coach. After describing the race run with the rival coachmen, he ends optimistically, "The Old Stage will run for ever!" But from his twenty-nine years as "coachman" he could forewarn young Sheridan that "the road is not all turnpike." The prologue to *Florizel and Perdita* (1756),[3] Garrick's revision of *The Winter's Tale*, begins with a statement of the comparison which he then developed through all its many applications:

> *TO various Things the Stage has been compar'd,*
> *As apt Ideas strike each humorous Bard:*
> *This Night, for want of better Simile,*
> *Let this our* Theatre *a* Tavern *be.*

Garrick contrived within the scheme of the simile to speak with admiration and regret of Quin, who had retired in 1751.[4]

3. The prologue was published with *Catharine and Petruchio* (1756), Garrick's revision of *The Taming of the Shrew*. The Advertisement reads:

> THE following PROLOGUE was spoken to the Dramatic Pastoral, called the *Winter's Tale*, and this Comedy; both of which are altered from *Shakespear*, and were perform'd the same Night.
> Some of the Lines of the PROLOGUE are only relative to the *Winter's Tale*, yet as the Publication of the Pastoral is defer'd for some time, and as the PROLOGUE has been particularly desir'd, it is hop'd that it will not be disagreeable to the Reader to see it prefix'd to this Comedy.

4. Quin was the Falstaff of the century. Wilkinson in comparing Quin and Henderson as Falstaff gives the preference to Quin, who "had every requisite from Nature." (*Memoirs*, IV, 79.) Discussing the first part of *Henry IV*, Davies says that the public would not have tolerated another

But shou'd you call for Falstaff, *where to find him,*
He's gone—nor left one Cup of Sack behind him.
Sunk in his Elbow-Chair, no more he'll roam;
No more, with merry Wags, to Eastcheap *come;*
He's gone,—to jest, and laugh, and give his Sack at Home.

The closing lines are an unconscious commentary on Garrick's muddled and conflicting principles about the revision and presentation of Shakespeare:

> *The Five long Acts, from which our Three are taken,*
> *Stretch'd out to sixteen Years, lay by, forsaken.*
> *Lest then this precious Liquor run to waste,*
> *'Tis now confin'd and bottled for your Taste.*
> *'Tis my chief Wish, my Joy, my only Plan,*
> *To lose no Drop of that immortal Man!*

This is the extended simile at its worst. Arthur Murphy, quoting the last line, wittily observed that in the revision of *The Tempest*, Garrick "lost a *tun* of him." [5] Garrick revived and altered the simile in 1769 for the prologue to *The Jubilee*, an amusing piece full of life, spoken by King.

The performance of the play itself was often used as the basis of the comparison. Motteux's prologue to Farquhar's *The Twin Rivals* (1702) begins with an extended description of the actors' undergoing enemy storm during the five divisions of the play. The first two acts are but hit-or-miss sallies; with the third,

> *Your Critick-Engineer's Safe under ground*
> *Blow up our Works, and all our Art confound.*

Falstaff while Quin was on the stage. (*Dramatic Miscellanies*, I, 233.) Quin retired in 1751, but made his last appearance at a performance of *Henry IV* for Ryan's benefit at Covent Garden on March 19, 1753. See Genest, IV, 374–375.

5. Murphy, *The Life of David Garrick*, I, 302.

The fourth act *"Brings on most Action"* and somewhat re-
gains lost ground, but

> *Then comes the last; the Gen'ral Storm is near,*
> *The Poet-Governor now quakes for fear;*
> *Runs wildly up and down, forgets to huff,*
> *And wou'd give all h'as plunder'd—to get off.*

After lauding the bravery and triumph of the English soldiers at Venlo and Liège, the prologue returns to the battle
between the dramatist and the audience:

> *Then grant 'em gen'rous Terms who dare to write,*
> *Since now—That seems as desp'rate as to fight:*
> *If we must yield—Yet e're the day be fixt,*
> *Let us hold out the Third—And, if we may, the Sixth.*

The proceeds of the third, sixth, and ninth nights went
to the author after the charges of the house were deducted,
but so few plays in the early years of the century reached
a ninth night that the author did not think of such success as a possibility.

Using the metaphor made famous by Swift in *A Tale of
a Tub,* Cibber's epilogue to Dennis's *The Invader of His
Country* (1719) describes the speaker's coming forward

> *T'appease the Critick, as when under Sail*
> *Ships throw an empty Barrel to a Whale.*

Mrs. Barry, speaking Garrick's epilogue to *Sethona* (1774),
is a gypsy telling the fortunes of the audience by reading
their faces; Mrs. Abington in the epilogue to Cumberland's *The Choleric Man* (1774) is an artist drawing portraits of the audience while in Garrick's satirical banter
she comments on their deficiencies. The anonymous epilogue to Kenrick's comedy, *The Widow'd Wife* (1767),
supposes Mrs. Clive, the speaker, a doctor feeling the pulse
of the audience. Dressed in *"a suit of velvet, plain,"* with

a golden button and a smart bag wig, she prescribes taking the play every night:

> *'Tis by* our *nostrums you are kept alive:*
> *Pursue the regimen of doctor* CLIVE.

The least subtle of metaphors was that in which the prologue was compared to a bill of fare, "SINCE *plays are but a kind of Publick Feasts.*" [6] Motteux's epilogue to Farquhar's *The Inconstant* (1702) [7] is the most thorough development of the comparison.

> LIKE *hungry Guests a sitting Audience looks:*
> *Plays are like Suppers: Poets are the Cooks.*
> *The Founders you; The Table is this Place.*
> *The Carvers, We; The Prologue is the Grace.*

Garrick was especially pleased with culinary prologues. He introduced the "bill of fare" metaphor into his epilogue to Murphy's *All in the Wrong* (1761), giving it a patriotic twist:

> . . . *if I gain my wish,*
> *I'll give you, Sirs, a downright English dish.*[8]

He used it by way of anecdote in the prologue to Colman's *The Musical Lady* (1762), spoken and published repeatedly, the printed prologue bearing as a very apt motto Bayes's recommendation for his prologue-epilogue in *The Rehearsal*: "*And, 'egad, it will do for any other Play, as well as this.*" The prologue to Bickerstaffe's *Daphne and*

6. Prologue to Cibber's *Love Makes a Man* (1700). With the culinary prologues compare the first chapter of *Tom Jones*.

7. A note published with the first edition of the play concerns the presentation of the prologue: "The prologue that was spoke the first night receiv'd such additions from Mr — who spoke it, that they are best if bury'd and forgot. But the following Prologue is literally the same that was intended for the Play, and written by Mr *Motteux*." The speaker was probably Pinkethman, noted for his improvising.

8. Murphy, *Works* (1786), III, 381–383.

Amintor (1765) begins by informing the audience that the "cook" has been pleased "To hash a piece of ven'son that was cold" and has added fresh ingredients.[9] The most flagrant of Garrick's prologues is that to *A Christmas Tale* (December 27, 1773), spoken by Mr. Palmer [1] in the character of Christmas, ushered on to the stage by several persons carrying "different kinds of dishes." The piece was directed to the upper gallery, who are admonished:

> *O make the neighb'ring roof with rapture ring;*
> *Open your mouths, pray swallow every thing!*

Boswell mentioned the play and prologue in his letter to Garrick, dated April 11, 1774. "You have enlivened the Town, I see, with a musical piece. The prologue is admirably fancied *arripere populum tributim*, though to be sure Foote's remark applies to it, that your prologues have a culinary turn, and that therefore the motto to your collection of them should be *Animus jamdudum in patinis*." [2]

These "culinary" prologues are of no importance except as they indicate the caliber of the gallery audience, *"honest hearty grinners"* who were entirely uncritical, but Garrick could, with considerable vigor, direct his prologues to the critics in the pit. In his epilogue to *The Suspicious Husband,* he inserted a fable to illustrate the hard lot of playwrights:

9. Bickerstaffe based *Daphne and Amintor. A Comic Opera* on Saint-Foix's *The Oracle,* already adapted to the English stage by Mrs. Cibber. See the Preface to *Daphne and Amintor.*

1. This was apparently William Palmer. See the cast of the play as it is given in the *Drury Lane Calendar,* p. 219. Commonplace and ridiculous though the prologue is, it gained the speaker popularity. "The Prologue, spoke in the Character of Christmas, is new and laughable. Palmer does it great Justice, and rises daily in the public Esteem." *St. James's Chronicle,* December 30, 1773–January 1, 1774. For reference to a print showing Palmer speaking the prologue, see above, p. 37.

2. Boswell, *Letters,* I, 202, and note 1. Garrick's collection of his own prologues and epilogues is owned by the Folger Library. Some of Ben Jonson's prologues also have a "culinary turn"; see prologues to *The Silent Woman* and *The New Inn.*

AN *Ass there was, our Author bid me say,*
Who needs must write—He did—And wrote a Play.
The Parts were cast to various Beasts and Fowl:
Their Stage a Barn;—The Manager an Owl!
The House was cramm'd at Six, with Friends and Foes;
Rakes, Wits, and Criticks, Citizens and Beaux.

The epilogue proceeds to show how the audience is *"A perfect Abstract of the Brute-Creation!"* Murphy, in his *Life of David Garrick,* describes this epilogue as "new in the kind" and quotes it entire, adding the immediate interpretation of the fable by Rich, under whose management Garrick acted at Covent Garden in 1746–1747: "An anecdote of old Rich on this occasion has been often told. He sat in the orchestra on the first night, and when Mrs. Pritchard spoke the words, *'The manager an owl,'* he turned to a friend, and whispered, *'He means me.'* "[3]

A writer often unified his prologue or epilogue by building it around the title of the play which it introduced. One of the most common devices was to present the title as a rhetorical question, or to give it an unexpected turn or playful application. Garrick ended the epilogue to Murphy's *All in the Wrong* (1761) with a lively song of nine stanzas, sung by two ballad singers, each stanza ending with a reference to the title:

YE *Critics above, and ye Critics below,*
Ye finer spun Critics, who keep the mid row,
O tarry a moment, I'll sing you a song,
Shall prove that, like us, you are all in the wrong.

Ye Poets, who mount on the fam'd winged steed,
Of prancing, and wincing, and kicking take heed:
For when by those hornets, the Critics, you're stung,
You're thrown in the dirt, and are all in the wrong.

3. *The Life of David Garrick,* I, 127.

Ye Actors, who act what these writers have writ,
Pray stick to your Poet, and spare your own wit;
For when with your own you unbridle your tongue,
I'll hold ten to one you are all in the wrong.

He directs his stanzas at the various theatre-goers—news-mongers, politicians, soldiers, and sailors in the upper gallery—until he arrives at his clever conclusion:

Ye judges of taste to our labours be kind,
Our errors are many, pray wink, or be blind;
Still find your way hither to glad us each night,
And our note we will change to you're all in the right.

Garrick devised the entire epilogue to Hugh Kelly's *The School for Wives* as a play on the title. Drury Lane is *"An* ancient College *to instruct the town."*

We've Schools *for* Rakes, *for* Fathers, Lovers, Wives.

The School for Scandal, which Garrick called "The School," was yet to be added to the number. Mrs. Mattocks, speaking Garrick's epilogue to Murphy's *Know Your Own Mind* (1777),[4] applies the title to the various persons in the audience who do not know their own minds and concludes with an appeal to the critics,

Be of one *Mind with me, and like this Play;*
Thence will two wonders rise: Wits will be kind,
Nay more—behold a Woman Knows her *Mind!*

In the closing years of the century, prologues and epilogues completely detached from the subject of their plays, except for the reference to the title, became increasingly common. Many of these were independent acting pieces, but they are chiefly distinguished by their approach to *vers de société.* An excellent example is the prologue to Mrs. Cowley's *Second Thoughts Are Best* (1781),[5] a revision of

4. Murphy, *Works*, IV, 181–182.
5. The *Gentleman's Magazine*, April 1781, p. 187.

her comedy, *The World as It Goes,* which had been performed at Covent Garden the preceding month, the opening lines referring to both plays and the alterations:

I'm sent to tell you—what's by all confest,
In every Act—our *Second Thoughts are best.*
Thus hath our Author form'd anew her Play,
And leaves the *World* to go its usual way;
In this, she hopes, you'll join in her support;
For second thoughts thro' country, city, court,
Amend the slips, which slanderers make their sport.

Each stanza recurred to the title and at the same time
afforded the speaker, Lee Lewes, a chance to delight the
audience by his impersonations.

The blusterer, who would fright us with his threats
Of swords and pistols, paying honour's debts,
Cries—"Dare you with a man of courage jest?
'I'll cut your throat—but *Second Thoughts are best.*"

Old Hoardly—listening to his starven heir,
Says—"I'll relieve your pain, your want, your care,
"Tarry but while I unlock yon iron chest—
"But stop!—I'm told that *Second Thoughts are best.*"

George Colman, the younger, in his epilogue to Edward
Morris's *The Secret* (1799), imparts a "secret" to the Drury
Lane family, the first line quoted, with its implication that
the "critic-parents" are also hangmen, being a parody of
Polly's famous song in *The Beggar's Opera:*

Ah! ponder well, thou Critic-Parent, dear!
And, be not on The Secret too severe!

.   .   .   .

But, ah! there is one Secret still behind,
Our Bard, to-night, has struggled hard to find.
'Tis one on which depends his Rise or Fall;—
It is the Secret—how to please you All.

Colman altered the last four lines from the conclusion to
Garrick's *Address to the Town,* a prologue that he spoke
soon after the half-price riots in 1763, before a performance of Mrs. Centlivre's *The Busie Body.*[6] This is one of
the many instances in which Garrick's prologues were
adapted without acknowledgment.

At the turn of the century, John Taylor, a facile and
prolific versifier, achieved success with the prologue as light
verse for which he needed to know nothing of the play
except the title.[7] His prologue to *Sighs* (1799), a comedy
adapted from Kotzebue, proves the theme of the play of
universal applicability,

> For where's the heart without its secret sigh!

The "scenic Muse" forever sighs in vain for something
new; the miser, lover, hero, and poet sigh.

> The Critic hunts for faults with eager eyes,
> And only o'er an author's beauties sighs.

As for the author,

> He fears, alas! the weakness of his cause,
> And sighs most anxiously for your applause.

Taylor's epilogue to Holman's *The Votary of Wealth*
(1799) is also a rhymed essay on the title, managed with
vivacity and playfulness. Such pieces are separated from
the trenchant, critical, and often indecent prologues of
the early years of the century by a revolution in the men-
tality, character, and taste of the audience. Written for

6. "Address to the Town" (the *London Magazine,* March 1763, p. 159)
ends:

> There is one secret still remains behind,
> Which ever did, and will distract my Mind—
> I'd give up all for that—nay, fix for ever,
> To find the Secret—to deserve your Favour.

7. Taylor's prologues and epilogues are collected in Volume One of his
Poems on Various Subjects (1827).

comedies and farces, they are artistically appropriate and in complete harmony with the gaiety and banter which they introduced or concluded.

Although Garrick was not the first to think of the epilogue as light verse built around the title, he surpassed his predecessors in the art and remained without a rival. His epilogue to Bickerstaffe's *'Tis Well It's No Worse*,[8] spoken by King, is one of the best of the century and is still alive with the excitement and suspense of the moment when the curtain was about to fall and the author given over to the critics:

INSTEAD of an epilogue, round, smart, and terse,
Let poor simple me, and in more simple verse,
Just handle the text—*It is well it's no worse.*

The brat of this night, should you cherish and nurse,
And hush it, and rock it, tho' you fill not his purse,
The daddy will say, that—*'Tis well it's no worse.*

Or shou'd his strange fortune turn out the reverse,
That his pockets you fill, tho' his play you shou'd curse,
Still our author will say—*It is well it's no worse.*

The town with each poet, will push, carte and tierce,
If the bard can so guard, that his buff you don't pierce,
Tho' you pink him a little—*'Tis well it's no worse.*

Should the play-house be full, tho' the criticks so fierce,
The managers, actors, and author asperse,
We shrug up our shoulders—*'Tis well it's no worse.*

But should you to damn, be resolv'd and perverse,
If quietly after, from hence you disperse,
We wish you good-night—and—*It's well it's no worse.*

8. Bickerstaffe wrote as the concluding paragraph of his Preface to *'Tis Well It's No Worse*: "To Mr. Garrick he is indebted for—every thing; but, as they were given in a moment of necessity and disappointment, he must particularly thank him for his Prologue and Epilogue; the value of the gift being in no sort lessened to the receiver, by the short time taken to produce them."

CHAPTER 4

THE AUDIENCE AS IT IS
REFLECTED IN THE PROLOGUES
AND EPILOGUES

The most marked characteristic of pro-
logues and epilogues is their liveliness and vitality. This
is true of Plautus's prologue to the *Menaechmi* and of
Terence's prologue to the *Andria*, of Marlowe's prologue
to *Tamburlaine*, of Shakespeare's prologue to *Henry VIII*,
of Dryden's prologue to *The Conquest of Granada*, of
Garrick's prologue to *The School for Scandal*, and of the
prologues by obscure scribblers of the eighteenth century.
Written to meet a practical demand and often ephemeral
by their very nature, the prologues are an undimmed and
vivid portrait of the society which produced them. Differing in scope from diaries and letters, they approached life
from all angles and depicted in bright, ever-changing and
yet ever-recurring patterns successive generations of theatre-goers. The vivacity of the prologues springs from the
close relationship of the speaker to the audience. This
relationship was most immediate on the platform stage of
the Elizabethans, but it remained as long as the speaker

could "come forward" on the apron to address the audience. Even as late as 1773 the speaker was sufficiently near his audience to single them out for raillery.

> *You, Sir, in blue, red cape—not quite so grave:*
> *That critick there in black—so stern and thin,*
> *Before you frown, pray let the tale begin—*
> *You in the crimson capuchin, I fear you,*
> *Why, Madam, at this time so cross appear you?* [1]

"Are you all seated—may I venture in?" asks Bannister, speaking the prologue to *The Captives* (1786). He bids the *"Noise behind"* to cease, and *"Advancing, points to the Pit doors":*

> But first—are both your pit doors shut, I pray?
> Or noise will drown my strictures on the play.

He is interrupted by *"Noise from front boxes opening doors and calling places,"* and he mimics the box-keeper, "Your seat, my Lord, is here—your La'ship's there."

> Truce then with your confounded clank of keys.

Pictures are static; prologues and epilogues are full of din and commotion. Arthur Murphy in his occasional prologue presented at Covent Garden on October 18, 1754, addresses the noisy house:

> You then, who in the upper regions fix,
> Suspend awhile the tumult of your sticks.
> Ye box-keepers, each ruder noise give o'er,
> And all be hush'd,—as fruit-girls were no more.
> Unbend ye critic brows, and O ye beaux,
> Forget the gay anxiety of cloaths.[2]

Miles Peter Andrews's epilogue to Frederic Reynolds's *The Dramatist,* performed at Covent Garden on May 16,

1. Garrick's prologue to *A Christmas Tale* (1773).
2. The *Gentleman's Magazine,* October 1754, p. 479.

1789, surveys the audience from the point of view of a late comer:

> What an overflowing House, methinks I see!
> Here, Box-keeper, are those my Places? No,
> Madam Van Bulk has taken all that Row;
> Then I'll go back—you can't—you can, she fibs,
> Keep down your Elbows, or you'll break my Ribs;
> Zounds, how you squeeze! Of what do you think one
>   made is?
> Is this your Wig? No, it's that there Lady's.[3]

A young rake in one of the side-boxes makes an assignation with an alderman's pretty wife. The alderman finally notices the beau:

3. Quoted by Allardyce Nicoll, *A History of Late Eighteenth Century Drama 1750–1800* (Cambridge, 1927), p. 10. Compare Garrick's description of the crowded house in the prologue to *New Brooms!*, spoken for the opening of Drury Lane on September 21, 1776:

> The Coachman Manager will sometimes please ye—
> But shou'd he stuff the Coach too full, and squeeze ye,
> You then begin to swear—"Zounds! shut the door,
> "We're cramm'd already—here's no room for more."

At the close of the century the theatre as it is represented in the prologues is always crowded, the reverse of the sad condition of the 1730's when the common theme of prologues was the neglect of the town. The opening lines of Mrs. Cowley's prologue to *The Town before You*, spoken by Mrs. Mattock's, describe the audience in 1794 (Nicoll, p. 10):

> Ah! ah! you're here, and comfortably tight?
> Well squeezed and press'd, I see—from left to right.
> Waiting the moment when the curtain rises,
> Gaping for plots, adventures, and surprises!

For extended discussions of the eighteenth-century audience, see James J. Lynch, *Box, Pit and Gallery; Stage and Society in Johnson's London* (University of California Press, 1953); Harry W. Pedicord, *The Theatrical Public in the Time of Garrick* (New York, King's Crown Press, 1954); John Loftis, *Comedy and Society from Congreve to Fielding* (Stanford University Press, 1959).

> Who's that scroudges? You shan't shove my wife,
> I shove her! A good Joke, upon my Life.

The following passages, chosen from hundreds equally
pertinent, illustrate that, turn to what part of the century
we will, the prologues and epilogues bring the audience
to life, often with unflattering realism. In 1700 theatre-
goers, in spite of the reformers, were still those of the
preceding age, including the "vizard masks" in the side-
boxes—

> Ye Side-Box Nuns, that hood-wink all your Graces,
> For Modesty won't let you shew your Faces.[4]

Charles Johnson, in the epilogue to Love and Liberty. A
Tragedy (1709), describes the critics "shooting" the ladies
through an "optic glass" instead of paying attention to the
play and forbids them to pass sentence on what they have
neither seen nor heard. Turning to the rest of the house,
the speaker continues:

> Nor barbarous Noises from the Gallery come,
> Nor Mask below to clap nor hiss presume:
> Let the Miss cackle at the Fops that flout her,
> Or cluck the Squires that hovering peep about her.

In 1719 the "vizards" were still frequenting the theatre in
Lincoln's Inn Fields, the prologue to The Younger Brother
then referring to them as "those bashful Ladies,"

> Who, with a hood-wink'd Face, the Play-house haunt.

Mrs. Oldfield, speaking Cibber's epilogue to Mrs. Centlivre's The Man's Bewitch'd (1709), casts her eyes over the
house to discover who has sent her the verses that she holds
in her hand:

<hr/>

4. Epilogue to Baker's Hampstead-Heath (1705).

Let's see! it can't be, sure! from th' upper Flight;
No, no—that's plain—for— None of them can Write:
Nor can I think it from the Middle fell;
For I'm afraid—as few of them can Spell:
Beside, their Haggling Passions never gain,
Beyond the Passage-walking Nymphs of Drury-Lane:
And then the Pit's more stock'd with Rakes and Rovers,
Than any of these senseless, whining Lovers.
The Backs o' th' Boxes too seem mostly lin'd
With Souls, whose Passion's to themselves confin'd.

The anonymous epilogue spoken by Peg Woffington in Covent Garden on January 8, 1755, after a performance of *The Suspicious Husband*,[5] also presents a straightforward picture, with the customary reference to the various levels of the house. There are the love-making pairs in the upper gallery; the prostitutes in the green boxes; the gallants in the pit; the effeminate beaux on the stage; and the fine ladies in the front boxes, who have reluctantly left "the dear society of cards" to be bored by a play. The epilogue is neither indecent nor comic; it analyzes the audience with critical brutality but also reveals an awareness of social responsibility.[6]

5. Genest, IV, 419.
6. "Epilogue *spoken by Mrs.* Woffington, *at the Theatre-Royal in* Covent-Garden; *after a Play for the Benefit of* The Lying-in Hospital for married Women." *The London Magazine,* January 1755, p. 36. The prologue may very well have been written by the speaker, whose character was a mixture of coarseness, generosity, and sympathy. On her death she endowed almshouses in Teddington. (Doran, *"Their Majesties' Servants,"* II, 13.)
    For other references to the green boxes, see the epilogue to *A Word to the Wise;* the stage directions to Isaac Jackman's *The Divorce* (1781); the prologue by George Colman, the younger, for the opening of the Haymarket, June 14, 1790; and the prologue to Charles Stuart's *The Distrest Baronet* (1787). The green boxes were not confined to the London theatres; for example, they are mentioned in the playbills for the Theatre-Royal in York, January 24, February 3 and 19, March 8, 10, 11, 1784, preserved in an extra-illustrated copy of James Boaden's *The Life of Mrs. Dorothy Jordan,* Vol. I, in the Theatre Collection at Harvard.

The inattention of the audience was a matter of continual comment in the prologues, but the author who was greeted by mere indifference was fortunate. Garrick's epilogue to *The Clandestine Marriage* (1766) is a playlet dealing with a group of stupid people who, out of idleness and dullness, are resolved to damn all plays. The fine lady, acted by Mrs. Abington, describes her company at the theatre:

> *In the first Act Lord George began to doze,*
> *And criticis'd the Author—through his Nose;*
> *So loud indeed, that as his Lordship snor'd,*
> *The Pit turn'd round, and all the Brutes encor'd.*

Garrick was particularly aware of the part of the audience who ignored the play and came only to be seen. Mrs. Cibber, presenting his epilogue to Samuel Crisp's *Virginia* (1754), asks:

> *May I approach unto the* Boxes, *pray—*
> *And there search out a judgment on the Play?*
> *In vain, alas! I should attempt to find it—*
> *Fine Ladies see a Play, but never mind it—*
> *'Tis vulgar to be mov'd by acted passion,*
> *Or form opinions, till they're fix'd by fashion.—*

In the prologue to *A Christmas Tale* (1773), the speaker remarks:

> *Don't think, fair Ladies, I expect that you,*
> *Should hear my tale—you've something else to do.*

Mr. Beecher Hogan tells me that these boxes were those nearest the top of the theatre; the more expensive lower boxes were usually trimmed in crimson. But green was the favorite color of the theatres; *cf.* the green-room and the green carpet used in the final acts of tragedies. Mrs. Barry, speaking Garrick's epilogue to *Alfred* (1778) asks:

> *If this green cloth could speak, would it not tell,*
> *Upon it's well-worn nap how oft I fell?*

The prologue to Thomas Baker's *Tunbridge-Walks: or, The Yeoman of Kent* (1703) is addressed to a motley audience—to *"dreadful Sons of War,"* who have come to *"fright fair Maids in Masks";* to the beaux, lacking in courage and brains; to courtiers

> . . . *who in Wit, and Judgment grow,*
> *For where the Money Ebbs, the Wit shou'd Flow.*

But added to these are the *"Citts,"* so brisk and plump,

> *Fatn'd with good* Quest-*Ale, and* Christmas *Cheer,*

a part of the audience increasing so rapidly in importance that by the middle of the century they could not be omitted from the prologues, and to them many of Garrick's pieces are addressed. In 1706 Baker again comments on the increase of the middle classes in the audience:

> *Some Cheapside-Bobbs too trudge it to our Play,*
> *Faith,* Jack, *this* Hay-Market's *a cursed way:*
> *What signifie the Quality or Wits,*
> *The Money,* Daniel, *rises from us Cits.*
> *Who, like Cock-Sparrows, hop about the Benches,*
> *And court, with Six-pences, fat Orange-Wenches.*[7]

Of less importance, but also growing in number, and different in character from Ralph in *The Knight of the Burning Pestle,* were the apprentices whom the epilogue to Mrs. Centlivre's *Love's Contrivance* in 1703 describes in terms that would fit George Barnwell:

> *The City Prentices, those upstart Beaus,*
> *In short spruce Puffs, and* Vigo *Colour Clothes,*
> *Who with a Brace of Trulls stole here to Day,*
> *And muster'd up a Crown to see this Play;*
> *Lewdness and Gaming will run them aground,*
> *And Masters Cash fall short a Hunded Pound.*

7. Epilogue to Mrs. Centlivre's *The Platonick Lady* (1706).

Apprentices who paid a crown for admission sat in the boxes, and the prologue to *The Dramatist* includes them among the heterogeneous audience in the side-boxes in 1789. Less affluent apprentices paid a shilling and sat with the footmen in the upper gallery.

For the author of the play the most important part of the audience was the dreadful jury of critics in the pit, and to them the prologuisers constantly referred. Ordinarily during the first night's performance the author stood behind the scenes, the speaker of the prologue pretending to be looking at him or even talking to him. The presence of the unseen author, alert to every hiss and shielded from damnation by the speaker alone, gave verisimilitude to the imaginary conversation:

> *I told the Bard—(ay, yonder he stands quaking,*
> *Alas! poor Soul, he's in a piteous Taking!)—*
> *I hope, Sir, you'll excuse what I shall say:—*
> *But truely, Sir, I tremble for your Play.*[8]

Arthur Murphy, dressed in traditional black, spoke Garrick's prologue to his farce, *The Apprentice* (1756), declaring himself *"The Culprit of this Night."*

> *Prologues precede the* Piece,—*in mournful Verse;*
> *As Undertakers—walk before the Hearse.*
> *Whose doleful March may strike the harden'd Mind,*
> *And wake it's feelings—for the Dead—behind.*

Garrick, in the character of the disappointed and drunken poet, delivering the prologue to Murphy's *The Desert Island* (1760), looks *"behind the Scenes,"* and says to the successful rival, *"Ay, you may frown."* In the prologue to Kelly's *False Delicacy* (1768), he assures the audience that regardless of how conceited the author may be,

8. Epilogue spoken by Miss Bellamy to Moncreiff's *Appius* (1755).

In three hours time, you'll bring him to his senses;
And well you may, when in your power you get him,
In that short space, you blister, bleed, and sweat him.

Fielding in the epilogue to Captain Charles Bodens's *The Modish Couple* (1732) pronounced the playwright braver than the soldier—"*One* Critic Clerk *wou'd rout an* Alexander." Nine nights of such torment, and the poet will "*dwindle to a Beau*":

His Pegasus, *when next he mounts, will know it,*
And wonder what's become of half *the* Poet.

Sometimes the author tried to mollify the pit by submission and modesty. The epilogue to Sir Hildebrand Jacob's three comedies, *The Nest of Plays,* described on the title page as "the first Play licenced by the Lord Chamberlain, since the late Act concerning the Stage," makes the usual reference to the author:

And now I come to plead for Master Bayes.
Doubtful, and pale, behind the Scenes *he stands;*
Yet hopes a gen'rous Pardon from your Hands.

But as he relates in his Preface, he received very different treatment, for the audience would not tolerate a licensed play. The prologue or epilogue often asked for mercy because the author was young or inexperienced as a dramatist; for example, Fielding wrote the epilogue to *Love in Several Masques* (1728) as a plea to the "*tremendous Criticks in the Pit,*" entreating them to be lenient with the first play of a very young author who in time might improve. All prologuisers, including Fielding, conclude such appeals with the supposition that the critics will turn a deaf ear, rise in wrath, and damn the play to insure themselves from further trouble with the aspiring young playwright and to warn off a host of scribblers. Pleas for the author's youth were too frequently abused to be effective.

Addison in the prologue to his comedy, *The Drummer; or, the Haunted-House,* performed anonymously in Drury Lane on March 10, 1716, three years after the triumph of *Cato,* describing the author as *"anxious for his Fame to Night,"* goes on to remind the critics that

> *Censure, when no Man knows who writes the Play,*
> *Were much good Malice merely thrown away,*

and then refers to himself as

> *A raw young Thing, who dares not tell his Name.*

If the play fails, he threatens to help hiss it off the stage, as Lamb almost a century later hissed *Mr. H.:*

> *But, if you're rough, and use him like a Dog,*
> *Depend upon it—He'll remain Incog.*
> *If you shou'd hiss, he swears He'll hiss as high,*
> *And, like a Culprit, join the Hue-and-Cry.*

But even when the appeal was false, the author's dread was sufficiently genuine. In 1700 Dryden began his prologue to the revision of Fletcher's *The Pilgrim* with a description of the poet baited by the audience as a bear at the stake is baited by dogs:

> *HOW wretched is the Fate of those who write!*
> *Brought muzled to the Stage, for fear they bite.*
> *Where, like* Tom Dove, *they stand the Common Foe;*
> *Lugg'd by the* Critique, *Baited by the* Beau.
> *Yet worse, their Brother* Poets *Damn the Play,*
> *And Roar the loudest, tho' they never Pay.*[9]

9. Dryden wrote both the prologue and epilogue for the play, performed just before his death. Both pieces "equal anything of the kind which he ever produced," and are excellent examples of the trenchant Restoration prologues and epilogues. See the prefatory note to *The Pilgrim,* in *The Works of John Dryden,* ed. Scott and Saintsbury (Edinburgh, 1882–1893), VIII, 480, and W. B. Gardner, *The Prologues and Epilogues of John Dryden* (New York, 1951), pp. 335–340.

Garrick in 1767 informs the "snarling" critics that they must be "muzzled" for the first performance of his dramatic romance, *Cymon*.[1] By a slight change in the metaphor, the critics become a pack of hounds pursuing the helpless author. In the prologue to *Eugenia* (1752) by Philip Francis, Garrick advises the critics not to destroy the game at once but wait, *"like other Sportsmen,"* till he grows older and can give them a good chase; in the epilogue to Mrs. Griffith's *The School for Rakes* (1769) the author is a hare, trembling

'Till she escapes this dreadful *pack of wits.*

George Colman, writing in 1780, compares the poet to a beggar followed not by one dog but by a whole pack of critic curs, snarling and howling.[2]

There is a unanimity in the playwrights' condemnation of the critic, expressed by the similarity of the comparisons used by widely different writers in every decade of the century. To Lord Lansdowne in 1701 the critics are vultures feeding on the carrion of plays. He particularly resents lack of intelligent criticism; every dunce who has money enough to get a seat in the pit may set himself up as a critic of a play that he cannot understand.[3] Nicholas Rowe in 1707 accuses the audience of damning his play, *The Royal Convert,* without listening to it:

Each puny Whipster here, is Wit enough,
With scornful Airs, and supercilious Snuff,
To cry, This Tragedy's such damn'd grave Stuff.[4]

1. *Cymon* . . . The Third Edition (1767). The prologue was not printed in the first and second editions.
2. Prologue to *A Chapter of Accidents* (1780).
3. "Prologue *to Mr.* Higgons's *excellent Tragedy, call'd* The Generous Conqueror." Quoted from *Poems upon Several Occasions.* The Third Edition (1721), pp. 108–109.
4. Prologue to *The Royal Convert* (1707).

Francis Godolphin Waldron, in the prologue to his first play, *The Maid of Kent* (1773), thinks of the critics as birds of prey ready with beak and talon to dig out the heart of the "melodious lark." In 1711 Charles Johnson devoted the entire prologue to his comedy, *The Generous Husband,* to a consideration of the critic. He concludes that poets have become so intimidated that they no longer dare to write honestly and hence it follows that the comic spirit is driven from the stage. He knows that the house is packed and he expects no justice:

> *The Law most wisely does those Trades exclude,*
> *From Pannels upon Life—who deal in Blood.*
> *Criticks are Butchers all—inur'd to Death,*
> *The Blood-hounds never give a Poet Breath.*

In 1775 the speaker of the epilogue to Dr. Thomas Francklin's *Matilda,* in pleading with the *"Tribunal of Old Drury,"* banishes the critic, for

> *Death is his Trade, and Damning—his Profession;*
> *Disqualify'd—because, to say no further,*
> *Butchers are never heard in case of Murther.*

The prologue to the anonymous, unacted comedy, *The Humours of the Road,* published in 1738, declares that an author would as readily find courteous treatment at Billingsgate or Hockley in the Hole as in a theatre, such is the critics' *"Brutish Love of doing ill."*

In the pit were the disappointed and jealous rival authors who came for the sole purpose of damning the successful playwright. Congreve refers to them in the epilogue to *The Way of the World* (1700) as *"Spys on Plays,"* coming to the pit in shoals. James Miller includes rival poets in his survey of the house in the epilogue to *The Humours of Oxford* as *"those who've Wrote themselves, but Wrote in vain,"* and therefore *"Usurp the Criticks Privilege, to*

Rail." Mrs. Yates, in Murphy's epilogue to *The Choice*
(1765), turns to the critics and suggests a reason for their
malice:

> . . . *amongst you here i' th' Pit,*
> *Are there no bards, who like an Inquest sit*
> *On murder'd plays, and rave, and fret, and foam,*
> *And* DAMN *this piece,—yet have a worse at home?* [5]

James Cobb's prologue to the comedy *The Projects* [6] (1786),
spoken by Bannister, is in the manner of Gay's *Trivia* and
gives a humorous turn to the jealousy of the rival poet:

> WHO has not been (just at his dinner hour)
> In London streets o'ertaken by a shower;
> And whilst a door receiv'd his straighten'd back,
> In vain has halloo'd to the passing hack;
> 'Till pinch'd with hunger, and his patience tir'd,
> Hoarse with the frequent call of "Coach unhir'd,"
> Desperate has sallied from his cold retreat,
> And dared the dangers of the dirty street;
> Where luckier friends, blest with a coach at last,
> Have nodded, smil'd, and splash'd him as they pass'd.
> But worse, alas! the dangers which surround
> The Bard, who ventures on dramatic ground.
> Who dares the critic storm, the sneering cough,
> The hiss—the ah! no more! and Off! Off! Off!
> While brother bards, snug in their boxes sit,
> Loll at their ease, and—splash him with their wit.

The inhumanity of the critics occasionally aroused bitter
personal comment in prologues and now and then an author made a plain statement of his hard lot. James Miller's
epilogue to *Art and Nature,* performed at Drury Lane on
February 16, 1738, is addressed to "Ye cruel bloody Criticks

5. *The Works of Arthur Murphy* (1786), IV, 387–388.
6. The *London Chronicle,* Feb. 21–23, 1786.

of the *Pit*," and reminds them of the author's labors in making his play perfect and of the diligence of the actors who "Forty Morns together" came shivering to rehearsals through cold and wet, "not to be heard at last." In these characteristic lines, Mrs. Clive, the speaker, voiced not only her own grievance but her concern for the difficulties into which the theatre had fallen. Hugh Kelly's prologue to *A Word to the Wise* (1770) bitterly advised the audience to damn the play so that the poet will remain destitute as poets should:

> What, tho some taylor's oft protracted bill
> May hang all trembling on the author's quill,
> Regard it not, remove the growing evil—
> A well drest poet is the very devil—
> Do taverns dun him—What, can scribblers treat?
> Fine times, indeed, when scribblers think to eat—
> Do justice then—to-night, ten minutes here
> May blast the bard's whole labour of a year.—

He urged the audience to remember that mercy is "the Briton's noblest crown," but the appeal, although made by Thomas King, was in vain and the play was damned. Holcroft's prologue to *Seduction* (1787) describes the disappointment and resentment attendant on the unmerciful lash of the critic who, with all the pain which he inflicts, cannot quite succeed in extinguishing genius.

Prologuisers gave much consideration to how they might best appease the critics:

> *Long have we thought, much Labour has it cost,*
> *What sort of Prologue 'tis wou'd please you most.*[7]

Some resorted to satire and invective, some met censure with disdain, and others tried submission and insidious flattery. Woodward, dressed as Harlequin, ended his clever

7. Prologue to *Hibernia Freed* (1722) by William Philips.

prologue to the anonymous farce, *An Hour before Marriage* (1772)—the title page giving the information: "as it was Attempted to be Acted at the Theatre-Royal in Covent-Garden"—by beseeching the audience to damn the play as it had usurped the place of pantomime. *Biographia Dramatica* records: "The audience seem too literally to have understood this ludicrous advice of the motley hero." [8]

In 1732 in the prologue to *The Old Debauchees*, Fielding ridiculed various prologue conventions, including the attack on the critics:

> *Perhaps, for Change, you, now and then, by Fits,*
> *Are told that Criticks are the Bane of Wits;*
> *How they turn Vampyres, being dead and damn'd,*
> *And with the Blood of living Bards are cramm'd.*

The prologue to *The Universal Gallant* (1735), spoken by Quin, is a serious consideration of the lack of critical standards. No playwright can please the critics, for they come determined to condemn:

> *Writing seems War declar'd against the Town.*

In a word, there is no criticism, and the decisions of the pit are merely the expression of insensibility and brutality:

> *'Tis not the Poet's Wit affords the Jest,*
> *But who can Cat-call, Hiss, or Whistle best.*
> *Can then another's Anguish give you Joy?*
> *Or is it such a Triumph to destroy?*
> *We, like the fabled Frogs, consider thus,*
> *This may be Sport to you, but it is Death to us.*

The Universal Gallant was damned, and Fielding repeated his accusations of the critics in the Advertisement to the published play.

8. *Biographia Dramatica*, II, 311. See also Genest, V, 331, for the unhappy fate of the play.

A boisterous description of the brutality of the critics is given in the prologue to *The Wedding Day* (1743), the last of Fielding's plays to be performed while he was living. Written and spoken by the actor, Charles Macklin, the prologue is one of the liveliest of the century and important because of its comments on Fielding as a dramatist and because of the vividness with which it sets before us the intimate relationship of speaker, author, and audience. Macklin begins by informing the audience that they will be deprived of the prologue that they expected:

. . . *If you please, your Money shall be return'd. But Mr.*
    Garrick, to day
Who performs a principal Character in the Play,
Unfortunately has sent word, 'twill be impossible, having
    so long a Part,
To speak the Prologue: He hasn't had time to get it by
    Heart.

He proceeds in doggerel, apparently improvising. When the author suggests that they begin without a prologue, the speaker warns him that such neglect would invite the audience to damn the play.

"Ha! damn my Play!" the frighted Bard replies:
"Dear Macklin, you must go on then and apologize."
Apologize! not I: Pray, Sir, excuse me.
"Zounds! something must be done: Prithee, don't refuse
    me:
"Prithee, go on: Tell them, to damn my Play, will be a
    damn'd hard Case.
"Come, do: You've a good long, dismal, Mercy-begging
    Face."
Sir, your humble Servant: You're very merry.—"Yes," says
    he; "I've been drinking
"To raise my Spirits; for by Jupiter! I found 'em sinking."

So away he went to see the Play.—O! there he sits:
Smoke him, smoke the Author, you laughing Crits.
Isn't he finely situated for a damning Oh—Oh! a—a shrill
Whihee? O direful Yell!
As Falstaff *says: Would it were Bed-time,* Hal, *and all were*
well!
What think you now? Who's Face looks worse, yours or
mine?
Ah! thou foolish Follower of the ragged Nine,
You'd better stick to honest Abram Adams, *by half.*
He, in spight of Critics, can make your Readers laugh.

Macklin then pretends to stumble through the "old Prologue Cant," making occasional gibes at the author and
ending with the conventional appeal to the jury of critics.

More efficacious than humor and cajolery was the subtle
flattery which proclaimed that the author felt no terror
of the pit as he valued only the judgment of men of
intelligence who were free from prejudice—a circuitous
way of calling all men who did not applaud the play
dunces:

> *Such* Cynics, *and such* Wou'd be*'s, give no Pain,*
> *Their Censure is Applause, their Praise Disdain.*[9]

Aaron Hill tried the device in the prologue to *The Tuscan
Treaty* (1733) and again in the prologue to Thomson's
Agamemnon (1738). The latter is a somewhat heavy piece,
spoken by Quin, and begins by describing the means by
which authors try to "bribe" applause:

> *Nor poorly fearful, nor securely vain;*
> *Ours would, by honest Ways, that Grace obtain:*
> *Would, as a Free-born Wit, be fairly try'd:*
> *And then—let Truth and Candour, fair, decide.*

9. The second prologue to Joseph Dorman's *The Female Rake* (1736).

He courts no Friend, who blindly comes to praise;
He dreads no Foe—but whom his Faults may raise.

Indulge a generous Pride, that bids him own,
He aims to please, by noble means alone:
By what may win the Judgment, wake the Heart,
Inspiring Nature, and directing Art:
By scenes, so wrought, so rais'd, as may command
Applause, more from the Head, than from the Hand.

He concludes by emphasizing the moral of the play. The similarity of Hill's prologue to *Agamemnon* to the closing lines of Johnson's prologue to *Irene* is apparent. Johnson's prologue conforms to the established pattern and yet is expressive of his character:

Be this at least his Praise; be this his Pride;
To force Applause no modern Arts are try'd.
Shou'd partial Cat-calls all his Hopes confound;
He bids no Trumpet quell the fatal Sound.
Shou'd welcome Sleep relieve the weary Wit,
He rolls no Thunders o'er the drowsy Pit.
No Snares to captivate the Judgment spreads;
Nor bribes your Eyes to prejudice your Heads.
Unmov'd tho' Witlings sneer and Rivals rail;
Studious to please, yet not asham'd to fail.
He scorns the meek Address, the suppliant Strain,
With Merit needless, and without it vain.
In Reason, Nature, Truth he dares to trust:
Ye Fops be silent! and ye Wits be just!

By the middle of the century, authors were attempting to control the audience by describing the pit as reformed and no longer ready to damn unjustly. In place of "Gothic Uproar," Candour, Patience, and Politeness rule the pit.[1]

1. Prologue to McNamara Morgan's *Philoclea* (1754).

The prologue to Dodsley's *Cleone* (1758) refers to former times when *"Prologues were but Preludes to engage"* and adds optimistically, *"Past are those hostile days."* The prologue to Richardson's *The Fugitive* (1792) begins with the usual allusion to the author,

> Actor and Author in one panic join'd;
> I quake before the curtain; he behind.—

But the writer adds:

> And yet, in modern times, th' aspiring Wit
> Braves but few perils from the well-dress'd pit.

Conditions are now altered, for the pit has grown civil, its "chequer'd crowds" including ladies. Tate Wilkinson, writing in 1790, observed that "at present, to save the audience trouble, the morning papers have taken most of the grand articles of setting up or knocking down into their own custody." [2]

Nevertheless, in 1789 Cumberland in the epilogue to *The Impostors* speaks of the author as going *"Stern foremost down the rapides of damnation,"* and in 1790 John Taylor refers to the critics as

> . . . the dragons, breathing hostile flame,
> Who watch th' Hesperian fruit of letter'd fame.[3]

These, and the passages quoted in the following discussion, suggest that Wilkinson's comment is a gibe at the newspaper critics rather than a description of a reformed pit. In 1703 Farquhar in his prologue to Francis Manning's

2. Wilkinson, *Memoirs*, IV, 82.

3. John Taylor's prologue to the farce, *Modern Breakfast; or, All Asleep at Noon*, by Henry Siddons. The play was published in 1790, with a dedication to Mrs. Piozzi. The prologue is much too long but justly pleads for clemency because of the author's youth, Henry Siddons being then just sixteen.

All for the Better expressed the settled opinion of play-wrights of the eighteenth century:

> *Rejoyce ye Criticks, who the Pit do Cram,*
> *For ye shall have a glut of Plays—to damn.*

The frequent references to catcalls, with which the "critics" armed themselves at new plays, are sufficient to prove that the poets' fears were grounded in a stark reality. The catcalls were the recognized instruments of damnation and struck the hidden author with terror. The epilogue to Brooke's *Gustavus Vasa*, published in 1739, pretends that the actors are met in the greenroom, debating what kind of epilogue will be most likely to save the play, when their meeting is suddenly interrupted by the sound of a catcall—the sign of a riot. In 1751 Woodward, "in the Character of a *Critic*, with a *Catcall* in his Hand," spoke the prologue to Moore's *Gil Blas*. This is an excellent commentary on the relationship of the playwright and his audience and on the odd but common notion that writers were criminals who must be exterminated. The speaker turns first to the pit and then to the author:

> *ARE you all ready? Here's your Musick! here!*
> *Author, sneak off, we'll tickle you, my Dear.*

The author, thoroughly frightened, asks if his play is to be damned. It certainly must be, replies the speaker, as it is a second offense. When the author vows he will write no more, the speaker assures him that the critics will damn him for that, too. The fact that the author is poor is no recommendation to the pit who have come not to be charitable but for the fun of a riot.

> *'Tis Death to him—What then?—'Tis Sport to us.*

Paul Whitehead in the prologue for the opening of Covent Garden in 1767 refers to the catcalls which seem thunder

in the ears of the playwright lost on the *"theatric main."* [4]
Colman in 1769 in the prologue to *The Sister* paraphrased
the prologue to *Irene:*

> *If lethargied by dullness here you sit,*
> *Sonorous catcalls rouse the sleeping pit.*

Hugh Kelly in the prologue to *A Word to the Wise* describes the wretched poet as fastened on the spit for the
amusement of the audience and basted with "cat-call
sauce." The prologue to Holcroft's *Duplicity* (1781) shows
a pit very little reformed, in which there are assembled
"cat-call-pipers, groaners, whistlers, grinners," and "gods"
armed with wooden thunder. Captain Edward Topham in
the prologue to Miles Peter Andrews's farce, *The Best
Bidder* (1782), refers to the failure of Andrews's comic
opera of the preceding year, the beaux and belles of the
pit turning "critics"—"An active audience, and a passive
stage"—to pelt the actors with apples and oranges, "sad
fruits of writing." The sound of catcalls rising above the
general confusion assails the author's ears, and the play is
damned:

> "Off! off! go on—encore! no more to-night!
> "Apology? over with him!"—'tis over with him quite." [5]

4. *The Rehearsal: with a Key, or Critical View of the Authors, and
their Writings. . . .* The Seventeenth Edition. As Acted at the Theatres
Royal, with the New Occasional Prologue, Written by Paul Whitehead,
Esq., On Opening Covent Garden Theatre, September the 14th, 1767.

5. *Lloyd's Evening Post,* December 25–27, 1782. Compare with this,
Boswell and his friends, Dempster and Erskine, determined to damn David
Mallet's tragedy, *Elvira* (Drury Lane, 19 January 1763). ". . . just as the
doors opened at four o'clock, we sallied into the house, planted ourselves
in the middle of the pit, and with oaken cudgels in our hands and shrill-
sounding catcalls in our pockets, sat ready prepared, with a generous
resentment in our breasts against dullness and impudence, to be the swift
ministers of vengeance." *Boswell's London Journal 1762–1763,* ed. F. A.
Pottle (New York, McGraw-Hill, 1950), p. 154. As the audience refused to
assist in their efforts to damn *Elvira,* Mallet's countrymen were deprived
of their pleasure.

The *Prelude* to Holcroft's *The German Hotel* (1790) is a
dialogue between an author, whose play is about to be presented, and a friend, who unaware of the authorship, has
armed himself and two others with catcalls, "because to
damn an author is damned high fun." The proposed victim observes that "An author on a first night is as happy
as Lucifer himself." In 1791 the "cat-call hurricane" is
still the dread of authors.[6]

The prologues are in themselves sufficient proof that
despite the long line of brilliant actors from Betterton to
Mrs. Siddons and despite Garrick's endeavor to raise his
profession to respectability, the theatre remained a savage
place in which author-baiting, hissing, and catcalls were
the most cruel but not the most dangerous sport. Goldsmith was not speaking in metaphor when in the epilogue
to *The Good Natur'd Man* he described the author as
biding "the pelting of this pit'less storm," for the *"ill-
condition'd oranges,"* and the *"bitter* apples" of the prologue to *Zobeide* often strewed the stage. *"The bravest
chiefs,"* says Smollett in the epilogue to *The Reprisal*
(1757) have *"been tam'd"* with missiles from the pit and
conquered by *"show'rs of hail"* from the gallery. James
Cobb's prologue to *The Female Captain* (1780) repeats
Smollett's observation:

Nor Alexander's self dare meet your rage,
When oranges and apples strew the stage;
And the world's victors, *here*—Oh, strange to tell!
Have fall'n the victims of a nonpareil.[7]

Catcalls and missiles were the bane of authors and actors;
riots, of managers. Woodward, speaking the prologue for
the opening of Covent Garden on September 20, 1773,
warns the "house" to beware of "faction":

6. Prologue to John Henniker's *National Prejudice,* the *European Magazine,* May 1791, p. 389.
7. *Lloyd's Evening Post,* September 18–20, 1780.

Oft have we seen, with Sadness and Surprize,
Th' assembl'd House in sudden Tumult rise;
Loud crack'd the Floor, the trembling Seats gave way,
And truncheon'd Heroes shudder'd at the Fray.

The prologue, *Bucks Have at Ye All,* made famous by both
King and Garrick, sets forth as axiomatic that *"Bucks
exist but in a Riot,"* and portrays the noisy confusion of
the audience, whether they make the theatre ring with
applause,

Or urg'd to Fury, tear the Benches down.[8]

Theatre riots were the final resort of the "packed
house," factions, political or social, attending for the purpose of supporting or damning the play. During the first
two decades of the century, prologues, almost as a matter
of course, lament that faction has invaded even the theatre
and protest that the author of the night is free from political interests. Generally the prologue declares that the
author has flattered no faction and is supported by no
party, although he is well aware that his play can succeed
only through such means.[9] The prologue to Dr. Joseph
Trapp's heroic tragedy, *Abra-Mule: or, Love and Empire,*
spoken by Betterton in his theatre in Lincoln's Inn Fields
in 1704, dwells on the anxieties which beset the author—
the fear of failure, the disappointment of a thin pit and
the dread of one that is full—

These are at best the anxious Writers cares:
But he, who now your fatal Censure fears,
Has no great Man to Countenance his Muse,
And shield him from the Arts which Rival Factions use.
No necessary Friends to start Applause.

8. *Lloyd's Evening Post,* March 4–6, 1771.
9. See, for example, the epilogue to Mrs. Pix's *The Double Distress*
(1701); to Oldmixon's *The Governour of Cyprus* (1703); to John Sturmy's
The Compromise (1723); to Havard's *Scanderbeg* (1733); and the prologue
to Shirley's *Edward the Black Prince* (1750).

Mrs. Manley's epilogue to *Almyna* (1706) describes the author as *"unknown, unfriended,"* and unsupported by any faction:

> *No Party made, at* Will's, *or* Tom's, *or* Sam's.

    Mrs. Centlivre's interest in politics caused the failure of her comedy, *The Perplex'd Lovers* (1712). She submitted the original epilogue to the licenser, who prohibited it. As it was impossible to conclude the play without an epilogue and too late to supply a new one, she sent the popular comedian, Henry Norris, "Jubilee Dicky," to placate the audience by improvising. He entreated them *"to excuse the Defect, and promised them an Epilogue the next Night."* The audience immediately supposed that Norris's extemporaneous remarks were the epilogue, and to show their resentment at being thus defrauded, they damned the play. On the next day the epilogue was licensed by the vice-chamberlain, but rumors had been spread about the town that it was a *"notorious whiggish Epilogue,"* and Mrs. Oldfield, who was to speak it, received letters warning her *"that there were Parties forming against it, and they advis'd her not to stand the Shock."* [1] Mrs. Centlivre published the epilogue, *"design'd to have been spoke the first Night by Mrs.* Oldfield," so that the reader could judge the innocence of her intentions. The panegyric to Marlborough and Prince Eugene with which the piece ends was her undoing. Norris appeared again the second night, this time in mourning, to speak a new epilogue, defending himself and Mrs. Centlivre and explaining the difficulties with the licenser:

> *Cou'd you no Credit to poor Scrub afford,*
> *Or cou'd you doubt your Brother* Dicky's *Word?*
> *I said you shou'd have an Epilogue to Day.*

1. Preface to *The Perplex'd Lovers* (1712).

But he could not cajole them into forgetting the affront, and the play was performed only three nights.

References to political factions—always less frequent than in the Restoration—reach their height with the Rebellion of 1715. Dr. George Sewell in his prologue to Mrs. Centlivre's *The Cruel Gift* (1716) informs the audience that Mrs. Centlivre's hope of success depends on their impartial judgment:

> *Not on confed'rate Clubs of clapping Friends,*
> *Dispos'd in Parties to support her Cause,*
> *And bully you by Noise, into Applause.*

The prologue and epilogue of Cibber's *The Non-Juror* (1717) are, in accordance with the play, openly defiant of the Jacobites. Rowe furnished Cibber with the prologue, beginning with the misleading statement that the play would offend neither Whigs nor Tories and setting forth Cibber's plot and purpose in a vivid picture of contemporary conditions. The epilogue, spoken by Mrs. Oldfield, is Cibber's defense of the comedy and an encomium of his temerity in creating political enemies:

> *Methinks to Write at all, is Bold enough,*
> *But in a Play to stand a Faction Buff!*

The Jacobites did not at that time show open resentment by damning *The Non-Juror,* but they did not forget the injury and opposed Cibber's later plays although they contained no political reference.[2]

Making the most of the excitement caused by *The Non-Juror,* Christopher Bullock produced *The Per-Juror* in 1717, but in his prologue informed the audience that the title was simply bait to draw them to the theatre and that

2. For the difficulties in which *The Non-Juror* involved Cibber, see his own account in his *Apology,* ed. Lowe, II, 185–191; Allardyce Nicoll, *A History of Early Eighteenth Century Drama,* pp. 14–15; and Joseph Knight's article on Cibber in the *Dictionary of National Biography.*

those who came expecting to see another Dr. Wolf, a *"furious* Whig," or *"Anabaptist Teacher"* will be disappointed: *"No; Politicks we cautiously disclaim."* The same ruse was used by Benjamin Griffin in 1720 in his *Whig and Tory,* the epilogue, spoken by a Trimmer, being designed to please all parties and offend none:

> *When* Tories *rule—I think the* Papists *civil,*
> *And frown, and give* Fanatics *to the Devil.*
> *But when the* Whiggish *Schemes at highest run,*
> *I cry,* What have the poor *Dissenters done?*

The anonymous epilogue to William Havard's *King Charles the First* (1737), admonishing the audience not to turn "regicides," insists that the play has no political bias and that the author will receive his "pension" on the third night. Garrick ended his prologue to *The Suspicious Husband* (1747) with the usual deprecatory compliment:

> *He asks no Friend his partial Zeal to shew,*
> *Nor fears the groundless Censures of a Foe;*
> *He knows no Friendship can protect the Fool,*
> *Nor will an Audience be a Party's Tool.*

This is a late reference to the packing of the house by political factions, and, of course, the practice still existed.

All through the century authors made up parties of friends to insure applause, and their enemies parties to insure damnation. In 1701 Steele packed the house for a favorable reception of *The Funeral,* a stratagem which he proudly published, and one considered not dishonorable. He ends the prologue—a piece full of earnest criticism of current drama and levelled against the shallowness of the audience—with the hope *"for a prevailing Party here":*

> *He knows h' has num'rous Friends, nay knows they'll*
>   *show it,*
> *And for the Fellow-Soldier save the Poet.*

Over a long period of years, parties made up at the Bedford Coffee House descended on the playhouse to terrorize the authors of new plays. In the Preface to *The Lady's Revenge* (1734) William Popple tells how on the fourth night of the play, eight or ten men from the Bedford Coffee House came in a body to Covent Garden to interrupt the performance: *"Accordingly Mr. Ryan coming on to speak the* Prologue, *they began their Uproar, but were soon silenced, and the* Prologue *was heard with Applause."* But the prologue did not prevent the rioters from being clamorous during the beginning of the play. At last Quin ascertained that most of the audience wished the performance to continue, and the disturbers left *"under the general Hiss of every Person then present."* In 1759 the epilogue to Paul Hiffernan's *The Lady's Choice* describes the critics from the Bedford Coffee House as *"A dreadful Legion to new-acted Pieces!"*

Two years after the enactment of the Licensing Act parties were still being formed to damn new plays. Thus *The Parricide* (1739) by William Shirley did not reach even a first night's hearing, for as he complains in the dedicatory letter to John Rich, bemoaning the tragedy as a "Rioted Play," a band of twenty or thirty persons, who knew nothing about either the play or the author, resolved to prevent its performance simply because it was new and had been licensed:

> That my Enemies came resolv'd to execute, before Trial, may be gather'd from their Behaviour ere the Play began; for at Five o' Clock they engag'd, and over-threw the Candles in the Musick-Room, and call'd a Council of War to determine whether they should attack the Harpsicord or not. . . .
> . . . I flatter'd myself my *Prologue* would, at least, procure me a patient Hearing, and gentle Treatment:

But Humility or Modesty has no Effect on dishonest
Minds. . . .

Arthur Murphy's prologue to *The Way to Keep Him*
(1760) describes the old prologuisers bidding defiance to
the critics,

"*Scatter'd like ratsbane up and down the pit,*"

and disdains either to intimidate or appease the author's
foes:

> *To govern here* no party *can expect;*
> *An audience will preserve its own respect.*[3]

In the prologue to *The Brothers* (1769) Cumberland
assured the audience that he sought "no station'd
friend . . . , no hir'd applause." Woodward, speaking the
prologue to Colman's *The Man of Business* (1774), in the
character of a disappointed poet, explains gleefully how
he has made his revenge certain:

> I've lin'd the house in front, above, below;
> Friends, like dried figs, stuck close in every row!
> Some wits in ambush, in the gallery sit;
> Some form a critick phalanx in the pit;
> Some scatter'd forces their shrill catcalls play,
> And strike the Tiny Scribler with dismay.
> O then my hearts! charge! fire, your triumph's certain
> O'er his weak battery from behind the curtain.

For the prologue to Mrs. Cowley's *Which Is the Man?*
(1782), Lee Lewes appears "*dress'd as an Officer*" to rec-
onnoitre the enemy territory. He looks into the pit and
fears a "treach'rous ambuscade," but the author himself
intends to fight a fair battle and has no "*puffing* miners"
in his pay;

3. Murphy's *Works* (1786), III, 3–4.

>No mercenary band who have been wont
>To hack and hew like pioneers in front!

Less important than the pit in saving or damning the play but still to be kept in good humor were the "gods" of the upper gallery or "Olympus," as Garrick calls it in his prologue for the benefit of the Theatrical Fund. Sitting in the least advantageous part of the house, the gods were a noisy crew. Dogget, presenting the prologue to Burnaby's *Love Betrayed* (1703), looks toward the upper gallery and observes that some can hear, *"Tho' they can't See."* During the first three decades, the upper gallery was in the possession of the footmen who accompanied their masters to the play or preserved their seats for them, an arrangement made by the infamous Christopher Rich, the manager of Drury Lane at the time when Betterton and his fellow actors seceded in 1695 to the theatre in Lincoln's Inn Fields. According to Cibber, Rich, in order to attract people of quality to Drury Lane, "resolv'd, at least, to be well with their Domesticks, and therefore cunningly open'd the upper Gallery to them *gratis.*" Previously no footmen had been admitted before the end of the fourth act. Rich thus established a custom which Cibber denounced as "the greatest Plague that ever Play-house had to complain of." The riot which occurred in Drury Lane on March 5, 1737, was caused by the footmen who were denied their usual privilege of admission. Three hundred of them broke open the door of the theatre, forced their way on the stage, and wounded twenty-five persons. The ringleaders were sent to Newgate, and a guard of soldiers was appointed to protect the theatre.[4] Thereafter the pro-

4. Cibber, *Apology,* I, 233–234. The *Gentleman's Magazine,* March 1737, p. [186], contains a description of the riot. From Newgate the ringleaders wrote a menacing letter to Fleetwood, the manager of Drury Lane, threatening to reduce the playhouse to the ground, "but a Guard of 50 Soldiers being appointed for several Nights, the Footmen made no farther Attempts."

logues make less frequent reference to the footmen, who were gradually replaced by Garrick's "honest hearty grinners." [5] Prologuisers held the footmen in contempt and addressed them with a sneer. Farquhar in the prologue to *Sir Harry Wildair* (1701) flays the several sections of the house and points out the footmen as examples of *"most nice Morality":*

> *To pleasure them his* Pegasus *must fly,*
> *Because they judge, and lodge, three Stories high.*

Mrs. Centlivre's epilogue to *Love's Contrivance* (1703), after dealing severely with the indigent beaux and the dishonest apprentices, turns to the upper gallery,

> *Our upper Friends, whose Height Respect denotes,*
> *Since Liv'ries too are not unlike lac'd Coats,*

and predicts that from frequently listening to prologues, they will learn to harangue the town and *"make ingenious Speeches when they're hang'd."* It should be noted that this and similar prologues lashing the house were conventional and had been prevalent since the Restoration; hence brutal humor of this sort was accepted as a customary part of the evening's entertainment.

Pinkethman literally played to the gallery in the prologue to Mrs. Centliver's *The Basset-Table* (1705), when he appeared in the part of Buckle, the footman, and addressed his *"—dear Brethren of the Upper Tire,"* giving a remarkable demonstration of his popularity with them.

> *Your thundering plaudit 'tis that deals out Fame,*
> *You make Plays run, tho' of themselves but Lame:*
> *How often have we known your Noise Commanding,*
> *Impose on your Inferior Masters Understanding;*
> *Therefore, Dear Brethren, (since I am one of you)*
> *Whether adorn'd in Grey, Green, Brown or Blue,*

5. Prologue to *A Christmas Tale.*

This day stand all by me, as I will fall by you,
And now to let—
The poor Pit see how Pinky's Voice Commands,
Silence—Now rattle all your Sticks, and clap your grimy
                                              Hands.

He defies the vainest author to show such power over pit or
boxes. Prior, in the epilogue to Mrs. Manley's *Lucius*
(1717), draws a ludicrous picture of the upper gallery who
divide their attention between tumult and love,

> *And whilst their Sweet-hearts their Attention fix,*
> *Suspend the Din of their damn'd clatt'ring Sticks.*

The price of admission to the upper gallery was a shilling—a fact seldom omitted by the jeering prologuiser. In
Garrick's epilogue to *The Orphan of China* (1759), the
upper gallery is the *"shilling party."* Murphy's epilogue to
The Choice (1765), spoken by Mrs. Yates, emphasizes the
difficulty the upper gallery had in hearing, even when they
paid attention:

> *. . . I strain these tender lungs, still willing*
> *To let you hear a little for your shilling.*

Frederick Pilon's epilogue to *He Would Be a Soldier*
(1786) invokes

> Ye gods above, high arbiters of wit,
> Who on your shilling thrones in council sit.

The second epilogue to Dennis's *Gibraltar* (1705) is spoken
by the "Serjeant," one of the minor characters of the play,
who, after some bitter observations on the injustice of his
superiors' receiving the reward for the battles which he
fights and on the fortune he could make if he turned states-
man and robbed the nation, or physician and plundered
and killed his patients, has a grim conclusion for *"my Mas-*
ters of that upper Tire":

Each of you paid a Shilling, that came in,
Which going out you shall receive again;
For on the Stairs twelve grim Tar-pawlins *stand,*
Who as you pass shall strike you in the Hand,
Till each is hurried by a lusty Tar,
From the Fictitious to true Gibraltar.

During the later half of the century, sailors took the place of the footmen as the object of banter directed to the upper gallery, and contempt was replaced by patronizing indulgence. Garrick points out the "jolly sailor" and his sweetheart,

Hearts full of love, and pockets full of fruit.[6]

Miss Younge, in the epilogue to Mrs. Cowley's *More Ways than One* (1783), directs the attention of the house to the upper gallery:

Momus is surely there, from all this racket,
Yonder he sits,—he's in a sailor's jacket;

and the epilogue to Charlotte Smith's *What Is She?* (1799), like most of its kind, comments on the sailors' simple and entirely uncritical taste:

That jolly Tar, by Kate from Rotherhithe brought—
With Bard or Critic ne'er disturbs *his* thought,
He only comes to make the Gallery ring
With "Rule Britannia," and "God save the King."

The prologues called upon the upper gallery to drown the hisses of the pit in applause when their tastes were at variance; for example, the prologue to Bickerstaffe's *The Absent Man* (1768) fears that the critical part of the audience will not suffer out the farce and commands the upper gallery,

In spite of their airs, laugh as loud as you can.

6. "Address to the Town," the *London Magazine*, March 1763, p. 159.

The usual conclusion of the author-mariner metaphor is illustrated by Andrew Franklin's prologue to *The Wandering Jew* (1797), which describes the author as being in danger of sinking under critic storms; then

[*Imploring Galleries.*] But should the Gods assume a milder
    form,
And with propitious beams dispel the storm;
He'll croud all sail—each grateful breeze he'll court—
Huzza!—and sail triumphant into port.

The attitude of the prologues to the upper gallery in the latter part of the century reflects the growth of sentimentalism and is based on the belief in the inherent goodness of the common man. Garrick's prologues represent the upper gallery as the part of the house most responsive to theatrical illusion—indeed, as being quite unable to distinguish it from actuality—and most susceptible to feeling, *"as Nature works."* The epilogue to *Virginia* (1754), from which these words are taken, pictures two *"honest Britons as e'er trod on leather,"* discussing with sorrow and indignation the proper punishment for Appius, and, incidentally, entirely puzzled by the tragedy. In Burgoyne's epilogue to *The Fugitive* (1792), the "faithful overseers in the clouds" roar for hornpipe to eke out a farce,

But still true nature, be it laugh or tear,
Finds with electric touch its centre there.
The pregnant sense of right disdains controul,
And the rough hand reports the honest soul.

Edward Jerningham's prologue to *The Siege of Berwick* (1793) says of the *"boist'rous inmates of the sky,"*

You ride the clouds, and are yourselves the storms;

but, on the other hand, they are the touchstones by which the truth of the play may be tested. If the play is founded on *"unerring Nature,"*

Your glowing soul has grasp'd the Author's cause,
And hurl'd around the thunder of applause.

The gradual change in the attitude of the prologues toward the upper gallery closely parallels social history. The sailor himself, as later discussion will show, became a stock sentimental character in prologues.

The members of the audience who underwent the least change from 1700 to 1800 were the beaux. Pit and gallery were feared by author and actor, but the beaux were merely tolerated and held up to continual ridicule. For a hundred years they remain indifferent to the play, self-centered and self-conscious. The charges brought against them from decade to decade are ever the same—vanity, effeminacy, cowardliness, and stupidity. Mrs. Centlivre in 1702, after marshalling more than the usual number of contemptuous epithets, adds that the rumor goes that beaux in the dressing room are hiring French masters to teach them not only to dance and sing but to smile. In 1726, Mrs. Younger, dressed as a beau, spoke the lively, indecent epilogue to Welsted's *The Dissembled Wanton*, ridiculing beaux for their affectation. They have no interest in plays and authors, for *"Poets are Slovens."*

But whatever their usual lack of intelligence, the beaux showed considerable ingenuity in defrauding the box-keeper. D'Urfey in the prologue to *The Bath, or, The Western Lass* (1701) makes an explicit comment about the reprehensible shifts by which they contrived to see the play without paying for it:

Laugh as you please, provided that you pay,
For here are sad Complaints, that Wits are dull that way.
I'm told that Beaus with Perukes cover'd o're,
Make such strange shift to save poor shillings four,
They'll in Side-Box three Acts for nothing sit,
At last sneak down for six-pence to the Pit.

166 PROLOGUES AND EPILOGUES

Thomas Baker's epilogue to *The Fine Lady's Airs* (1708) also mentions the difficulty with which the gatherers extorted money from the evasive and brazen beaux:

> Side-Boxes *wou'd with Ladies Foibles play,*
> *But they themselves stand Buff to all we say,*
> *For nothing strikes them Dead, but*—Please to Pay.

In Garrick's epilogue to *The Suspicious Husband* (1747), the agile monkey, representing the beau, skipped from box to box and *"bilk'd ev'ry Box-keeper."*

The beau was too trivial to demand serious satire, but his affectations and vanity were the subject of constant amusement and raillery. The prologue to Charles Coffey's *The Female Parson: or, Beau in the Sudds* (1730), in which the beau imitates Cibber in Sir Novelty Fashion, is a finished caricature, preserving the beau's affectations of speech as well as of dress:

With Snuff-Box, powder'd Wig, and Arms a-kimbo,
Cane, Ruffles, Sword-Knot, Burdash, Hat and Feather,
Perfumes, fine Essense, brought from Lard knows whither.

These, he says, are his weapons, for he is a thorough-going coward:

The Devil take me,—'tis an odious Sight
To see a finish'd Beau—lug out to fight,
When, rat me, he had rather bid good Night.
Ladies, Gad's Curse, let each one guard her Heart,
For when I come just now to play my Part,
Demme,—each am'rous Glance shall prove—a fatal Dart.

The similarity between Coffey's Modely and Garrick's Sir Anthony Branville has already been noted.[7]

Degeneracy and cowardice are the most constant charges brought against the beaux. Philip Frowde's epilogue to

7. See above, Chapter 3, p. 96, n. 5.

The Fall of Saguntum (1727) deals disdainfully with fops who neglect civic responsibilities to spend their time gaming and who consider public spirit a troublesome virtue which died with ancient Rome. Mrs. Clive presented a lively epilogue to Shirley's rampantly patriotic drama, *Edward the Black Prince* (1750), in which she deplored the degeneracy of the times. Englishmen in King Edward's reign were heroes,

> . . . *But now, O dire Disgrace!*
> *Lo, half their Offspring lost in Silk and Lace.*

Her final admonition to the "*arrant Beaux, so trim, so degagée*" is that they ". . . *harden into Manhood back again.*"

In Mrs. Centlivre's *The Stolen Heiress* (1702), the part of the silly pedant was played by Dogget, who retained the character for the epilogue. He describes the "*finish'd Beau*" as one who devotes himself to piquet, gaming, and dress and affects to despise the classics which he has acquired only by rote,

> *For Learning is a Thing requires Brains;*
> *And that's a perquesite the Gentleman disdains.*

Fielding commended *Love in Several Masques* (1728) to the beaux:

> *From you then—ye Toupets—he hopes Defence:*
> *You'll not condemn him—for his want of Sense.—*

Garrick in the epilogue to *Barbarossa* (1754) makes Woodward say of the fine gentleman whom he is impersonating:

> *When Thoughts arise I always game, or drink,*
> *An* English *Gentleman shou'd never think.—*

A stock complaint against the beaux is that they sleep through the play, "*then wake, to hang the Knave.*" [8] Field-

8. Epilogue to Theobald's *The Perfidious Brother* (1716).

ing in the prologue to *The Temple Beau* (1730) laments
the decline of the theatre and ascribes it to the increase of
dull beaux:

> Will*'s has resign'd its old Pretence to Wit,*
> *And Beaux appear, where Criticks us'd to sit.*
> Button *himself, provok'd at wit's Decline,*
> *Now Lets his House, and swears he'll Burn his Sign.*

If, Fielding continues, the theatres followed Button's example and closed because their patrons lacked wit, players
and authors would then starve together. *"Ye Beaux,"* in
Garrick's prologue to *The School for Rakes* (1769), scorn
all writing because they cannot understand it, their minds
being quite suited to their bodies. In his epilogue to *The
School for Wives* (1773) the beaux are *"true stoicks, and
high bred,"* who

> *Come, but ne'er know what's done, or sung, or said;*
> *Should the whole herd of criticks round them roar,*
> *And with one voice cry out,* encore! encore!
> *Or louder yet,* off, off; no more! no more!
> *Should Pit, Box, Gall'ry with convulsions shake,*
> *Still are they half asleep, nor t'other half awake:*
> *O, ladies fair! are these fit men to wed?*
> *Such husbands,* half, *had better be* quite *dead.*

Farquhar's epilogue to Gildon's *The Patriot* (1703) was
spoken by Pinkethman dressed as a stage beau and reveals
vividly the attitude that young men about town had or
pretended to have toward literature. The beau has in an
idle minute written the epilogue for the play:

> *We don't pretend to write, with Wit, nor Care;*
> *But only, as we Dance, we write, with Air;*
> *With careless sliding Stile; just like our Gate;*
> *But Gay, and Modish, Thoughtless, as our Pate.*

The beaux often write prologues and epilogues—thereby, incidentally, gaining free admission to the theatre—but, alas, the actors refuse to speak their pieces. Farquhar then puts into the mouth of the beau a delightful gibe at himself and his fellows who were a constant source of annoyance to the actors by their presence on the stage:

We, that support their House! alack a day!
We, make more Comedy, on the Stage, than they.

But in spite of all his grievances, he can't see the *"poor Rogue"* of an author have his play lost for want of an epilogue.

In 1792 Colman, the younger, in the prologue to *Cross Partners,* presents a less dandiacal beau, a Dickensian young man, long since driven from the stage to the green boxes, but in all other respects like his predecessors:

What play, or whose, he little cares, so he
Sports but his figure at the comedy.

Miles Peter Andrews's epilogue to *Better Late than Never* (1790), an acting piece for Mrs. Jordan, ridicules the beau of past generations, "rather unlike the Smart of present days,"

For I defy all History to shew,
One thing in Nature, like a Modern Beau;
Hat slouch'd, short Stick, Knee Trappings, that bring back,
The Memory of renown'd Sixteen String Jack:
Eternal Boots, and Collar, you'd suppose,
Cut, in kind contact, with his Buckship's Nose.

But, here again, barring external appearance, the modern beau would have been quite in his element in the first decade of the century:

Thus trimly deck'd each night among the Doxies,
He storms the Lobby, and assails the Boxes;

With Gait and Manner—something in this way,
Proves his rare Taste, and descants on the Play—
"Here, Box-keeper! why don't the Rascal come?
Halloa—Tom Gerkin! can you give us room?
What this?—The Farce—Macbeth—an Opera?—Oh!
Came out last Season—stupid stuff—damn'd low.

The chief complaint against the beaux was their presence on the stage and behind the scenes. The first lines to
D'Urfey's epilogue to *The Modern Prophets* (1709) are
addressed to the gallants on the stage, within arm's reach
of the speaker,

> . . . —*you roaving Beaus,*
> *Who for your Pleasure now sit here in Rows.*

Continuing an Elizabethan practice, they disrupted the
play, as Farquhar's beau complaisantly observed in the
passage quoted from the epilogue to Gildon's *The Patriot.*
Pinkethman delivered this epilogue surrounded by the
beaux whom he is ridiculing:

> *You side-box Beaux, I've orders, to engage*
> *From all us, Brother Beaux, here on the Stage.*

He invites them to make up a party at White's for the
poet's benefit night. From the stage the beaux sauntered
behind the scenes, as they had done since the reign of
Charles II. Dryden, in the epilogue to *The Pilgrim* (1700),
proposes what he apparently considered an impossible reform:

> *What wou'd you say, if we shou'd first begin*
> *To Stop the Trade of Love, behind the Scene.*

Managers were torn between their wish to restrict the
greenroom, wings, and stage to the performers and their
fear of offending their patrons. They added requests, sup-
plications, and commands to the announcements of plays

in the newspapers and to playbills, but such appeals were made in vain. The epilogue to Charles Beckingham's tragedy, *Scipio Africanus*, spoken by Mrs. Bullock at Lincoln's Inn Fields in 1718, is a flippant piece of raillery, during which she points to the wings and says:

> . . . *pert and noisy Sparks stand peering here.*
> *Our private Scenes are grac'd with powder'd Beaus,*
> *Who, judging wrong laugh at our Tragic Woes,*
> *And prove their Want of Sense to shew their Cloaths.*

The epilogue to Thomas Cooke's *The Triumphs of Love and Honour* (1731), spoken by Cibber's daughter, Mrs. Charlotte Charke, describes the "dangler,"

> . . . *that Species of the Beaus*
> *Whose Commendation most is in his Cloaths,*

and is printed with the instructions: "Pointing to those behind the Scenes." It is noticeable that when John Rich in 1731 drew up his Proposals for the shareholders of the Covent Garden Theatre, then being built, he specified that the subscribers should have the liberty to see the plays "in any part of the House excepting behind the Scenes." [9] Cibber boasted that he and his fellow patentees banished the beaux from the scenes and the stage and accomplished the reform "at the Hazard of our Lives." [1] His achievement was temporary, for when Garrick assumed the management of Drury Lane in 1747, his epilogue for the opening night announced his resolution to forbid the beaux admittance to the greenroom, scenes, and stage. He hoped to placate the audience by treating the reform lightly and by the pretence that the actress herself was indignant:

9. Henry Saxe Wyndham, *The Annals of Covent Garden Theatre* (1906), I, 23.
1. Cibber, *Apology*, I, 234.

No Beaux behind the Scenes!—'tis Innovation!
Under the specious Name of Reformation!
Public Complaint, forsooth, is made the Puff,
Sense, Order, Decency, and such like Stuff.

.   .   .   .

Can it be thought this Law will ever pass,
While Doors are only Wood, and Windows Glass?

The epilogue ends with a line-for-line parody of *Othello,*
III, 345–357, Garrick's most prolonged offence of the kind,
sufficiently illustrated by the following passage:

"We had been happy, though the House had fail'd,
"Masters and all, had not this Scheme prevail'd.
"For ever now farewell the plumed Beaux,
"Who make Ambition—to consist in Cloaths.

Garrick was explicit as to the seriousness of his intention,
but the opposition was too strong and the "innovation"
did not endure. The *Drury Lane Calendar* records that
during a performance of *Harlequin's Invasion,* given as an
afterpiece to *Othello,* March 28, 1761, "Miss Piercy in
running off the Stage, which was greatly crowded, fell
down and broke her arm." [2]
Finally in 1762 Garrick and Lacy enlarged the Drury
Lane Theatre so that the house provided space for the
audience even on benefit nights, and "From that time
scarce any but the performers were permitted to visit the
scenes of the playhouse." [3] Garrick's epilogue to Hannah
More's *Percy,* performed at Covent Garden on December
10, 1777, reminds the audience that *"gentlemen are now
forbid the scenes"* and, in mock derision of the chivalry of
the play, promises *"to drive these ballad-heroes from the
stage."*

2. *Drury Lane Calendar,* p. 81.
3. Davies, *Life of David Garrick,* I, 348–349.

On benefit nights it was customary to build on the stage
a semi-circular bank of seats and after these were filled to
allow spectators to crowd into whatever space was left.
Although this seriously hampered the actors, they could
not entirely disapprove of it as it increased their profits,
and it was not until the theatre was enlarged that they were
willing to forego the audience behind the curtain. Tate
Wilkinson has left a first-hand description of the stage on
benefit nights and of the difficulties the actors suffered in
threading their way among the audience. The "building"
was so high that it reached to the "clouds." Persons "of
menial cast" sat on the floor, and "beaux and no beaux"
obstructed the entrances.[4] Davies had seen the battle of
Bosworth Field "fought in a less space than that which
is commonly allotted to a cock-match." [5] For the performance of Mrs. Cibber's masque, *The Oracle,* at Covent
Garden on March 17, 1752, the audience on the stage
formed a serious impediment for the actors. The prologue,
spoken in the midst of the spectators, informs them that
The Oracle, not to be outdone by Woodward's *Queen
Mab,* boasts a fairy as one of its characters:

> *And Ours, were but this magic circle free,*
> *Cou'd shew some pretty tricks, as well as She;*
> *But, for this time, your very goodness foils*
> *Our fairy's art, and half your pleasure spoils:*
> *On this full stage, (we see it with glad hearts)*
> *Our Statue-dancers cannot shew their parts;*
> *But what you lose for this one crouded night,*
> *Whole years of best endeavour shall requite.*

The playbills for benefit nights or for first nights of
unusual performances frequently bore the announcement
that the boxes are "to be open'd to the Pit." This could

4. Wilkinson, *Memoirs,* IV, 109 ff.
5. Davies, *Garrick,* I, 347.

be readily done, as the last seats of the pit were almost level with the first seats of the boxes opposite the stage, the seats, whether in pit or boxes, being backless benches. The "sermon" epilogue to Foote's *The Minor* (1760) describes the house on benefit nights when no distinction was made between pit and boxes:

> For foremost rows in side-boxes you shove,
> Think you to meet with side-boxes above?
> Where gigling girls, and powder'd fops may sit,
> No, you will all be cramm'd into the pit,
> And croud the house for Satan's benefit.

During the reign of Queen Anne, it became the fashion to end prologues with exaggerated compliments to the ladies in the boxes and with special tributes to the Queen.[6] It was to the ladies that the "culprit" appealed for mercy when he was sentenced by the jury of the pit; a beam from their eyes would guide the lost mariner safe into harbor. With what elegance the compliment could be managed is illustrated by the closing lines to Addison's epilogue to Granville's operatic drama, *The British Enchanters,* performed at the Queen's Theatre in the Haymarket in 1706. The prologue is a panegyric on the complicated stage machinery which will adorn the music, "but," adds the speaker, turning to the boxes,

---

6. See, as a few examples chosen from many, Farquhar's epilogue to *The Twin Rivals* (1702); Steele's epilogue to *The Lying Lover* (1703); William Taverner's epilogue to *The Faithful Bride of Granada* (1704); and Motteux's prologue to *Thomyris, Queen of Scythia* (1707), ending with the gallant and patriotic sentiment which concluded the majority of prologues spoken during the first decade of the century:

> *AS* Britain's *Beauties all the World's excel,*
> *Great* ANNA's *Reign disdains a Parallel.*

> *But howsoe'er, to please your wand'ring Eyes,*
> *Bright Objects disappear and brighter rise:*
> *There's none can make Amends for lost Delight,*
> *While from that Circle we divert your Sight.*

The author frequently declares that he has no regard for the critics in the pit as he wrote his play only for the ladies in the boxes—

> *Our Muse, ye snarling Cynicks, scorns your Favour,*
> *'Tis that Illustrious Ring must damn or save her.*[7]

Fielding ends the epilogue to *Love in Several Masques* with a similar defiance. He has had, as previous quotations from the epilogue show, a fling at the critics and the beaux;

> *Lastly, to you ye Charmers, he applies,*
> *For in your tender Bosoms Mercy lies,*
> *As certain, as Destruction in your Eyes.*
> *Let but that lovely Circle of the Fair,*
> *Their Approbation, by their Smiles declare,*
> *Then, let the Criticks, Damn him—if they dare.*

This is a conventional ending to prologues, and the efficacy of the ladies' decision was apparently slight.

Garrick's prologues have some very unflattering observations about the ladies in the audience, but although the compliments to the boxes became less frequent in the latter part of the century, they were never entirely abandoned. The epilogue to Mariana Starke's *The Widow of Malabar* (1790), spoken by Mrs. Mattocks, is a noisy, blustering piece. The speaker enters *"as if pushed upon the Stage by the Prompter, to whom she addresses the two first Lines."*

7. Epilogue to James Sterling's *The Rival Generals* (1722). See also the epilogue to Hughes's *The Siege of Damascus* (1720).

Dispatch'd, in so much haste, from the Green-room,
To find out—if I can—this WIDOW's doom!

The piece is cleverly built up on the subject of the play;
the speaker hopes that none of the "gods" will hurl a "hissing" bolt and consume her. Certainly the ladies in the
boxes—fair English ladies—will spare her. She bids them
to

Break Criticism's shaft, quench Rancour's fire,
Nor light our trembling AUTHOR's Funeral-Pyre.

George Colman, the elder, who took all prologue conventions for his own and improved upon them, wrote an
amusing epilogue to William Cooke's revision of *The
Capricious Lady* (1783), addressed to the ladies. Describing
the haughty demeanor of Elizabethan ladies, presumably
the ladies of the sonnets, he compares them to their suc-
cessors:

Their virtue nought could shake, no siege could alter,
A rock, impregnable as *Gibraltar!*

.   .   .   .

While they, bright stars, above all weak comparison,
Shone forth the female ELIOTS of the garrison.

The speaker, Mrs. Abington, was particularly well-suited
to epilogues which turned on compliments to the boxes, by
her caprice and graces cajoling into applause not only the
ladies but the entire audience.

Colman's bantering reference to the ladies in the boxes
illustrates how readily the prologues and epilogues, sometimes through a mere topical allusion—"the female Eliots
of the garrison"—help us visualize the audience of the
eighteenth century. With the clarity and perception of
Hogarth, they set before us generations of theatre-goers—
the alert and hostile critics, the self-centered beaux, the

ladies adorning the boxes, the sailors asleep in the upper gallery. But they have an additional liveliness in their constant appeals, admonitions, denunciation, and cajolery. This auditory quality gives the pieces their unique value in recreating the audience in its relationship to the playwright and actor.

CHAPTER 5

"THE DRAMA'S LAWS
THE DRAMA'S PATRONS GIVE"

There was a continual recognition in the prologues of the eighteenth century that the drama had fallen into decline, that tragedy, in particular, could no longer succeed unsupported by comedy, farce, or lesser forms of amusement, and that the audience could be held only by opera, pantomime, and miscellaneous entertainment. The great number of plays presented for only one night and the newspaper announcements in which the play is buried beneath descriptions of dancers, singers, and contortionists confirm these charges. Whether the unsuccessful plays deserved more favorable reception is doubtful, but the rival amusements were certainly a continual vexation and threat to the serious dramatists.

The theatre announcements in the early numbers of the *Daily Courant,* with their detailed accounts of the acrobatics, dancing, and music by which the plays were overwhelmed, fully justify the complaints made in the contemporary prologues. Against what opposition authors and actors strove is shown by the following advertisement from the *Daily Courant* for Monday, April 26, 1703:

> FOR the Benefit of Mr. *William Pinkeman* at the
> Theatre Royal in *Drury-lane* to Morrow being *Tues-*

day the 27th of *April*, will be presented a Play call'd
Oroonoko, in which will be perform'd several Italian
Sonatas by Signior *Gasperini* and others. And a new
Entertainments [*sic*] of Instrumental Musick, com-
pos'd by Mr. *Keller*, in which Mr. *Paisible*, Mr. *Banister* and Mr. *Latour* perform some extraordinary
Parts on the Flute, Violin, and Hautboy, with several
new Dances by Mr. *Du Ruel*, and Mrs. *Campion*.
Likewise the famous Mr. *Evans*, lately arriv'd from
Vienna (where he had the Honour to perform before
Prince *Eugene* of *Savoy*, and most of the Nobility of
that Court) will Vault on the manag'd Horse, where
he lyes with his Body extended on one Hand in which
posture he drinks several Glasses of Wine with the
other, and from that throws a Sommerset over the
Horses head, to Admiration. To begin exactly at half
an Hour after five by reason of the length of the
Entertainments.

All this was necessary to lure an audience to so famous a
play as Southerne's *Oroonoko* and to insure the success of
Pinkethman's benefit.[1] Similar notices appeared for other
performances not only at Drury Lane but at Dorset Garden, Lincoln's Inn Fields, and, later, at the Opera House
in the Haymarket, which was supposed to have an aris-
tocratic audience.

The usurpation of the theatre by miscellaneous entertainment was a problem of utmost concern to playwrights
and authors alike, and the prologues were the obvious
means of voicing their fear and anger. John Dennis in the
prologue to *Iphigenia* (1700) represents the Genius of
England as attempting to restore the Tragic Muse who has
fled from the British stage for *"twenty rolling Moons,"*

1. Pinkethman, being himself a showman as well as an actor, was
probably far from objecting to the "Entertainments" that swelled his
benefit.

while in her place have flourished foreign and effeminate arts. Abandoning enslaved Italy, servile France, and abject Spain, the Tragic Muse had hoped to establish herself in England:

> *Once more I thought t' inspire* Athenian *flights,*
> *And once more tower to* Sophoclean *heights.*

But she still finds no promise in the British stage:

> *Here Song and Dance, and ev'ry Trifle reigns,*
> *And leaves no room for my exalted strains.*

The Genius of England cries out:

> *This said the Muse, my* Brittons, *against you:*
> *Oh Supreme* Jove! *And is th' Indictment true?*
> *It is.*

The constant accusation of the prologuisers is that the public has lost its ability to appreciate drama and can only enjoy debased amusements,

> *The far-fetch'd Trash of* Italy *and* France.
>
> .   .   .   .
>
> *Yet these please now your vitious Pallates more*
> *Than your wise Sires the Tragick Muse of Yore.*[2]

"That Novelty is *taking,* be the *Puppet-Shew* a Witness," observes Aaron Hill in the Preface to *Elfrid: or, The Fair Inconstant* (1710)—an Augustan tragedy adhering strictly to the unities, as Hill boasts.

Steele is speaking for all his fellow playwrights when he begins his prologue to Vanbrugh's *The Mistake* (1705) with an arraignment of the audience:

> OUR *Author's Wit and Raillery to-Night*
>
> *Perhaps might please, but that your Stage-Delight*
> *No more is in your Minds, but Ears and Sight.*

2. Prologue to *The Conquest of Spain* (1705) by Mrs. Pix.

Steele vigorously denounced stage machinery and spectacle that were stifling the drama; for example, his prologue to *The Funeral: Or, Grief A-la-mode* (1701) begins with protest and reproof:

Nature's Deserted and Dramatick Art,
To Dazle now the Eye, has left the Heart;
Gay Lights, and Dresses, long extended Scenes,[3]
Daemons and Angels moving in Machines,
All that can now or please or fright the Fair
May be perform'd without a writer's Care,
And is the Skill of Carpenter, not Player;
Old Shakespear's Days could not thus far Advance,
But what's his Buskin to our Ladder Dance?

. . . .

Fie, Let confusion on such Dulness seize.
Blush you're so Pleas'd, as we that so we Please.

With scorn and anger, Oldmixon in the prologue to Gildon's adaptation of *Measure for Measure* (1700) advises poets to "*study the* Smithfield-Bards" to mollify the town's resentment of true poetry,

Or, you must Starve, and we shut up our Booth.

His prologue to *The Governour of Cyprus* (1703) emphasizes the conflict between authors who see their best efforts slighted and the audience who are pleased with "*Farce and Fustian*," and he adds that to the audience the art of filling the house is evidence of first-rate genius. Granville introduced the spectacular devices of *The British Enchanters*, with a severe rebuke to the audience for their willingness to accept such entertainment as he was about to provide them. Let no "vain fool" of a poet labor over style or plot, for the audience cares for neither. He himself has kept carefully to nonsense, but if any line deviates,

3. "Scenes," *i.e.* "flats."

> *Forgive him,* Beaux, *he means you no Offence,* ⎫
> *But begs you, for the Love of Song and Dance,* ⎬
> *To pardon all the Poetry and Sense.* ⎭

Taverner's prologue to *The Maid the Mistress* (1708) accuses the audience of turning the stage into a Smithfield
Fair:

> *To what you like we must of course submit,*
> *We dare not quarrel with a crowded Pit,*

but he has nonetheless attempted to present a play without "Italian *Airs, or Steps from* France."

Dramatists might draw a faint consolation from remem-
bering that the theatre of ancient Rome had also suffered
from rival entertainment. Terence began the earlier of the
two prologues to the *Hecyra* by recalling indignantly that
when it was first acted it could be neither heard nor seen
because the audience was distracted by a rope-dancer. In
the second prologue the speaker, the veteran actor-
manager, Lucius Ambivius, is even more specific: he is
now once more trying to present the *Hecyra* for which he
has never been allowed a silent hearing because of the
storm that "nipped it in the bud": "quom primum eam
agere coepi, pugilum gloria, comitum conventus, strepitus,
clamor mulierum, fecere ut ante tempus exirem foras." [4]
Charles Molloy makes this incident the basis for the prologue to *The Half-Pay Officers* (1720) and draws the obvious parallel. As if to illustrate the comparison, Molloy's
prologue introduced not only his play but a jig danced by
an aged actress, one Mrs. Fryer.[5]

Fielding frequently used his prologues to express his

4. *Terence*, (Loeb Classical Library, 1912), II, 128.
5. For Mrs. Fryer's success, see Thomas Whincop, *Scanderbeg: or, Love
and Liberty . . . To which are added A List of all the Dramatic Authors,
with some Account of their Lives; and of all the Dramatic Pieces ever
published in the English Language, to the Year 1747* (1747), p. 262.

contempt of miscellaneous entertainment and of the public who supported it. In the prologue to his second comedy, *The Temple Beau* (1730), he names the theatre in Goodman's Fields as the refuge for playwrights who have the courage to defy the public and write unadulterated drama:

> HUMOUR *and Wit, in each politer Age,*
> *Triumphant, rear'd the Trophies of the Stage:*
> *But only Farce, and Shew, will now go down,*
> *And* Harlequin's *the Darling of the Town.*

He continued the attack on rant and fustian in the prologue to *The Author's Farce* (1730). In the delightful prologue to *Tom Thumb*, first spoken on May 1, 1730,[6] he satirizes "modern" tragedy, describing it as a kind of farce and therefore acceptable to the mirth-loving audience. His ridicule of opera and pantomime will be mentioned below in this chapter.

The prologues not infrequently attributed the decline of the drama to the incompetence of the authors rather than to the depraved taste of the audience. Thus the prologue to *The Artful Husband* (1717) by William Taverner commiserates the audience on the inferior plays of the age and commends the critics for their forbearance to *"the pale Ghost of poor departed Wit."* Two years later in the prologue to *'Tis Well if It Takes* he makes the usual lament over the deserted theatre:

> *Well, Time was once—(When will those Days return?*
> *That* Golden *Age the Stage must ever mourn!)*
> *When Authors were both good, and very few;*
> *And Plays successful, and deserv'd it too:*
> *When Prologue-Players the full House addrest,*
> *Like Champions at a Coronation-Feast;*

6. Wilbur L. Cross, *The History of Henry Fielding*, III, 291. The prologue and epilogue are published in the second edition of *Tom Thumb* (1730).

> *Dar'd Censure and Detraction's Power defy,*
> *And, e'er the Critick snarl'd, pronounc'd the Lye.*

Fettiplace Bellers for the prologue to *Injur'd Innocence* (1732) followed the device of tracing the history of the drama from Greece to the Drury Lane Theatre,[7] declaring that the *"establish'd names,"* Shakespeare, Dryden, Otway, Congreve, Southerne, and Rowe, still drew *"applauding tears,"* but just as Greek drama fell into decay, so British drama had run its course. Bellers admonished the audience to receive his play with pity, if not with admiration:

> *Banish not all, because the best are gone;*
> *Each age will not produce an* Addison.

James Miller's prologue to *The Mother-in-Law* (1734) also placed the blame on the authors as well as on the public, both of whom had abandoned sense for sound and show.

In 1740 Cibber in his *Apology* set forth the fundamental rule of the theatre, a rule recognized by the prologuisers of the entire century: ". . . whenever the general Taste is vulgar, the Stage must come down to it to *live.*—But I ask Pardon of the Multitude, who, in all Regulations of the Stage, may expect to be a little indulg'd in what they like: If therefore they *will* have a May-pole, why, the Players must *give* them a May-pole. . . ." [8]

The prologuisers admitted the necessity of bowing before public taste, but in general they did not share Cibber's easy compliance. The fallen estate of the theatre and the debased interests of the audience are the chief concerns of the prologues to *The Mock Lawyer* (1733); *Fatal Falshood* (1734); *The Rival Milliners* (1736); William Havard's

7. The most amusing of the prologues giving an outline of history is by Ambrose Philips to his tragedy, *The Briton* (1722), quoted below in Chapter 6.

8. Cibber, *Apology* (ed. Lowe), II, 140.

King Charles the First (1737); and finally of Johnson's prologue for the opening of Drury Lane under the management of Garrick in 1747—a prologue which, says Boswell, "for just and manly dramatick criticism, on the whole range of the English stage, as well for poetical excellence, is unrivalled." [9] The great distinction of this prologue lies not in its originality but in the finality and dignity with which it states the critical dicta of eighteenth-century prologuisers:

> Hard is his Lot, that here by Fortune plac'd,
> Must watch the wild Vicissitudes of Taste;
> With ev'ry Meteor of Caprice must play,
> And chase the new-blown Bubbles of the Day.
> Ah! let not Censure term our Fate our Choice,
> The Stage but echoes back the publick Voice.
> The Drama's Laws the Drama's Patrons give,
> For we that live to please, must please to live.
>
> Then prompt no more the Follies you decry,
> As Tyrants doom their Tools of Guilt to die;
> 'Tis yours this Night to bid the Reign commence
> Of rescu'd Nature, and reviving Sense.

Johnson concluded by admonishing the audience to banish opera and pantomime—"the Charms of Sound, the Pomp of Show"—and to support drama, the purpose of which is to inculcate virtue and truth. He saw very clearly that the basis of the struggle between the actors and rival entertainment was economic. It follows that the lament for the decline of the drama is, as the passages already cited illustrate, almost invariably associated with a belligerent condemnation of the popular distractions corrupting the stage.

Beyond the scorn of unspecified miscellaneous entertainment—

9. Boswell, *Life of Johnson*, I, 181.

> To Sound and Show at first we make Pretence,
> In Time we may regale you with some Sense [1]—

the wrath of the prologuisers was usually directed toward
rival foreign entertainers, especially French dancers and
Italian singers, and the rivalry was made the basis of a
specious patriotism. The ridicule of French dancers was
a corollary of the "patriotic" prologue and inseparable
from it, the defects of the foreigners being a foil to native
virtues.[2] Conversely, the enjoyment of foreign entertainers
was a blot on an English audience. In Higgons's absurd
prologue to Granville's *The Jew of Venice* (1701) the Ghost
of Shakespeare is deluded by the magnificence of the audience at Drury Lane; the Ghost of Dryden disillusions him:

> *With all the outward Lustre, which you find,*
> *They want the nobler Beauties of the Mind.*
> *Their sickly Judgments, what is just, refuse,*
> *And French Grimace, Buffoons, and Mimicks choose.*

Rowe's prologue to *The Ambitious Step-Mother* (1700), an
excellent introduction to the "she-tragedy" bidding the
audience not to withhold their tears, ends:

> *O cou'd this Age's Writers hope to find*
> *An Audience to Compassion thus inclin'd,*
> *The Stage would need no Farce, nor Song nor Dance,*
> *Nor Capering Monsieur brought from Active* France.

Steele in his prologue to Vanbrugh's *The Mistake,* from
which I have quoted in this chapter, took occasion to chide
the fashionable audience of the Haymarket for preferring

1. Congreve's *Epilogue at the Opening of the Queen's Theatre in the
Hay-Market, with an Italian Pastoral* . . . (1705).
2. The patriotic prologue is discussed in the following chapter.

the elaborate costumes of tragedy to plot or fine acting, and he adds:

> *The other Style you full as well advance;*
> *If 'tis a Comedy, you ask—Who dance?*
> *For oh! what dire Convulsions have of late*
> *Torn and distracted each Dramatick State,*
> *On this great Question, Which House first should sell*
> *The New French Steps, imported by Ruel?*

A Prologue to the Town (1721) by Leonard Welsted describes the audience as entirely given up to "foreign Modes" and "foreign Nonsense," sitting "three long Hours" to watch French tumblers.[3]

The threat of usurpation by French dancers was less frequently the subject of prologues after the 1720's, but the hatred remained. The public demonstrated that they agreed with the playwrights and actors when Garrick attempted to produce his elaborate "Chinese Festival" in 1755. Patriotic zeal triumphed over love of spectacle, and the audience broke into destructive riots and drove the dancers from the stage.[4]

With the success of the famous dancer, Vestris, who appeared in London in 1781, criticism of French dancers revived in the prologues. Edward Topham had in mind not only the upper gallery when he wrote the epilogue to Andrews's *The Reparation* (1784), prophesying a "female patriot,"

---

3. Welsted's prologue and Steele's epilogue written for a performance of *Measure for Measure* (Genest, III, 55) were published together, the title reading: *A Prologue to the Town, As it was Spoken at the Theatre in Little Lincoln's-Inn-Fields. Written by Mr. Welsted. With an Epilogue on the same Occasion, By Sir Richard Steele. . . .* 1721. [Price 4 Pence].

4. Davies, *Life of David Garrick*, I, 186–192. See also, Deryck Lynham, *The Chevalier Noverre* (London, The Sylvan Press, 1950), Chapter II, "Noverre and David Garrick."

> *Whose taste the rage for Opera can defy,*
> *And bear to live—tho'* Pacchierotti *die:*
> *With strange ill-bred indifference can view*
> Vestris *on one leg, or,* the Dogs *on two.*

Since the time of Betterton, one of the chief grievances against the French dancers had been the excessive salaries paid them.[5] Farquhar in the *Prologue on the propos'd Union of the two Houses* records a disastrous attempt to entice the public:

> Vast Sums of Treasure too we did advance,
> To draw some mercenary Troops from *France;*
> Light-footed Rogues, who when they got their Pay,
> Took to their Heels—*Alons*—and run away.[6]

Vestris and his troop were engaged by Sheridan and his fellow proprietors of the Opera House for twenty thousand pounds. London was swept with excitement and enthusiasm, and public acclaim for Vestris confirmed the managers in their extravagance. Sheridan made the engagement of the French dancers the subject of his epilogue to Samuel Jackson Pratt's *The Fair Circassian* (1781), using the contemptuous terms of his predecessors and making the same appeal to patriotism. He rehearsed the dangers threatening the "dramatic state":

> What hosts of foes her tottering realms invade,
> By fashion muster'd, and by folly paid:
> While *Taste,* her old ally, unmov'd we see,
> And Spleen preserves an *arm'd neutrality*—

the "arm'd neutrality" being a clever reference to French maritime policy. He ridiculed Italian singers, "all arm'd

5. See Downes, *Roscius Anglicanus* (ed. Montague Summers, n.d.), p. 46, for the ruinous prices Betterton was forced to pay for his foreign entertainers.

6. *The Works of Mr. George Farquhar . . .* (1742), I, 38.

in whale-bone hoops," waging their traditional war against sense, and then he turned to the triumphant dancers and their ballet, *Jason and Medea*,[7] composed by Noverre, who, incidentally, had devised Garrick's "Chinese Festival":

Allied with these—in hostile bands advance
The light-heel'd legions of invading France.
To point her thunders on our British coast,
Year after year, has been vain Gallia's boast.
Their troops embark—their bold attempt is plann'd—
Their *heroes threaten*—and their *dancers land.*—
These only put their threats in execution,
And lay all London under contribution.

. . . .

And, modern Jasons, as of old in Greece,
Sail home triumphant with the golden fleece.

Obviously Sheridan, who was one of the persons responsible for the appearance of Vestris, was not serious in his indignation.

But whatever the policy of managers might be, the complaint of the actors and playwrights remained as it had been in 1703 when D'Urfey put it baldly in his prologue to *The Old Mode & the New:*

If *Comick Scenes cou'd please like capring Tricks,*
Or could be sounded with Italian Squeaks,
We might suppose this Play would last six Weeks.

. . . .

. . . .

In time of War, when Gold's of use to some,
1000 l. given tunefully from home,
Shews us the richest Fools in Christendom.

7. *The Plays & Poems of Richard Brinsley Sheridan*, ed. Rhodes (Oxford, B. Blackwell, 1928), III, 283. For *Jason and Medea*, see also Lynham, *op. cit.*, p. 102. For Sheridan's authorship of the epilogue to *The Fair Circassian*, see above, Chapter 3, p. 115, n. 5.

> *Ah! sad, sad times, for since these things must be,*
> *What is become, good Sirs, of Comedy?*

Pinkethman, speaking D'Urfey's prologue, sadly admitted
to the audience that he feared for his own fate since he
could not sing Italian opera, although to be sure,

> *Each Ditty, chanted by the dear bought fair,*
> *Is Arabick to all the Judges there.*

This fear was reiterated by a long line of actors, for
Italian opera and foreign singers aroused protest throughout the entire century. Sometimes the prologuisers abandoned reproof for flattery, contrasting sterling English
sense with meretricious Italian sound; for example, Dennis
in his prologue to *Gibraltar* (1705) assures the audience
that he has drawn slight help from music and dance, his
success depending on their brains rather than on their ears.
Addison sponsored Edmund Smith's *Phaedra and Hippolitus* (1707) by an apologetic prologue—

> *Our Home-spun Authors must forsake the Field,*
> *And* Shakespear *to the soft* Scarlatti *yield*—

but Smith was a "home-spun author."

Prologues by Cibber are full of scorn and jealousy of
foreign singers, and he speaks as both actor and playwright. In the epilogue to *The Careless Husband* (1704)
he describes the actors as starving while the singers prosper.
For *The Lady's Last Stake* (1707) he wrote and sang a
parody epilogue which achieved not a little popularity,
showing how he and his family would sing their hunger
in recitative when he, a mere player, is utterly undone by
Italian opera.[8] Considering the actor's hard lot, he thinks,

8. A similar epilogue was sung after a performance of Langford's *The
Lover His Own Rival* (1736), emphasizing the economic basis for the hatred
of opera:

> *Perhaps great Caesar, who the World commanded,*
> *May snuff the Opera Candles when disbanded.*

He then demonstrates how "Seignior Cibberini" might draw crowds. The piece read today is silly enough, but apparently Cibber designed his Italian singer as an acting part akin to Sir Novelty Fashion. His prologue to *Love in a Riddle* (1729), a ballad opera following in the wake of *The Beggar's Opera,* is a defense of English singers as opposed to foreign singers, and the epilogue, the liveliest that he ever wrote, is a song for Harper, with a chorus to be sung by the audience. The chief interest of *Love in a Riddle* is that the part of Phillida was sung by Miss Raftor, later Kitty Clive, who waged ceaseless war against the "invaders."

As to the genuineness of Mrs. Clive's hatred of Italian singers, her epilogues leave no doubt. From beginning to the end of her career, she delighted in mocking, defying, and flouting them. Her hatred was primarily professional, based on the fact that effeminate foreign singers, whom she held in personal contempt, took away the livelihood of honest native actors.

> Orpheus *drew Stones with his inchanting Song,*
> *These can do more, they draw our Gold along,*

she exclaims in the epilogue to *The Intriguing Chambermaid* (1734).

Fielding satirized opera in his burlesques and denounced it in his prologues and epilogues. He ends the prologue to *The Universal Gallant* (1735) with a plea for native actors, and in the epilogue to *Pasquin* (1736) he bids the audience,

---

> Even Songs in old *English* are so much disdain'd,
> That *Italians* come flocking from *Rome,* Sir;
> Until by their Squeeking your Pockets are drain'd,
> They'll ne'er think it time to go home, Sir.

"Banish all Childish Entertainments hence." They should at least divide their attention between foreign sound and English sense:

> *But let those Singers, who are bought so dear,*
> *Learn to be civil for their Cheer at least;*
> *Nor use like Beggars those who give the Feast.*
> *And tho' while Musick for her self may carve,*
> *Poor Poetry, her Sister-Art, must starve;*
> *Starve her, at least, with Shew of Approbation,*
> *Nor slight her, while you search the whole Creation,*
> *For all the Tumbling-Scum of every Nation.*

By the 1730's ridicule of Italian opera was so much a part of the evening's entertainment that Elizabeth Cooper in the prologue to *The Rival Widows* (1735) described *"Veteran Bards"* as those who *"Bully in Prologues,"* defy the pit, and *"lash the sing-song Age"*—Mrs. Cooper being one of the very few dramatists to defend Italian opera. Prologuisers did not inquire if the art they were attacking had any merit, and the audience expected contempt unsupported by proof. Francis Lynch introduced his comedy, sufficiently characterized by the title, *The Independent Patriot: or, Musical Folly* (1737), by comparing himself to a knight attacking a monster: *"At Musick's Trunk the furious Ax he drives."*

In 1754 Foote in the prologue to *The Knights* ridiculed the Italian burlettas being performed at Covent Garden:

> *I have a Plan to treat you with Burletta,*
> *That cannot miss your Taste,* Mia Spiletta.[9]

Twenty years later in the prologue for the new theatre in Birmingham under the management of Yates, Foote pretends to rejoice in his escape from London theatres:

9. "Spiletta" is a character in *Gli Amanti gelosi* (Covent Garden, 1753). Cf. Wilkinson, *Memoirs,* IV, 199.

FROM fiddling, fretting, Monsieur and Signior,
And all the dangers of the Italian shore;
From squeaking Monarchs and chromatic Queens,
And Metastasio's mix'd, and mangl'd scenes,
Where fashion, and not feeling, bears the sway,
Whilst sense and nature coyly keep away,
I come.[1]

John Hoole, the translator of Metastasio, introduced his tragedy, *Cyrus* (1768), with a prologue acknowledging his source, and, by way of describing his plot, ridiculed Italian opera! For the opening of the New Theatre Royal in Edinburgh in 1769, David Ross, the manager, spoke a prologue in which he dedicated his theatre to drama: "May Shakespeare triumph, and may Opera die." [2] But opera continued to flourish. In 1792 the comic actress, Mrs. Jordan, speaking Burgoyne's epilogue to Richardson's *The Fugitive,* carried on the tradition established by Kitty Clive in imitating the inanities of Italian opera for those who delight in "Words of soft nothing, by soft nothing sung."

For the serious dramatists of the eighteenth century, pantomime was a more formidable enemy than Italian opera. Pantomime was an enthusiastically accepted part of the English theatre, written by English writers and performed by English actors. In the prologue for the opening of Drury Lane under Garrick's management, Johnson described the drama of the Restoration as supplanted by pantomime:

But forc'd at length her antient Reign to quit,
She saw great *Faustus* lay the Ghost of Wit: [3]

1. The *London Chronicle,* July 5–7, 1774.
2. The *Scots Magazine,* December 1769, p. 652.
3. Thurmond's famous pantomime, *Harlequin Doctor Faustus,* was first presented at Drury Lane in 1723.

Exulting Folly hail'd the joyful Day,
And Pantomime, and Song, confirm'd her Sway.

Johnson knew the audience whom he was addressing, and
he was a realist:

Perhaps, where *Lear* has rav'd, and *Hamlet* dy'd,
On flying Cars new Sorcerers may ride.
Perhaps, for who can guess th' Effects of Chance?
Here *Hunt* may box, or *Mahomet* may dance.[4]

During the first three years of his management, Garrick
succeeded in making Shakespeare the chief dramatist of
his repertory, and between September 1747 and June 1750,
he produced thirteen of Shakespeare's plays. The *Drury
Lane Calendar* for those years records one hundred forty-
seven performances of Shakespeare, the other main productions being Elizabethan and Restoration revivals and
adaptations, earlier eighteenth-century plays, and new
plays. It was taken for granted that the theatre would include dancing, and Garrick employed a French ballet
master. The ballet, "The Savoyard Travellers," was performed on November 9, 1749, and thereafter was frequently part of the evening's entertainment. It was also
taken for granted that a theatre would include pantomime,
and before 1750 Garrick produced a number of pantomimes; for example, Mrs. Behn's *The Emperor of the*

4. As early as 1654 there was a rope-dancer called the "Turk," performing at the Red Bull playhouse. Mr. Leslie Hotson in his *The Common-
wealth and Restoration Stage* (Cambridge, Mass., 1928), p. 86, quotes four
entries from the newssheet, *Mercurius Fumigosus*, regarding the Turk's
acrobatics, one of the entries reading: "*News from St Johns Street* is, That
the *Turk* the other day, dancing so high, in capering on the upper Rope,
discovered a *Myne of Gold* in the *Ayre*" [23–30 August, 1654]. The issue
for 30 August–6 September comments that the Turk's discovery is
"thought but a meer fable, his meaning being, *by shewing his tricks in
the Aire, he would quickly gather much gold to himself*" [30 August–
6 September, 1654].

Moon in which Henry Woodward played Harlequin.[5] He
presented some musical entertainments and, as a tribute to
"exulting Folly," the bottle-conjurer skit, *Don Jumpedo*.
It should be remembered that these diversions were used
as afterpieces and that some of them, such as *The Dragon
of Wantley*, with Mrs. Clive as the heroine, had merit of
their own. But the *Drury Lane Calendar* proves that Garrick in the first years of his management did not depend
on music or pantomime for his afterpieces but on farces
of high dramatic quality.

When Garrick delivered his occasional prologue for the
opening of the season of 1750–1751, he announced a
change of policy and declared himself compelled to cater
to public taste:

> Sacred to SHAKESPEARE, was this spot design'd
> To pierce the heart, and humanize the mind.
> But if an empty house, the actor's curse,
> Shews us our *Lears,* and *Hamlets,* lose their force;
> Unwilling, we must change the nobler scene,
> And, in our turn, present you *Harlequin;*
> Quit poets, and set carpenters to work,
> Shew gaudy scenes, or mount the vaulting *Turk*.[6]

5. Genest (IV, 263) notes that the pantomime had not been produced
for twenty years.

6. The *Gentleman's Magazine*, September 1750, p. 422. For the "vaulting
Turk," compare note 4 above. As to the "gaudy scenes," according to Tate
Wilkinson, "The very idea of a triumphal procession at Covent-Garden,
struck terror to the whole host of Drury, however big they looked and
strutted on common occasions." (Wilkinson, *Memoirs*, IV, 201.) Garrick
frequently tried to surpass Covent Garden. In addition to pantomimes and
musical entertainments, he devised the "Coronation" in 1761, admonishing
the pit in his epilogue to Delap's *Hecuba*:

> *Sneer not, ye critics, at this rage for shew,*
> *That honest hearts at coronation glow!;*

The Jubilee in 1769, and *The Institution of the Garter* in 1771. These
justify the charge made in the occasional prologue for the opening of
the Theatre Royal in Edinburgh in 1771:

In the answering prologue for the opening of Covent
Garden,[7] Barry made a defiant and brazen retort to Gar-
rick's threat of presenting Harlequin "in our turn," by
boasting that they had recourse to superior pantomime—
Harlequin being Rich's great accomplishment. But in
Woodward Drury Lane had not only a rival Harlequin
but the century's most skilful deviser of pantomimes. On
December 26, 1750, Garrick presented Woodward's *Queen
Mab,* and thereafter pantomime flourished at Drury Lane.[8]

How far Garrick moved from the position taken at the
beginning of his management can be seen from his prologue to *The School for Lovers* (1762). He represents himself in an imaginary argument with the author of the play,
to whom he is expounding the superiority of stage machinery to the unities:

> *Lord, Sir, said I, for gallery, boxes, pit,*
> *I'll back my Harlequin against your wit.*

In *Cymon,* the New Year's entertainment for 1767, he
backed stage devices and scenery against wit, plot, and
character. King, speaking the prologue to the upper gallery, disclaims *Cymon* as drama:

> *As for the Plot, Wit, Humour, Language—I*
> *Beg you such Trifles kindly to pass by;*

> Let rival Theatres seduce the nation,
> With the mock trumpery of Installation;
> Disgrace the Muses, and debase the age,
> And make a *walking Wardrobe* of the Stage.

(*Lloyd's Evening Post,* Nov. 29–Dec. 2, 1771.) For the humiliating failure
of Garrick's "Coronation," see Davies, *Life of David Garrick,* I, 336–338.
The Covent Garden "Coronation" devised by Rich even surpassed the
expectation of the public. (Genest, IV, 647.)

7. The *Gentleman's Magazine,* October 1750, p. 472.

8. For the performances of Woodward's pantomimes, see *Drury Lane
Calendar* under *Queen Mab* (1750); *Harlequin Ranger* (1751); *The Genii*
(1752); *Fortunatus* (1753); *Proteus; or, Harlequin in China* (1755); *Marplot
in Lisbon* (1755); and *Mercury Harlequin* (1756).

The most essential Part, which somewhat means,
As Dresses, Dances, Sinkings, Flyings, Scenes,—
They'll make you stare. . . .

George Keate concluded his epilogue to *Cymon* with a
critic's snarling:

"The drama's lost!—the managers exhaust us
"With *Op'ras, Monkies, Mab,* and *Dr. Faustus,*"

but he pronounced it the duty of a manager to satisfy all
varieties of public interest. Woodward, delivering Garrick's epilogue to *Barbarossa* (1754), in the character of a
"fine gentleman," banishes Shakespeare to France and reserves for the British stage "*A Farce or two—and* Woodward's *Pantomimes!*" [9] Woodward's departure from Drury
Lane in 1758 was a severe blow to Garrick.[1] The following year he devised his own pantomime, *Harlequin's Invasion,* which long remained popular. The evidence of
the prologues is that as patentee and manager Garrick was
governed by expedience, not principle; he committed himself to pleasing the audience, and therefore his prologues
and epilogues, of which there are over one hundred and
sixty extant, present no consistent dramatic theory. Like
Sheridan's epilogue to *The Fair Circassian,* they often were
sops to the audience.

9. Delight in pantomime was by no means restricted to the upper gallery.
In Garrick's burlesque, *A Peep behind the Curtain* (1767), the Fuz family
are waiting to see Mr. Glib's play. Their interest in drama may be judged
by their conversation:

> *Lady Fuz.* Don't let us lose time, Mr. Glib; if they are not ready for
> the rehearsal, suppose the manager entertains us with thunder and
> lightning; and let us see his traps, and his whims, and his harlequin
> pantomimes.
> *Sir Toby.* And a shower of rain, or, an eclipse; and I must beg one
> peep at the Patagonians.

1. Wilkinson, *Memoirs,* II, B.

As Garrick had declared in 1750, his compliance with public taste was in large measure due to the success of Rich's pantomimes. Opposed as these were to the nature of drama, yet their luring the audience away from Shakespeare was not quite another instance of Old Hunks and *Hamlet*. In spite of Pope's description in *The Dunciad* (III, 227–272) of the childish machinery and tawdry settings which enchanted the audience—"Here shouts all Drury, there all Lincoln's-inn"—Rich's pantomimes frequently called forth admiration from competent critics. A panegyric by Thomas Davies suggests that Rich's pantomimes deserved the acclaim they received. Speaking of Rich as Harlequin, Davies says: ". . . his gesticulation was so perfectly expressive of his meaning, that every motion of his hand or head, or any part of his body, was a kind of dumb eloquence that was readily understood by the audience. Mr. Garrick's action was not more perfectly adapted to his characters than Mr. Rich's attitudes and movements to the varied employment of the wooden-sword magician."[2] John Jackson, the author of *The History of the Scottish Stage,* who saw Rich only in his old age, is as laudatory as Davies and gives a detailed and appreciative picture of his "hatching of *Harlequin* by the heat of the sun."[3] After seeing the pantomime, *Robinson Crusoe* (1781), Walpole remarked: ". . . how unlike the pantomimes of Rich, which were full of wit, and coherent, and carried on a story."[4]

2. Davies, *Garrick,* I, 339. See also, Paul Sawyer, "John Rich; a Biographical Sketch," *Theatre Annual,* XV, 55–68.

3. John Jackson, *The History of the Scottish Stage* (Edinburgh, 1793), pp. 367–368. The pantomime described is Theobald's *Harlequin a Sorcerer.* Cf. Pope, *The Dunciad,* III, 1.248:

> Lo! one vast egg produces human race.

4. *The Letters of Horace Walpole,* ed. Toynbee (Oxford, The Clarendon Press, 1903–05), XII, 359.

In the prologue to *Harlequin's Invasion*, Garrick expressed his admiration of Rich's ability in the part with which he had identified himself for fifty years:

When Lun appear'd, with matchless art and whim,
He gave the pow'r of speech to ev'ry limb;
Tho' mask'd and mute, convey'd his quick intent,
And told in frolic gesture all he meant.
But now the motley coat, and sword of wood,
Requires a tongue to make them understood.[5]

Paul Whitehead's prologue for the opening of Covent Garden in 1767 lists the various kinds of entertainment to be offered the audience the coming season. Far from decrying pantomimes, the managers boast that they will support the tradition which Rich created for his theatre:

Here all the Gods of Pantomime shall rise:
Yet 'midst the pomp and magic of machines,
Some plot may mark the meaning of our scenes;
Scenes which were held, in good King Rich's days,
By sages, no bad epilogues to plays.[6]

Weaver gives the date of Rich's first pantomime as 1717,[7] and by the second decade of the century, authors were

5. *The Poetical Works of David Garrick* (1785) I, 158. From the remainder of the prologue—of which only the passage quoted has ever been printed—it is apparent that this was an introduction to a Christmas performance of *Harlequin's Invasion*, first produced in 1759. The prologue, in manuscript in the Folger Library, describes the entertainment as a "Xmas Pye,"

Made up of Trick, Song, Dance, of Prose & Rhyme,
A Tragic-Comic-Operatic-Pantomime.

6. See above, Chapter 4, p. 152, n. 4, for Whitehead's prologue.
7. John Weaver in 1728 published *The History of the Mimes and Pantomimes*, a pamphlet which included a list of twenty-two performances from 1702 to 1726. For these early pantomimes, see Nicoll, *A History of Early Eighteenth Century Drama*, pp. 252-253.

looking with fear upon the intruder. Gay's epilogue to *The Captives* (1724) states the case of the neglected play-wrights who had been defeated even at Drury Lane by the success of *Harlequin Doctor Faustus:*

> *Will Poets ne'er consider what they cost us?*
> *What tragedy can take, like Doctor* Faustus?

According to the prologue to *Bays's Opera* (1730), no play could succeed unless it ended with a jig and a pantomime. The author of the epilogue to *The Spend-Thrift* (1731) reflects with bitterness on the plight of the dramatist:

> *Were he compleat in* Action, Place, and Time,
> *Why, what are all these three—to Pantomime?*
> *He fairly owns throughout his every Scene,*
> *He has not the Address—of* Harlequin.

Between 1730 and 1737 Fielding through his burlesques, prologues, and epilogues attacked pantomime. The pro-logue to the mock tragedy in *Pasquin* (1736) informs the audience that Common-Sense will on that night make her appearance as a rival to Harlequin: *"Oh! Love her like her Sister Monsters of the Age."* The author of the re-hearsal play in *The Author's Farce* (1730) amazes the player by telling him that a cat is to speak the epilogue to rival the dumb-show in *Perseus and Andromeda,* a panto-mime revived by Rich and then playing at Lincoln's Inn Fields.

Rich was a man undisturbed by hostile criticism and possibly even oblivious to it. His production of panto-mimes was no concession to the public, for he considered them superior to drama. He did not deign to answer ques-tions such as that asked by Joseph Reed in the prologue to *The Register-Office* (1761): *"Pray what's the Use of full-pric'd Pantamime?"* He cared nothing for Reed's con-temptuous description of his dancing:

> *When wriggling* Harlequin, *the Magic Sage,*
> *In horn-pipe Amble traverses the Stage!*

Rich died in November 1761, but the rage for pantomime continued. In 1774 Hugh Kelly's prologue to *The
Romance of an Hour* declares pantomime still the most
popular of dramatic entertainments and makes a spectator
say, with enthusiasm, regarding *Cato:*

> "I never miss that play at any time,
> "If 'tis but added to a pantomime."

Kelly ridicules machines and stage devices—tempests,
lightning,

> A grand collection of dramatic dishes,
> Of dragons, giants, forests, rivers, fishes.

He denounces the audience as dull, uncritical, and gulli-
ble, excited only by scenery and claptrap:

> Shakespeare is great—is exquisite—no doubt—
> But then our carpenters must help him out.
>
> .   .   .   .
>
> Let critics proudly form dramatick laws,
> Give me, say I, what's sure to meet applause;
> Let them of time, and place, and action boast,
> I'm for a devil, a dungeon, or a ghost—

Kelly states specifically that he is referring to the demands
of pit, boxes, and gallery.

Conway's epilogue to Jerningham's *The Welsh Heiress*
(1795) also denounces the audience for their lack of taste.
His accusation is exactly that made in the first decade, and
he uses almost the same terms:

> 'Tis said your taste for Comedy is flown;
> That darling child you once were proud to own:

That Shakespeare's fires no more your senses rouse;
Congreve and Vanbrugh seldom fill the house.

Instead the audience delights in pantomime, spectacle, and opera. Far from understanding the turmoil that they demand, they are left to guess where the action is supposed to occur and what has caused the alarms and excursions,

Till by the friendly banners we are told,
There Macedon's, there Persia's chief behold!

Thus with place names supplying the lack of plot, the childish pageantry proceeds, accompanied by noise, pyrotechnics, and the general confusion of machinery:

There demigods by entrechâts advance,
And Carthage flames demolish'd in a dance.

Following the pattern that Johnson had established, Charlotte Smith wrote a critical prologue for her comedy, *What Is She?* (1799), tracing the drama from its infancy, when authors, actors, and stage carpenters gained equal fame, through the Restoration, the most mature period of the English stage, during which plot, wit, and verse needed no extraneous help,

But all must change—behold the Muses mourn,
And, drooping, see Taste's infancy return;
Again the Bard calls forth red stocking'd legions,
And show'rs of fire from the infernal regions;
Again, storms darken the Theatric sky,
And strung on ropes the fearful Cupids fly:
Again pale ghosts stalk tunefully along,
And end their visit, just as ends the song.
The siege, th' explosion, nightly concourse draws,
And castles burn and fall—with vast applause!

Some of the trumpery ridiculed by Miss Smith was the necessary setting for the current "horror" plays and is similar to the stage devices prescribed by Matthew Gregory Lewis in his epilogue to Holcroft's *Knave, or Not?* (1798) for the young dramatist who wishes to succeed: "Give us Lightning and Thunder, Flames, Daggers and Rage." Many other late prologues and epilogues reveal a compete loss of critical standards in both prologuisers and dramatists; for example, the prologue to Miles Peter Andrews's *The Mysteries of the Castle: A Dramatic Tale* (1795) recommends the play to the audience from pit to gallery because it is a hodge-podge of music, pantomime, and *"a dash of terror."*

In 1799 an anonymous mock prologue, published with *A Critique on the Tragedy of Pizarro,*[8] holds up to scorn an audience that supports such hodge-podges. The prologue, "To Be Spoken by Any Body, in the Character of a Puppet-Show Man," ridicules the fustian and heroics of *Pizarro,* then being presented at Drury Lane:

> *Grown* gentlemen and ladies, pray walk in;
> Our puppet-show's "just going to begin;"
> My little mistresses, and masters too,
> Walk in, the entertainment's fit for you.

The writer describes Sheridan's tragedy as nothing but scenery and noise, remarkable only for its length:

> In this at least our pantomime is *new,*
> We give you *five* long acts instead of *two;*
> Five *ling'ring* acts stuff'd full of stage *devices,*
> Five acts of pantomime—at *playhouse prices!!!*

8. *A Critique on the Tragedy of Pizarro, as Represented at Drury Lane Theatre with Such Uncommon Applause. To Which is Added, a New Prologue, That Has Not Yet Been Spoken.* The Second Edition (1799). R. Crompton Rhodes, *Harlequin Sheridan* (Oxford, B. Blackwell, 1933), pp. 183-184, prints the prologue. For a summary of the prologue to *What Is She?* see Nicoll, *Late Eighteenth Century Drama,* pp. 25-26.

Eighty years had passed since the epilogue to Dennis's *The Invader of His Country* drew a striking comparison between the banishment of Coriolanus by the Roman rabble and the banishment of tragedy by the English audience. Just as Coriolanus led the enemy to attack Rome, so tragedy will join forces against the British theatre and, uniting with the invaders, farce, opera, and tumblers, destroy it. If we substitute "pantomime" for Dennis's "invaders," the mock prologue to *Pizarro* reads like a commentary on this prophecy. The dramatists of the late eighteenth century had reason to protest against the increasing number of pantomimes. Professor Nicoll's "Hand-List of Plays, 1750–1800," shows that of the one hundred and fifty-seven pantomimes written in the last half of the century over two-thirds fall between 1780 and 1800.[9]

The quotations in this chapter prove that from Betterton to Sheridan the perversity and dullness of the audience were among the chief themes of the prologuisers. They were right in decrying the intrusion of pantomime and spectacle into serious drama, and in denouncing the audience for their childish delight in miscellaneous entertainment and stage machinery. But such denunciation is not necessarily a proof of critical discernment, for the prologuisers also urged the audience to applaud wooden Augustan tragedies and sentimental comedies. Their concern here was not with the detached weighing of the intrinsic or relative merit of various forms of drama, but with the relationship of those forms to the playwrights, actors, and audience, and to the immediate problems of the theatre.

9. Nicoll, *A History of Late Eighteenth Century Drama*, pp. 232–348.

CHAPTER 6

THE PATRIOTIC PROLOGUE

Vituperation of Italian opera and French dancers was only one expression of the pervasive contempt of foreigners, augmented throughout the century by a long series of wars. An obvious and common stratagem of the prologue was to win the audience by appeals to national prejudice. Although there are prologues expressing honest and justifiable patriotism, the majority of patriotic prologues were simply ruses to capture the favor of the audience and thus incline them to extend their enthusiasm to the play itself. The writer of prologues could be sure of winning applause by references to victories in battle and to popular heroes; he could also be sure that scorn of the French would meet boisterous approval; and by emphasizing the general superiority of the English, he could reconcile even the upper gallery to accept a translation from the French.

In the first decade of the century many prologues celebrated the victories of Marlborough, the popularity of such pieces being attested by newspaper announcements; for example, the *Daily Courant* for Friday, August 11, 1704, after announcing a revival of *The Emperor of the Moon,* adds: "Also a new Prologue, occasion'd by the good News that arriv'd yesterday, of the Great Victory gain'd

over the French and Bavarians, by his Grace the Duke of
Marlborough." The prologue to *Zelmane: or, The Cor-
inthian Queen* (1705) exhorts the victors of all ages to lay
their trophies at the feet of Queen Anne, who alone has
fought for justice. An "armed" epilogue to the play was
spoken by Mrs. Bowman, *"drest like* Victory":

> I Victory *from* Danube's *Banks appear,*
> *Laurels unknown, to* English *Arms I bear.*

Both the prologue and the epilogue to Dennis's *Appius and
Virginia* (1709) are patriotic. The prologue flatters the
audience by comparing their courage to that of the Romans and illustrates the point by the heroism displayed
at Oudenarde:

> *Be witness that eternal Day which quell'd*
> *The vanquish'd Gaul upon the wond'ring* Scheld.
> *Like* Hannibal *the crafty* Vendome *fled,*
> *While* Britain *fought like* Rome, *like* Scipio Marlborough
>   *led.*

The epilogue ends with adulation of Queen Anne, who
is England's Virginia, Lucretia, and Portia in one. The
dramatic opera, *Alarbas,* published in 1709, is also provided with a patriotic epilogue, recounting the blessings
bestowed by the reign of Queen Anne: *"Witness* Hockstet,
Ramillies, Audenard."

The authors of such prologues had not infrequently to
defend themselves against the accusation of being inspired
by Whiggish principles. Dennis published his tragedy,
Liberty Asserted (1704), with a Preface insisting that the
prologue and epilogue, as well as the play itself, were not
political, as the critics thought, but patriotic. The epilogue enforces the apology by asserting that Dennis wrote
the tragedy to prove that savages—the play is laid in Can-

ada and extols the valor of the Iroquois—are more natural in their affections than are European tyrants:

> To reclaim such our Author bad me say
> He wrote this English and no Party Play:
> He minds not who's of Whig or Tory Clan
> But who for Lewis is, or who for ANN?

Mrs. Centlivre, a zealous Whig, came to grief because of a single line lauding Marlborough, then in disgrace, in the epilogue to The Perplex'd Lovers (1712).[1]

With the Rebellion of 1715 prologuisers hastened to express fervent loyalty to the House of Hanover and fear of Jacobites and their machinations. Anti-Jacobitical prologues range from pleasant trifles such as Thomas D'Urfey's Prologue Spoken like a Scotch Highlander with a Sword and Target,[2] celebrating the defeat of the rebels at Preston, to such furious tirades as Bartholomew Paman's prologue to Ambrose Philips's Humfrey, Duke of Gloucester (1723), a warning of the horrors following submission to prelates and Rome.[3] Three prologues chosen from many will serve to illustrate the writers' abhorrence of the Jacobites, their loyalty to the Protestant Succession, and their reverence for the memory of King William. The first of these is Philips's prologue to The Briton. A Tragedy (1722), an amusing but highly prejudiced condensation of history, written to prove the thesis:

1. For Norris's improvised epilogue, and for political factions in the audience, see above, pp. 155–156.

2. Thomas D'Urfey's Wit and Mirth (1719), II, 348.

3. For other Anti-Jacobitical pieces, see Rowe's prologue to The Tragedy of Lady Jane Gray (1715), a panegyric of King William and the Protestant Succession; Rowe's epilogue to Mrs. Centlivre's The Cruel Gift (1716); Beckingham's prologue to The Tragedy of King Henry IV of France (1719); Dennis's prologue to The Invader of His Country (1719); Pack's prologue to Sewell's Sir Walter Raleigh (1719); Hughes's prologue to The Siege of Damascus (1720); Sterling's prologue to Giffard's Merlin: or, The British Inchanter (1736); and Miller's prologue to Mahomet the Impostor (1744).

> Britons, . . .
> *The Love of Freedom is your ancient Glory.*

The Roman invasion under Caesar introduced luxury and imposed servitude, thus crushing the *"Native Vertue"* of the ancient Britons, until the Saxons revived "British *Manliness of Soul."* Then with the Restoration,

> *. . . another Set of* Romans *came;*
> *And brought worse Slavery:—Though they chang'd the*
>   *Name:*
> *Tamed us with Luxuries of a different Kind;*
> *And made plain Truth distasteful to the Mind.*
>   *By* Nassaw's *Aid, at last, we drive Them, hence;*
> *And, once again, return, to* common Sense.
> *In* Britain, *ever may It keep Possession!*
> *Establish'd, by the* Protestant Succession.

Rowe's *Tamerlane,* written shortly before the declaration of the War of the Spanish Succession, is a political allegory in which the hero represents William III and the proud but conquered Bajazet, Louis XIV.[4] The prologue extols William as a warrior heroically sacrificing his own safety for his people and as a just prince, greater in peace than in war. For many years *Tamerlane* was performed annually in the theatres of London and Dublin on November 4, William's birthday, and also occasionally on November 5, the anniversary of his first landing in England.[5] For the performance of *Tamerlane* at Covent Garden on November 4, 1746, Horace Walpole wrote an epilogue, to be spoken by Mrs. Pritchard in the character of the Comic Muse, to celebrate the suppression of the Rebellion of 1745.[6] He begins with the usual appeal:

4. See Johnson's *The Lives of the English Poets,* ed. Hill, II, 66–67.
5. *Biographia Dramatica,* III, 318–319.
6. *The Works of Horatio Walpole* (1798), I, 25–27.

> Britons, once more in annual joy we meet
> This genial night in freedom's fav'rite seat,

and proceeds with a description of the dangers they have
so narrowly escaped. Had the Rebellion succeeded, the
Lord Chamberlain's office would have been turned into an
inquisitorial chamber in which *Henry VIII, The Spanish
Fryar, Cato,* and

> Ev'n Tamerlane, whose sainted name appears
> Red-letter'd in the calendar of play'rs,

would be burnt as heresy. Mrs. Pritchard's banter is a sort
of burlesque of the virulent Anti-Jacobitical prologues of
the earlier part of the century. The prologue ends with
the prediction that William, Duke of Cumberland, will
share the military and civil laurels of his great predecessor.

Fielding, who parodied numerous prologue conventions,
set forth Tom Thumb in all the glamor of the patriotic
hero. The mock prologue to *Pasquin* (1736) introduces the
heroine, Common-Sense, with the admonition:

> Britons, *attend; and decent Reverence shew*
> *To her, who made t'* Athenian *Bosoms glow.*

In the prologue to *The Author's Farce* (1730) Fielding
ridicules both the ranting actor and the appeal to patriotism as a device to win applause:

> *Or, when in Armour of* Corinthian *Brass,*
> *Heroick Actor stares you in the Face,*
> *And cries aloud with Emphasis that's fit, on*
> *Liberty, Freedom, Liberty and* Briton;
> *While frowning, gaping for Applause he stands,*
> *What generous* Briton *can refuse his Hands?*

He turns to the earnest recommendation of the farce with
the comment: *"But Handkerchiefs and* Britain *laid aside."*

Fortunately Fielding's satire did not give the *coup de grâce* to patriotic prologues; they continued through the Napoleonic Wars as excellent expressions of public opinion.

Edward Phillips, the author of *Britons, Strike Home* (1739), instructs the audience that the subject of his play is a very proper reason for its being enthusiastically received:

> *From Crisis of the Times and where he lays*
> *His Scene, he thinks himself insur'd of Praise.*

The scene of the comedy is the battleship, the St. Joseph, and the characters British sailors; therefore the prologue bids the critics:

> *Suspend to Night at least Theatrick Laws,*
> *And kindly view the Characters he draws;*
> *Instead of Rules and Language, Plot and Art,*
> *Accept the Tribute of a* British *Heart;*
> *And let not your least Triumph over* Spain
> *Conduce to give one* Englishman *a Pain.*

Phillips declares in the epilogue that every right-minded person will be ready to substitute national prejudice for critical acumen.

> *The Taking o' th'* St. Joseph *who will damn?*
> *To every* Briton *That must Joy afford,*
> *And sure we have no* Spanish *Dons aboard:*
> *None then with Malice will our Scenes arraign,*
> *But they who hate* Old England, *and love* Spain.

Shirley in the prologue to *Edward the Black Prince* (1750) uses like reasoning: as the play presents "*genuine* English *Feats*" and "*just historic Truths,*" the audience is forced to applaud:

> *And sure that Tale must have for* Britons *Charms,*
> *That shews you* France *subdu'd by* British *Arms:*

Our Lions traversing their ravag'd Plains,
Their Armies broken, and their King in Chains.

The patriotic prologue frequently included a panegyric
of the king or a current hero. In the epilogue to Brooke's
The Earl of Essex (1761), spoken by Mrs.
Pritchard as Queen Elizabeth, Garrick celebrated the accession of
George III—"*Born amongst Britons, and by Britons
taught*"—and prophesied for him a long reign of peace.
On June 4, 1761, the King's birthday, Garrick closed the
season at Drury Lane by a prologue ending with a rapturous tribute. He proudly declared in the prologue to
the command performance of *Much Ado about Nothing*,
November 14, 1765: "*'Tis for my King, and, zounds, I'll
do my best!*" [7]

One of the most popular of Garrick's prologues, and his
last but one, written to introduce Colman's alteration of
Bonduca (1778),[8] is a patriotic address containing a eulogy
of Pitt, who died the year the play was performed. Beginning with the usual praise of the heroic ancient Britons,
Garrick bids the audience recall that the same dauntless

7. The *London Chronicle*, December 7–10, 1765.
8. The prologue to *Bonduca* was printed in the usual newspapers and
magazines—the *St. James's Chronicle*, Aug. 4–6, 1778, and in the *London
Chronicle* on the same day; in *Lloyd's Evening Post*, Aug. 7–10, 1778; in
the *London Magazine*, Aug. 1778, pp. 377–378. It was not printed with the
first edition of the play, but appears in the 1808 edition, "regulated from
the prompt book." For conflicting opinions about the merits of this prologue, compare the *Diary and Letters of Madame D'Arblay*, ed. Charlotte
Barrett (1893), I, 23, in which Johnson is reported as saying that he could
not read the piece because of its dullness: "I don't know what is the
matter with David; I am afraid he is grown superannuated, for his prologues and epilogues used to be incomparable," with *The Private Correspondence of David Garrick*, II, 313, where Hannah More writes in a
letter to Garrick: "I congratulate you, dear Sir, on your prologue to
Bonduca: it is admirable! I happened to dine at our Bishop's the day it
came out; he was quite in raptures, and read it to me till he could repeat
the best part of it." Johnson's condemnation to the contrary, the prologue
is better than most of its kind.

spirit was displayed by Edward III at Crécy and that courage in times of danger has always been England's chief
glory:

> To the mind's eye let the Fifth Harry rise,
> And in that vision boasting *France* despise.
> Then turn to later deeds, your sires have wrought,
> When Anna rul'd, and mighty Marlb'rough fought.

He invokes the spirit of Pitt to guide the country through
the coming years of war and to inspire her to scorn threats
of French invasion.

The patriotism of the prologues, even in times of peace,
was usually accompanied by disdain of foreigners, especially the French. Occasionally a prologuiser admits that
France rivals England in the arts and graces. Mrs. Cibber,
appearing as the Tragic Muse in Thomson's epilogue to
Tancred and Sigismunda (1745), describes the humanizing
effect of tragedy in Greece and Rome.

> *On* FRANCE *and* YOU *then rose my brightning Star,*
> *With social Ray—The* ARTS *were ne'er at War.*
> *O as your Fire and Genius stronger blaze,*
> *As yours are generous Freedom's bolder Lays,*
> *Let not the* Gallick *taste leave yours behind,*
> *In decent Manners and in Life refin'd.*

But even here Thomson qualified his praise by the couplet
emphasizing England's superiority in manliness. The reluctant acknowledgments commonly paid the French are
illustrated by such pieces as the prologue to Miller's *The
Humours of Oxford* (1730). Miller admits that every nation may boast some special blessing or peculiar art—

> *'Tis* Britain's *Glory, she enjoys 'em all.*
> *Her Native Fire with* French *Politeness grac'd,*
> Rome's *ancient Liberty, and modern Taste.*

Then comes the prologuiser's alchemy by which the recognition of merit in the French as a nation, the importation of French goods, the adaptation of French plays are all made acceptable, even to the upper gallery:

> By Foreign Arts your Taste may be refin'd,
> But Home-bred Sense alone can feast a British Mind.

Along with common sense, certain other characteristics are peculiar to England and cannot be borrowed from foreign lands. Most important is the dauntless courage inherited from the ancient Britons, a courage always controlled by manliness and tempered by mercy. "*They'll bravely conquer*," says Charles Shadwell in the prologue to *The Humours of the Army* (1713), "*and as bravely spare.*" The prologue to *Buthred* (1778) presents a clear picture of the usual concept of the ancient Britons:

> Rough were their manners, but unstain'd with guile,
> Their anger ne'er was hid beneath a smile;
> Tho' furious, when resisted, soon appeas'd:—
> The prostrate foe their gen'rous mercy rais'd.

> Such Britons were, and such their sons remain,
> While polish'd France succeeds the barb'rous Dane.

All prologues agree that the chief characteristic of the English is surliness concealing a kindly heart.

Contrasted to them are the trivial, effeminate French, whose only resolute quality is perfidy. They are weak and absurd and, like Dr. Caius, express themselves in excited jargon. Steele devoted the epilogue to *The Tender Husband* (1705) to an attack on opera as Jacobitical, effeminate, opposed to the "*Manly Wit*" that should flourish on the stage, and possibly treasonous, as it is sung in a foreign tongue. He concludes his denunciation by urging:

> Let those Derision meet, who would Advance
> Manners, or Speech, from Italy or France;

Let them learn You, who wou'd your Favour find,
And *English* be the Language of Mankind.

James Sterling's prologue to *Merlin: or, The British Inchanter* (1736), a piece which runs so true to pattern that it is a paradigm of the "visionary" patriotic prologue, commends the play as fit for "British Palates" and introduces the Ghost of Merlin, an ancient Briton arisen to rescue the stage from effeminacy by "superior Magic" and "manly Charms." Farquhar built his epilogue to *The Recruiting Officer* (1706) around a drummer's beating the *Grenadier March,* music excellently suited to the "Genius of the *English*." "Gentlemen, this piece of Musick, call'd an *Overture to a Battel,* was compos'd by a famous *Italian* Master, and was perform'd with wonderful Success, at the great *Opera's* of *Vigo, Schellenberg,* and *Blenheim;* it came off with the Applause of all *Europe,* excepting *France;* the *French* found it a little too rough for their *Delicatesse.*" Garrick's epilogue to Colman's *The Spanish Barber* (1777),[9] a play adapted from Beaumarchais, describes France as a nation of friseurs, simpletons, and rascals, whose chief delight is marital infidelity.

The France of the prologues is constantly denounced as corrupting with her effeminacy the rough, manly Britons. "Where," demands Rowe in the epilogue to Mrs. Centlivre's *The Cruel Gift* (1716),

Where are the tough brave BRITONS *to be found,*
With Hearts *of* Oak, *so much of Old renown'd?*

Certainly they are not to be found among the "spritely" fops *"to Froth and France inclin'd"* of John Hewitt's prologue to *A Tutor for the Beaus* (1737) or among the "powder'd Coxcombs" of Cumberland's epilogue to *The Brothers* (1770):

9. The *London Magazine,* September 1777, pp. 480–481.

Ill would their mincing minuet steps agree
With the deep roll of a tempestuous sea;
Ay, there's the stage on which we tutor France,
There not she us, but we taught her to dance.[1]

The "honest tar" of Pilon's prologue to *The Invasion*
(1778) scorns French threats of invasion and looking to
the upper gallery exclaims:

Invade us, boys! why sluice my English blood,
And send me home with all my timbers wood;
If I, Ben Block, with half the British fleet,
Would not these Parley-vous most soundly beat!

Even French food was held in contempt by the prologuisers. As roast beef was proper food for Englishmen, so
"froth" was proper for Frenchmen; or, as Elijah Fenton remarked in the prologue to Southerne's *The Spartan Dame*
(1719), "Cressy *was lost by Kickshaws, and Soupe meagre.*"
Fielding extended his dislike of foreign entertainment to
the entertainers and in the epilogue to *The Universal Gallant* (1735) denounced the beaux for imitating them in
their dress and manners.

French *only with their Palates will go down.*
French *Plays Applause have, like* French *Dishes, got,*
Only because you understand them not.
Happy Old England, *in those glorious Days,*
When good plain English *Food and Sense could please.*

He urges the ladies to shun all fops *"asham'd of being*
Britons *born."*

More delightful to the upper gallery than mere ridicule
was caricature through impersonation. Garrick, introducing a performance of *Harlequin's Invasion,* defies Vol-

1. *Lloyd's Evening Post,* February 12–14, 1770. For authorship and date
of the epilogue, see the *Public Advertiser,* February 10, 1770.

taire's adverse criticism of Shakespeare, "Shall we, the hearts of Oak, give up Parnassus?" and then describes the hero of the evening, "Monsieur Harlequin," through whom the French are to be satirized—"He's somewhat crafty, somewhat too absurd." [2] King in Garrick's prologue to *Albumazar* (1773) declares that the English are the only human beings who know how to laugh, and he demonstrates how Frenchmen grin. The point of Colman's prologue to *Bon Ton* (1775) is the contrast between the affected and artificial refinement of the French and the hearty, honest vulgarity of the citizen's wife:

> *Ah! I loves life, and all the joys it yields—*
> *Says Madame Fussock, warm from Spital-fields.*
> *Bone-Tone's the space 'twixt Saturday and Monday,*
> *And riding in a one-horse chair o' Sunday!*
> *'Tis drinking tea on summer afternoons*
> *At Bagnigge-Wells, with China and gilt spoons!*

Madame Fussock was a foil to the obliquity of the Englishman Frenchified by studying Chesterfield's *Letters*, the "graces" concealing his black heart. Both characters were designed to be acted by King.[3]

The more serious and the more smug patriotic prologues assert that the love of liberty is the chief and unique passion of the English. Samuel Madden in the epilogue to *Themistocles* (1729) reminds the audience that a Frenchman would be hanged for advancing principles such as those of the play:

> *But you, rough* Britons, *with your cursed Bravery,*
> *Have such a vile Antipathy to Slavery;*
> *You'd rather die like Fools, in Freedom's Cause,*
> *Than once survive your Liberties and Laws.*

2. Garrick MSS., the Folger Library.
3. See above, pp. 58–59. Garrick's epilogue to Hannah More's *The Inflexible Captive* (1774) also criticizes adversely Chesterfield's *Letters*.

Henry Brooke's prologue to *Gustavus Vasa* (published
1739), a play prohibited by the licenser for political reasons, is an excellent example of the earnest patriotic prologue. Brooke by implication draws a parallel between
the corruption and national depravity of Sweden in the
sixteenth century and the abuses of the Walpole government. He describes Gustavus rising to liberate a people
who, like the ancient Britons, had a passion for freedom:

> *Ask ye what Law their conq'ring Cause confess'd?*
> *Great Nature's Law, the Law within the Breast,*
> *Form'd by no Art, and to no Sect confin'd,*
> *But stamp'd by Heav'n upon th' unletter'd Mind.*

In a scathing attack on Walpole and his administration,
Johnson condemned the Lord Chamberlain for prohibit-
ing *Gustavus Vasa* and offered the prologue as sufficient
proof that Brooke's principles could be nothing but ab-
horrent to the ministry.[4] In emphasizing man's innate
goodness, Brooke was a forerunner of the prologuisers of
the early years of the French Revolution. Arthur Murphy
supplied Brooke with a prologue to *The Earl of Essex*
(1761), a rather solemn and lugubrious piece, well-fitted to
the speaker, Thomas Sheridan.[5] Murphy exhorts the audience to receive the play kindly because it concerns English history, their *"own domestic woe."* If France—even
France—can shed tears over the fall of heroes,

> *Much more should you—from freedom's glorious plan,*
> *Who still inherit all the rights of man.*

4. "A Complete Vindication of the Licensers of the Stage, from the
Malicious and Scandalous Aspersions of Mr. Brooke, Author of Gustavus
Vasa . . . By an Impartial Hand," *The Works of Samuel Johnson* (Ox-
ford, 1825), v, 329–344.

5. The epilogue by Garrick, discussed above in this chapter, is also
admonitory and heavy. The tragedy was printed for Thomas Davies, who
played the part of Cecil.

Prologuisers hailed the fall of the Bastille with rapture mingled with condescension. William Meyler exclaimed in his epilogue to *Earl Goodwin* (1789) by Anne Yearsley, the celebrated milkwoman of Bristol,

> Lo! the poor Frenchman, long our nation's jest,
> Feels a new passion throbbing in his breast;
> From slavish, tyrant, priestly fetters free,
> For *Vive le Roi,* cries *Vive la Liberte!*
> And daring now to act as well as feel,
> Crushes the Convent, and the dread Bastille.[6]

The lines were omitted in the "recital" by the command of the Lord Chamberlain and indeed Meyler's whole effusion in its Protestant zeal is remarkably like the broadsides of the days of Titus Oates. More dignified but not less patronizing is Conway's prologue to his comedy, *False Appearances* (1789), which he adapted from *Les Dehors Trompeurs* of de Boissy, as he avows in the Preface to the play. Using a common ruse, which will be discussed below in this chapter, Conway defends his borrowing by adverse criticism of the original play and then turns to the freedom promised by the Revolution:

> And shou'd the Genius of this happy isle
> On Gallia's sons at length propitious smile;
> While in each breast the patriot spirit glows,
> We'd hail as brothers, whom we've met as foes:
> To the same point their generous ardor tends;
> The friends to Freedom, must be Britain's friends.

Thomas Bellamy's occasional prologue spoken by Palmer in November, 1789, is a more rapturous outburst:

> And, oh, forever be the hand ador'd
> Who first the Bastile's horrid cells explor'd,

6. The *European Magazine,* November 1789, pp. 380–381.

Free'd each pale inmate from a wretched doom,
And fix'd their fame for ages yet to come! [7]

"France is blest with England's Liberty." The writer attributes the French Revolution solely to the example set by England's love of freedom.

As it became clear that the Revolution was turning into anarchy, the effusions eulogizing liberty came to an end, and, following the course of history, the prologuisers qualified "liberty" by "law." The change in attitude is humorously expressed in Captain Edward Topham's epilogue to Reynolds's *The Rage* (1794). The piece is a series of imaginary conversations about the war, ending with a speech by "English Tom Blunt, a dealer in small wares," who does not admire the methods of the French:

"I does not relish freedom—when one's dead;
"So once for all my means and resolution
"Go, to stand by the good old Constitution."

Panegyrics of the Hanoverian kings had always been tempered by emphasis on the social contract; for example, an occasional prologue published in the *Gentleman's Magazine,* October, 1732, with the censorious title: *On his* MAJESTY's *Birth-day, a Prologue, spoken at* Goodman's-Fields *Theatre; which we insert instead of, as preferable to, the* Laureat's ODE *on the same Occasion.* The author, describing George II as,

Lord of a Train of Virtues all his own,

deplores the lot of the French struggling under a despotic monarch,

While Our's bestows ev'n more than we would crave,
To make us Free—Himself the greatest Slave.

7. *Ibid.,* p. 382.

Prologues introducing plays ultimately derived from the classics or from classical history frequently begin by comparing the equal readiness of modern British and Greek and Roman heroes to die for liberty, but they make it clear that the ideal has always been liberty under law. The anonymous prologue to Home's *Agis* (1758), spoken by Garrick, announced that the sole purpose of the tragedy was to inspire heroism and a love of freedom, and it assumed that the audience would be moved to tears, *"If Kings asserting liberty can charm."* William Duncombe recommended his tragedy, *Junius Brutus* (1734), as an adaptation of Voltaire's *Junius,* arguing that a theme *"Which warm'd with* British *Fire a* Gallic *Breast"* could not fail to win an audience *"so happy to be rul'd by Laws."* It was therefore no innovation for the Honorable John St. John to end the prologue to his opera, *The Island of St. Marguerite* (1789), emphatically, "LIBERTY IS LAW!," or for John Taylor in the prologue to *The World in a Village* (1793) to contrast with the terror and carnage of the French Revolution British liberty dwelling "in fair monarchic form," supported by three pillars—Justice, Mercy, and the Social Contract.

After war was declared, the prologues were still more insistent upon loyalty and the happiness and security arising from obedience to the laws. The laments for the course of the Revolution are often unaccompanied by any expression of triumph other than gratitude that England, holding firmly to monarchy and law, is safe from the bloodshed and anarchy which have overwhelmed France.

Prologues such as that for the opening of the new Drury Lane Theatre in 1794 reflect as clearly as any literature written during the French Revolution the revulsion of public feeling and the stability of a people exalting law as the basis of liberty.[8] A couplet from Taylor's prologue to

8. The *European Magazine,* May 1794, pp. 384-385.

Disinterested Love (1798) sums up the change in emphasis in the prologues after the disillusionment:

> May Britons still those glorious laws revere,
> Aloof from innovation's mad career! [9]

Topham in the epilogue to *The Rage,* quoted above, summarized with less dignity the results of the Revolution:

> Poor *Jean François* who shouts for Liberté
> Finds Slavery still the Order of the Day!

Many of these prologues regard France as a victim, a fallen nation that must be lifted to self-respect through English intervention.[1]

But whether France met with contempt or commiseration in the prologues, from beginning to end of the century the audience disliked adaptations from the French. In spite of this animosity there were adapters who made honest acknowledgment of indebtedness to French authors. James Miller in the prologues to three of his plays—*The Mother-in-Law* (1734), *The Man of Taste* (1735), and *The Picture: or, The Cuckold in Conceit* (1745)—emphasizes that he is presenting adaptations of Molière, whom he praises unstintedly. In the prologue to *The Miser* (1733) Fielding also paid tribute to Molière. Sometimes, as in Steele's prologue to *The Distrest Mother* (1712) or in John Kelly's prologue to *Timon in Love* (1733), the writer stresses the popularity of the original play. Holcroft's prologue to *The Follies of a Day; or, The Marriage of Figaro* (1784) reminds the audience of the extraordinary acclaim with which the comedy was received in Paris and adds as a

9. Taylor, *Poems on Various Subjects,* 1, 61.
1. See, for example, Edward Jerningham's epilogue to *The Siege of Berwick* (1793); Watson's epilogue to *England Preserv'd* (1795), printed in the *European Magazine,* April 1795, p. 268; Boscawen's occasional prologue to the same play, the *European Magazine,* February 1798, p. 110; and Cumberland's epilogue to *First Love* (1795).

final recommendation a picture of the French stage, with
its appreciative grenadier:

> Where the grim Guard, in nightly rapture, stands,
> And grounds his musquet to get at his hands.

But whole-hearted acknowledgment and unrestricted
acclaim are exceptions, and the provoking or fostering of
Anti-Gallic prejudice the rule. The least subtle means of
rousing the audience was the appeal to history, such as
appears in the prologue to Mrs. Pix's *The Double Distress*
(1701):

> *Our Ancestors without Ragou's or Dance,*
> *Fed on plain Beef, and bravely conquer'd* France:
> *And* Ben *and* Shakespear *lasting Laurels made*
> *With Wit alone, and scorn'd their wretched Aid.*

Pope concluded the prologue to *Cato* (1713) with a patriotic appeal for native drama.

> Britains *attend: Be Worth like this approv'd,*
> *And show you have the Virtue to be mov'd.*
> *With honest Scorn the first fam'd* Cato *view'd*
> Rome *learning Arts from* Greece, *whom she subdu'd;*
> *Our Scene precariously subsists too long*
> *On* French *Translation, and* Italian *Song.*
> *Dare to have Sense your selves; Assert the Stage,*
> *Be justly warm'd with your own Native Rage.*
> *Such Plays alone should please a* British *Ear,*
> *As* Cato's *self had not disdain'd to hear.*

The admonition, like all others of its kind, is entirely uncritical; no one asked if there might not be an adaptation
superior to a native play. Gay referred to the prevalence
of translations and adaptations in his prologue to *Three
Hours after Marriage* (1717), denouncing adapters as

"graceless Owlers," who smuggled their rules from France
and their plots from Spain.

But Wit, like Wine, from happier Climates brought,
Dash'd by these Rogues, turns English *common Draught:*
They pall Moliere's *and* Lopez' *sprightly strain,*
And teach dull Harlequins *to grin in vain.*

When these bunglers are damned, they have the arrogance
to shift the responsibility to the original authors. Having
made this trenchant attack, Gay followed the usual pattern of recommending the play on the score of its being
native.

The number of such prologues and their constant appearance in every decade of the century is a continual admission of the dependence of English dramatists on the
French. In 1774 Hugh Kelly in the epilogue to *The Romance of an Hour* used a different metaphor but made the
same strictures Gay had made in 1717:

How many authors of our modern stage,
Affect to rise the wonders of the age,
By bare translations from Molière, Corneille,
Racine, and numbers needless here to tell—
Yet each a jackdaw, drest in foreign plumes,
On his own beauty saucily presumes;
Looks on the parent bird with haughty eyes,
From whom entirely he purloin'd his dyes;
Or solely tells us when he comes to print,
Tho' *all* is *stolen*—He *borrow'd* but a *hint*—

the last line being an odd comment on Kelly's Advertise-
ment to the play, which minimizes his debt to Marmontel.
As for the upstart crows beautified in French feathers,
Kelly exclaims:

Ah that these daws were fortunately tost on
Thy coasts Connecticut, or thine O Boston!

Garrick urged the audience to support Murphy's *The Apprentice* (1756) because it was original:

No smuggled, pilfer'd Scenes from France we shew,
'Tis English—English, Sirs!—from Top to Toe.

Colman's entertaining prologue to *The Spanish Barber* (1777) also repeats Pope's criticism, making a humorous exposition of the art of performing French plays on the English stage. If the piece succeeds, the English author takes all the glory of having transformed (as well as translated) the play; if it fails, the fault lies with the French. The prologue was spoken by Parsons in the character of the enterprising tailor, Paul Prig, of Foote's comedy, *The Cozeners*. The tailor has just returned from Paris, where he has studied French fashions, one of which he intends to display:

A little weaver, whom I long have known,
Has work'd it up, and begs to have it shewn—
But pray observe, my friends—'tis not his own.
I brought it over—nay, if it miscarries,
He'll cry—" 'tis none of mine—it came from Paris."
But should you like it, he'll soon let you know
'Twas spun and manufactur'd in Soho.[2]

Colman shifted the basic metaphor to make it serve for the prologue to Johnstone's *The Disbanded Officer* (1786). "In Days of old" there was a heavy tax laid on imported luxuries, but in these more enlightened times, importation is encouraged by the government.

2. The *London Magazine*, September 1777, p. 480. Compare Garrick's prologue to Foote's comedy, *Taste*, with its "antiques" from Herculaneum, manufactured in the Strand. For Parsons in the prologue, see above, p. 37.

Teas, now a drug so cheap, with draughts bewitching,
Imperial, Congou, Hyson, charm the kitchen.

Fortunately the government controls importation, and
thus no one dares to palm off foreign goods as native:

Ah! were our plays thus wisely supervis'd!
Humours and passions gag'd, and plots exis'd,
What frauds would be unveil'd! Sophistication,
Much contraband, and much adulteration!
Neat as imported is the constant boast,
Though smuggling smacks and cutters crowd the coast.
At many a pilfer'd scene you've cry'd and laugh'd,
And oft, for home-brew'd, balderdash have quaff'd.
Plays from French vineyards drawn, have learnt to please,
Run, like Southampton port, on claret lees;
While the bard cries, to smuggling no great foe,
    " 'Tis English, English, Sirs, from top to toe." [3]

The dramatist of the evening makes no such boast; the
comedy is translated from Lessing,

His plays as much applauded in Vienna,
As here the *School for Scandal*, or *Duenna*.

Dramatists, disavowing foreign influence and insisting
upon their originality, constantly make such disclaimers
as Mrs. Centlivre's in the epilogue to *A Bold Stroke for a
Wife* (1718):

3. Colman's declaration served other prologuisers until the end of the
century; thus John Taylor in the prologue to Reynolds's *Management*
(1799) is confident that in spite of the current popularity of Kotzebue, his
comedy will be greeted with "patriotic pride," because

    'Tis English! English, Sirs! from top to toe!

An illuminating commentary on public taste and prejudice is contained in
the epilogue to *The Disbanded Officer* (an adaptation of *Minna von Barn-
helm*). After unrestricted approbation of the preposterous characters and
plot, Johnstone condemns French comedy as immoral and represents the
French as the source of all folly, dissoluteness, and the present degeneracy
of the stage!

Our Plot is new, and regularly clear,
And not one single Tittle from Moliere,

or as James Worsdale's in the prologue to *A Cure for a
Scold* (1735), an adaptation of *The Taming of the Shrew,*
deploring the tendency of British playwrights

To alter, mend, transpose, translate and fit
Moliere's *gay Scenes to please an* English *Pit.*

Cumberland introduced his comedy, *The Brothers* (1769),
with a condemnation of his fellow playwrights who find
their plots in current novels and in English classics, especially Shakespeare, and of those others who

to foreign Climes and Kingdoms roam,
To fetch for what is better found at Home:
The recreant Bard, oh! scandal to the Age!
Gleans the vile refuse of the Gallic Stage.

To lend force to the disclaimers of foreign sources the
prologuisers added that native history and native heroes
offered the only proper plot and characters for the British
stage. Aaron Hill's prologue to *Elfrid* (1710) flattered the
audience by reminding them that the heroes of the tragedy
were their own ancestors and the plot part of their own
history. The opening couplet of Rowe's prologue to *Jane
Shore* (1714) likewise emphasizes the superiority of native
history as the source of drama:

Tonight, if you have brought your good old Taste,
We'll treat you with a downright English *Feast.*

William Havard in the prologue to *King Charles the First*
(1737) declared himself

So much a Briton—*that he scorns to roam*
To Foreign Climes, to fetch his Hero home—
Conscious, that in these Scenes is clearly shown
Britain *can boast true Heroes of her own.*

Garrick's epilogue to Ralph's *The Astrologer* (1744) runs
the gamut of devices to win the applause of the upper gallery—patriotic appeal; denunciation and ridicule of the
French in rabble-rousing terms; alarm at the prevalence of
French fashions and manners; scorn of dramatists who
"pilfer" from Molière; the superiority of native sources for
British drama.

How a determined writer could transmogrify a foreign
source is shown in Thomson's prologue to *Sophonisba*
(1730). It is perfect of its kind because it is entirely conventional: it follows the usual pattern of tracing the history of the play from ancient times, omitting the "dark"
ages; it declares the heroic theme as most suited to the
British stage, and names the love of freedom as the chief
British virtue.

> WHEN *learning, after the long* Gothic *night,*
> *Fair, o'er the western world, renew'd his light,*[4]
> *With arts arising* Sophonisba *rose:*
> *The tragic muse, returning, wept her woes.*
> *With her th'* Italian *scene first learnt to glow;*
> *And the first tears for her were taught to flow.*
> *Her charms the* Gallic *muses next inspir'd:*
> Corneille *himself saw, wonder'd, and was fir'd.*
>
> *What foreign theatres with pride have shewn,*
> Britain, *by juster title, makes her own.*
> *When freedom is the cause, 'tis hers to fight;*
> *And hers, when freedom is the theme, to write.*
> *For this, a* British Author *bids again*
> *The heroine rise, to grace the* British *scene.*
> .   .   .   .
> *To night, our home-spun author would be true,*
> *At once, to nature, history, and you.*
> *Well-pleas'd to give our neighbours due applause,*

---

4. Johnson had these lines in mind when he wrote the first couplet of
his prologue for the opening of Drury Lane in 1747.

He owns their learning, but disdains their laws.
Not to his patient touch, or happy flame,
'Tis to his British *heart he trusts for fame.*
If France *excel him in one free-born thought,*
The man, as well as poet, is in fault.

Two months after the performance of *Sophonisba*, Fielding wrote his parody prologue to *Tom Thumb*, satirizing in general prologues demanding native heroes and in particular the prologue to *Sophonisba:*

> Britons, *awake!—Let* Greece *and* Rome *no more*
> *Their Heroes send to our Heroick Shore.*
> *Let home-bred Subjects grace the modern Muse,*
> *And* Grub-Street *from her Self, her Heroes chuse:*
> *Her* Story-Books *Immortalize in Fame,*
> Hickathrift, Jack the Giant-Killer, *and* Tom Tram.
> *No* Venus *shou'd in Sign-Post Painter shine;*
> *No* Roman *Hero in a Scribler's Line:*
> *The monst'rous Dragon to the Sign belongs,*
> *And* Grub-Street's *Heroes best adorn her Songs.*
> *To-Night our Bard,* Spectators, *would be* true
> *To* Farce, *to* Tragedy, Tom Thumb, *and* You.

Fielding again parodied the conventional summary of literary history in the opening lines of the prologue to *The Covent-Garden Tragedy* (1732); as to the characters of the play, they are native—all culled from Covent Garden.

The insistence on native and original plots drove playwrights to practice various ruses to reconcile the audience to adaptations. For example, the prologue could omit or disguise the immediate French source. Thus Whitehead in the prologue to Murphy's *The Orphan of China* (1759) does not mention Voltaire's *L'Orphelin de la Chine*, but the Chinese. Kemble in the prologue to Murphy's *The Rival Sisters* (1793), an adaptation of Thomas Corneille's

Ariane, commends the play as drawn *"from ancient stores"* and concludes with a comparison of George III to Minos. In the Preface to the printed play Murphy specifically names his French source.

The most common stratagem of the prologuisers was to acknowledge the French original with contempt and to avert the hostility of the audience by patriotic sentiment. Charles Johnson in the prologue to *The Sultaness* (1717) admits that his play is adapted from Racine but instructs the audience that England having conquered France in battle should appropriate her arts just as the conquering Romans plundered Greece. James Miller, denouncing the machinations of foreigners and Jacobites, ends the prologue to *Mahomet the Impostor* (1744) by admitting that he took the play from Voltaire, who, in turn, was indebted to Shakespeare. He therefore urges the audience,

> *E'en send our* English *Stage a Privateering:*
> *With your* Commission, *we'll our Sails unfold,*
> *And from their Loads of* Dross, *import some Gold.*

Aaron Hill had practiced similar legerdemain in the prologue to *Alzira* (1736). He extols Voltaire's *Alzire,* which had proved its merit before French audiences, a whole people weeping Alzira's woe:

> *Thrice thirty Days,* All Paris *sigh'd, for—*SENSE!
> *Tumblers—stood* still—*and thought!—in* WIT's *Defence!*

Surely an English audience, always pleased with foreign dancing and opera, will not leave the appreciation of *"solid* Sense, *to* France!"

> No—*That's impossible,—'tis* Britain's *Claim,*
> *To hold no* Second *Place, in* Taste, *or* Fame.
> *In Arts, and Arms,* alike victorious *known,*
> *Whate'er deserves Her* Choice, *she makes her own.*

Hill had driven the audience into a not uncommon trap. Thomas Vaughan's prologue to Mrs. Inchbald's *Next Door Neighbours* (1791), adapted, as the title page reads, "From the French Dramas *L'Indigent & Le Dissipateur*," makes an outrageous defense of borrowing:

> And as for those with whom she makes so free
> They'll ne'er complain of English Liberty;
> But glory to behold their Tinsel shine,
> Through the rich Bullion of the English Line.

Accused of smuggling in his play, *The English Merchant* (1767), an adaptation of Voltaire's *L'Écossaise*,[5] Colman admitted the charge and answered in the prologue that English poets, like English merchants, may bring home rich cargoes from all the corners of the earth:

> *With the rich Stores of ancient* Rome *and* Greece,
> Imported Duty-free, *may fill their Piece:*
> *Or, like* Columbus, *cross th' Atlantick Ocean,*
> *And set* Peru *and* Mexico *in Motion.*

He appeals to the weavers in the audience to justify him in declaring that although the thread and pattern are imported, " '*Tis* English *Silk when wrought in* English *Loom.*"

In 1755, when the nation was seething with hatred of France, Garrick produced a revival of Aaron Hill's *Zara*, an adaptation of Voltaire's *Zaïre*. In order to make the "importation" acceptable to the audience, he produced with it Mallet's masque, *Britannia*, he himself speaking the prologue "in the character of a Sailor, fuddled and talking to himself." [6]

5. Colman dedicated *The English Merchant* to Voltaire.
6. See above, pp. 101–102. The prologue is printed in *The Works of David Mallet* (1759), I, [185]–187.

> *For shall we sons of beef and freedom stoop,*
> *Or lower our flag to slavery and soop?*
> *What! shall these Parly-vous make such a racket,*
> *And we not lend a hand, to lace their jacket?*

Addressing all his acting to the upper gallery, he "reads the playbill of Zara," and painfully spells out the title:

> *I'm glad 'tis Sarah—Then our Sall may see*
> *Her namesake's Tragedy: and as for me,*
> *I'll sleep as sound, as if I were at sea.*

He then triumphantly discovers the masque:

BRI-TA-NIA—*oh* Britania! *good again—*
Huzza, boys! by the Royal George *I swear,*
Tom *coxen, and the crew, shall strait be there.*
All free-born souls must take Bri-ta-nia's part,
And give her three round cheers, with hand and heart!

Thus Garrick cajoled the upper gallery into accepting an adaptation from the French.

The prologue to James Solas Dodd's *Gallic Gratitude; or, The Frenchman in India* (1779), spoken by Mrs. Jackson in the character of Britannia, denounces France as a base violator of treaties and a nation of slaves. The purpose of the tragedy is to prove that

> *. . . deep sorrow will on those intrude,*
> *Who e'er depend on* GALLIC GRATITUDE.

Dodd made no mention in the prologue that he filched the play from the French, but to the Dedication he appended an acknowledgment: "The story of this Comedy is taken from a little French Farce of one act: how far I have extended or improved it, will be seen on comparing this piece with *La Naufrage,* written by M. Lafont, and published in the year 1710."

In prefaces and on title pages dramatists did not hesitate to give the French sources of their plays—an illuminating commentary on the distinction made between audience and reader. They assumed that most of the audience would agree with "old Meynell's observation, *For anything I see, foreigners are fools.*" [7] This conviction, strengthened by the prevalence of war, accounts for the success of the patriotic prologues and epilogues. Their writers had an unrivalled opportunity of controlling the audience and of evoking applause.

7. Boswell, *Life of Johnson*, IV, 15. For political and patriotic plays and prologues, see Nicoll, *A History of Early Eighteenth Century Drama*, pp. 19–23, and for complaints against adaptations, pp. 143–144. See, too, Nicoll, *A History of Late Eighteenth Century Drama*, pp. 17–19, 59–60, and James J. Lynch, *Box, Pit and Gallery*, Chapter XIII.

CHAPTER 7

CRITICAL THEORY AND THE
STANDARD DRAMATISTS

The writers of prologues and epilogues were concerned primarily with the relationship between the speaker and the audience, but not infrequently they made passing comment on dramatic theory, usually to stress the fact that the play of the evening followed a conventional pattern. The only critical theory given continued support by the prologuisers is the concept of Jonsonian comedy. Insistence that comedy is fundamentally satirical conflicted with the principles of the reformers; it ran counter to the admiration of Shakespeare and to the temporary triumph of Goldsmith's "laughing" comedy; even among the prologuisers it had a determined competitor in the drama of sensibility, but, as the illustrations given below will prove, it survived. Even to the end of the century prologues introducing satirical comedy have vigor and force. The prologues also contain considerable discussion and weighing of the unities and a worried recognition that the audience was wiser than the critics—a perception confirmed by the homage paid to Shakespeare. Lastly they refer to the works of the elder dramatists who formed a criterion for the present.

The relative state of tragedy and comedy is clearly set forth in Thomas Baker's prologue to his successful comedy, *Tunbridge-Walks,* performed at Drury Lane in 1703. Pinkethman is speaking, but that the speaker is a comedian does not prejudice the author's observations:

> *The Comick Writer still Supports our Stage,*
> *We live by the Good-Nature of the Age.*
> *Let others be with Tragick Lawrel's crown'd,*
> *Where undisturb'd the Heroe struts around,*
> *And empty Boxes echo to the Sound.*

If farce, opera, and various kinds of miscellaneous entertainment are omitted, this was true, and, in spite of such exceptions as Rowe's popular "she-tragedies," or *The Distrest Mother, Cato,* or *The London Merchant,* it remained true.

In 1703, Richard Estcourt, the comedian, offered some exceptionally pertinent criticism of current plays, then under attack by the reformers. His prologue to *The Fair Example* points out that there could be but one refutation to their charges—the production of great drama:

> *Wou'd but some happier Hand at length appear*
> *The sinking Beauties of the Stage to rear,*
> *With genuine Wit and well digested Rage*
> *To lash the headstrong Follies of the Age,*
> *Vile fulsom Farce no longer wou'd go down,*
> *Nor shou'd we dread the stern Reformers Frown:*
> *The Stage its Primitive Use shou'd know, design'd*
> *At once to please, and to instruct Mankind.*

The dictum pronounced by Horace was the first tenet of the dramatists as they express themselves in the prologues, with the emphasis usually on instruction rather than on delight. The writers of comedy therefore should strive to identify their art with satire:

THIS *Night our Author means to bring to view*
A Group of Figures to the Stage are new,
Yet to keen Satire's Lash who've long been due.

So the prologue to *The Projectors* in 1737, and this continued to be the prologuisers' definition of comedy. An
occasional prologue to a performance of Mrs. Centlivre's
The Wonder: A Woman Keeps a Secret in 1764 emphasizes the corrective purpose of the theatre:

The *comic Muse* from Follies wou'd reclaim:
And, lashing Vice, throw round her lasting Shame.
    Strong is the Influence of the modern *Stage*,
To check our Foibles, and amend the Age.[1]

Fielding began the prologue to *The Coffee-House Politician; or, The Justice Caught in his own Trap* (1730)
with a tribute to the fearlessness of classical comedy and
maintained that it is the duty of comedy to attack stupidity, greed, and corruption, especially in high place.

Long hath this gen'rous Method been disus'd,
For Vice *hath grown too great to be abus'd;*
By Pow'r, defended from the Piercing Dart,
It reigns, and triumphs in the Lordly *Heart;*
While Beaux, *and* Cits, *and* Squires, *our Scenes afford,*
Justice *preserves the* Rogues *who weild her Sword;*
All Satyr *against her Tribunal's quash'd,*
Nor lash the Bards, *for fear of being lash'd.*

Fielding's prologues make it evident that he thought of
his plays as effective weapons against social ills, and like
his plays they present an ugly picture of society. He excited loathing rather than indignation, but his purpose
was as he states it in the prologue to *The Modern Husband* (1732) to prove vice detestable, to reflect the life of

1. *Lloyd's Evening Post,* December 10–12, 1764.

the town *"vicious, as it is,"* and to restore the stage to its proper function, *". . . to divert, instruct, and mend Mankind."*

The most trivial farces and ballad operas were fortified by solemn pronouncements on the corrective power of comedy; for example, John Kelly introduced his ballad farce, *The Plot* (1735), by reminding the audience that

> *Notorious Falshood, Avarice, and Rage,*
> *May well expect the Satyr of the Stage.*
> *Satyr looks round, with keen impartial Eyes,*
> *On Vice, and Folly seizes as its Prize;*
>
> . . . .
>
> *The Stage applauds the Wise, the learn'd, the Good,*
> *But Knaves and Fools are properly our Food.*[2]

The occasional prologue for the opening of Covent Garden in September 1777 shows how habitually managers and audience thought of comedy as satire:

> Of all the lesser morals her's the school,
> Folly her game; her weapon Ridicule.
> Are any here who into error fall?
> Beware! her humour sly unmasks ye all.[3]

Charles Johnson's epilogue to *The Gentleman-Cully* (1701) describes the persistent method of comedy:

> *Our Author has a Sett of Coxcombs chose,*
> *Their various Faults and Follies to expose.*

The epilogue to Southerne's *The Fate of Capua* (1700) characterizes poets as *"fool-mongers,"* dealing in knaves, dunces, and sots. They pretend that they are *"charitable Quacks,"* who hope to mend their patients; whereas in

2. Genest, III, 446, observes of *The Plot*, "—the Prologue is much better than the piece itself."
3. *Lloyd's Evening Post*, September 26–29, 1777.

fact they are "Bedlam *Doctors,*" more willing to exhibit their victims than to cure them.

Samuel Foote set forth a special reading of Shakespeare in his prologue for the opening of Yates's theatre in Birmingham in 1774. He extends his own conception of comedy to Shakespeare and represents him as writing to "correct the heart," his purpose being:

> Of folly's sons t' explore the ample train,
> The sot, the fop, the vicious, and the vain;
> Hypocrisy to drag from her disguise,
> And affectation hunt thro' all her lies:
> Such was your bard.[4]

Foote always represents himself in his prologues as a corrector of vice, or, as Garrick describes him in the prologue to *The Cozeners* (1774), a watchman guarding the morals of the town:

> Dramatick writers were, like watchmen, meant
> To knock down Vice. . . .
> .   .   .   .
> 'Twas you cried *watch!* I limp'd at your command.

Foote held that in ridiculing not types but persons, and especially well-known persons, he was practising comedy in its primitive and unspoiled state. When "Thespis first sung ballads in a cart," the gaping crowd rejoiced in recognizing the mimic features, but in a more complicated society the art is not unattended with danger. Foote's loyalty to the principle resulted in all his characters being taken for insulting caricatures, although he sometimes wrote more generalized satire; for example, the epilogue to *The Lyar* (1762), one of his most clever pieces, is a discourse on the social necessity of lying:

4. The *London Chronicle,* July 5–7, 1774.

Consider, Sir, if once you cry it down,
You'll shut up ev'ry coffee-house in town:
The tribe of politicians will want food;
Ev'n now half famish'd—for the public good.

The abolition of lying would ruin newspaper editors and
all the legal profession. He finally puts to the pit the ad-
visability of so extraordinary a measure:

Is it your pleasures that we make a rule, ⎤
That ev'ry lyar be proclaim'd a fool,   ⎬
Fit subjects for our author's ridicule?   ⎦

In the prologue to *The Knights* (1754) Foote pretends to
look with envy at writers of tragedy, who deal with such
unfamiliar figures as heroes, kings, and queens; whereas
he must dare the anger of the audience by presenting
them characters they know only too well. At least, as he
observes in the prologue to *The Author* (1757), the writer
of comedy has unlimited choice:

Fresh Characters spring up as heretofore—
Nature with Novelty does still abound;
On every Side fresh Follies may be found.

Or, as the prologue to *Dr. Last in His Chariot* (1769),
written by Garrick and spoken by Foote, succinctly put it:
". . . the quacks are mankind."

There were certain protests against the corrective theory
of drama. Mrs. Centlivre, for example, maintained, as
Goldsmith did later, that the purpose of comedy was not
to instruct but to amuse, as she explained in the epilogue
to *Love's Contrivance* (1703), and therefore she preferred
the comedy of incident and intrigue. She is more explicit
in the prologue to *The Man's Bewitch'd* (1709), in which,
denying the charge that she is the author of a paper called

The Female Tatler, she entrusts to "Bickerstaff" the task of lashing vice and folly and reserves for herself that of mere entertainment:

> *In short, what e'er your Darling Vices are,*
> *They pass untouch'd in this Night's Bill of Fare.*

In the prologue to *The Artifice* (1722) plot, humor, and business are named as the three ingredients of comedy, but even Mrs. Centlivre, as a later quotation will show, could define comedy in terms of the stock characters of satire.

Cibber, while not departing from the corrective function of comedy, objected to its concentrating on the dregs of society.

> *OF all the Various Vices of the Age*
> *And Shoals of Fools Expos'd upon the Stage,*
> *How Few are lasht, that call for Satyrs Rage.*
> *What can you think to see our Plays so full*
> *Of Madmen, Coxcombs and the Driveling Fool;*
> *Of Citts, of Sharpers, Rakes, and Roaring Bullies,*
> *Of Cheats, of Cuckolds, Aldermen, and Cullies?*

These are beyond the reach of satire and need the hangman's whip, Newgate, or Bedlam. The lines, from the prologue to *The Careless Husband* (1704), introduce a plea for the comedy of manners, in which the characters are persons of breeding, susceptible to amendment by satire.

Cibber's theory of comedy met a sharp refutation in the prologue to Fielding's *The Miser* (1733), which asserts that characters are no longer drawn from nature and are lacking in vitality.

> *TOO long the slighted Comic Muse has mourn'd,*
> *Her Face quite alter'd, and her Art o'erturn'd;*

That Force of Nature now no more she sees,
With which so well her Johnson *knew to please.*
No Characters from Nature now we trace,
All serve to empty Books of Common-Place.

Modern dramatists, who "*regard not what Fools do, but
what Wits say,*" produce comedy without moral, plot, or
real wit, and think it sufficient if their speeches, no matter
how dull, are supposed to imitate the conversation of lords
and ladies. To this the prologue opposes the characters of
Molière,

Moliere, *who Nature's inmost Secrets knew,*
Whose justest Pen, like Kneller's *Pencil drew.*

It was the Jonsonian character, supported by classical
precept and practice, that won the favor of the prologuisers.
To the majority of the audience the limits laid down by
the epilogue to *The Successful Pyrate* (1712) were the accepted bounds of comedy:

So in the fourth of Horace, *Let your Bully,*
Says that Wit-Lawyer, *rage and beat his Cully;*
Old Soldiers brag, Slaves lie, and Clowns be dull,
And each Man in his Character a Fool.

Gay in the prologue to *Three Hours after Marriage*
(1717) uses a comparison which exactly illustrates the nature of satirical comedy:

Poets make Characters as Salesmen *Cloaths,*
We take no Measure of your Fops and Beaus;
But here all Sizes and all Shapes ye meet,
And fit your selves—like Chaps in Monmouth-street.

The anonymous prologue to Garrick's *Miss in Her Teens*
(1747) is significant in describing the kind of comedy
Garrick thought most likely to succeed in the middle years

of the century. He has culled from "real Life" two cowards, *"The vap'ring Bully, and the frib'ling Beau."* They were types, and yet they had their counterparts in the audience.

Hamlet's definition of the purpose of playing remained a commonplace of prologues throughout the century. The writers continued to regard comedy as a mirror in which man by studying his unflattering reflection might correct his defects. Charles Johnson's prologue to *The Generous Husband* (1711) describes what the stage was once and still should be:

> *Th' affected Fool and Knave wou'd blush to see,*
> *In this true Glass their own Epitome.*

In 1796 W. T. Fitzgerald began the prologue to Morton's comedy, *The Way to Get Married,* with the dictum:

> THE stage should be, to life, a faithful glass,
> Reflecting modes, and manners as they pass,

and then presents a thoroughly amusing and new "reflection" of the current beau.

Allied to the metaphor of the mirror, and as obvious, was that which considered the stage a canvas whereon the dramatist drew lifelike pictures of the endless comic types. The best dramatist, like the best painter, most closely followed "nature," *i.e.*, the archetypes of absurdities and folly. Comedy was, as William Taverner said in the prologue to *The Maid the Mistress* (1708), a *"moral School":*

> *Instructive Satyr shall the Town Survey,*
> *And draw its Monsters in each artful Play:*
> *The Fop, the Rake, the Country Squire and Cit,*
> *The real Blockhead and conceited Wit,*
> *The Jilting Mistress and the Faithless Wife*
> *Shall see themselves all painted to the Life.*

It is significant that although this and similar prologues of the time were perhaps intended to placate or hoodwink the reformers, yet they made only the ancient claims.

The theory of the archetypes was made the basis for the revival of comedies. *The Astrologer* (1744) by James Ralph was explained and defended by a prologue spoken by Garrick, lamenting the fact that dramatists had departed from the pattern set them by Shakespeare and Jonson, to whom the stage was a faithful mirror, shocking the vicious into reformation. Warned by the failure of his contemporaries whose plays with difficulty last three nights—*"a modern Play's Eternity,"*—Ralph presents no plot of his own but one which has survived a century, *The Astrologer* being a revision of Tomkis's *Albumazar*.

> *Tho' old the Draught, each Portrait yet may claim*
> *A living Likeness—Fools are still the same.*[5]

Colman, using the same comparison, arrived at a different conclusion in the prologue to his revision of *The Silent Woman* (1776). He comments on the difficulty of writing comedy which will endure and on the equal difficulty of reviving comedy which, no matter how popular in its own time, is now antiquated. The writer of tragedy deals with permanent emotions or with heroes who are part of our intellectual heritage; but comedy deals with the transient and topical:

> Whose pencil living follies brings to view,
> Survives those follies, and his portraits too.

The similarity between artist and playwright frequently recurs in Colman's prologues,[6] usually, as in the prologue

5. The audience was not interested, for a short prefatory note reads that on the second night of the play, the manager was "obliged to shut up his Doors, for want of an Audience."

6. The comparison was not new with either Colman or Garrick. Charles Johnson's epilogue to *The Gentleman Cully* (1701) begins:

to *Ut Pictura Poesis* (1789), in connection with a panegyric of Hogarth. Two years after Hogarth's death Garrick commemorated him in the prologue to *The Clandestine Marriage* (1766), inspired according to both Garrick and Colman by *Marriage-a-la-Mode,* although the likeness is not apparent, the play being entirely different in tone and plot from the remorseless set of pictures.

> POETS *and Painters, who from Nature draw*
> *Their best and richest Stores, have made this Law:*
> *That each should neighbourly assist his Brother,*
> *And steal with Decency from one another.*
> *To-night, your matchless Hogarth gives the Thought,*
> *Which from his Canvas to the Stage is brought.*
> *And who so fit to warm the Poet's Mind,*
> *As he who pictur'd Morals and Mankind?*

Colman wrote a lively prologue for Charlotte Lennox's *Old City Manners* (1775), an alteration of *Eastward Hoe,* beginning:

> IN *Charles the Second's gay and wanton days,*
> *When Lords had wit, and Gentlemen wrote plays,*

and ending with a rather long comparison between the moral purpose of drama and Hogarth's pictures, in this instance, *Industry and Idleness.* The Elizabethan dramatists drew *"city portraits,"* marking vice and virtue:

> Painters *with Poets bear an equal Strife,*
> *Which can best copy Nature to the Life.*

It had been an Elizabethan commonplace:

> . . . *None denie,*
> *Poets and Painters hold a sympathy.*

(Prologue to a revival of *Love's Cure, or the Martial Maid* in *The Works of Francis Beaumont and John Fletcher,* ed. A. R. Waller, ([Cambridge University Press, 1909], VII, 164.)

Artists, like these (old Ben the chief!) to-night,
Bring idleness, and industry to light;
Their sketch by time, perhaps, impair'd too much,
A female hand has ventur'd to retouch;
Hence too our Hogarth drew, nor scorn'd to glean,
The comic stubble of the moral scene.

.   .   .   .

Such be henceforth each comick artist's aim,
Poets or painters, be their drift the same.

In 1783 in the epilogue to an unpublished comedy, *A Friend in Need,* Colman again extols Hogarth for his "pencil'd satire" and "comedy on canvas," describing in detail the first of the series, *The Harlot's Progress.*[7]

Moralizing, the inevitable result of comparing the stage to mirror and canvas, was fostered by the activity of the reformers and by the growth of sensibility, but there still persisted prologues that represented the dramatist ranging the city for comic types to hold up to the unmitigated scorn and mirth of the audience. Farquhar's prologue to Mrs. Centlivre's *The Platonick Lady* (1706) expresses the joy of the playwright who after long trudging about London captures a prize fop or possibly picks up a whole set of fools *"to furnish out a Play."* In the prologue to *The Beaux' Stratagem* (1707) Farquhar compares the city to a field, where *"Rain, or Shine, the thriving Coxcomb grows"*:

A Weed that has to twenty Summer's ran,
Shoots up in Stalk, and Vegetates to Man.
Simpling our Author goes from Field to Field,
And culls such Fools, as may Diversion yield.

There is little break between Farquhar's prologue and that to Edward Morris's farce, *The Adventurers* (1790), describing the dramatist still searching the city for embodiments of the spirit of satire:

7. *Lloyd's Evening Post,* July 16–18, 1783.

Wide o'er the field dramatic scribblers range,
From gay St. James's, to the sober Change.

A common convention of the prologues was the pretense that the playwrights of the Restoration had exhausted the comic types. These fortunate predecessors had
unlimited choice, for, as Addison says in the prologue to
The Tender Husband (1705), *"the whole Herd of Fops
was all their Own,"*

Cuckolds, and Citts, and Bawds, and Pimps, and Beaux.

Then in lines which foreshadow *The Spectator* he portrays the modern playwright forced to pick and cull a
chance fool:

Long e'er they find the necessary Spark;
They search the Town, and beat about the Park:
To all his most frequented Haunts resort,
Oft dog him to the Ring, and oft to Court;
As Love of Pleasure, or of Place invites:
And sometimes catch Him taking Snuff at White's.

Addison admits that present fools have originality, and he
promises that the author has collected an entertaining variety. Mrs. Centlivre, contrary to her usual adherence to
action, introduces *Mar-Plot; Or, The Second Part of the
Busie-Body* (1710) with an envious look at the playwrights
of the Restoration because

Scowrers, and Rakes, and Debauchees are o'er,
Beaus are extinct, and Bullies are no more.

Therefore as the town affords her little choice, she has
gathered a set of foreign fools. John Taylor writing the
prologue to Frederic Reynolds's *Cheap Living* (1797)
makes a similar complaint in very different words. There
are no more "bold originals"; the day of "strong featur'd
characters" is over, and the dramatist must now be

Content to pick up, as he saunters along,
Some anomalous beings, that start from the throng.

The prologue to Reynolds's *Laugh When You Can* (1798)
is a trifling inquiry into the decline of the comic spirit,
coming to the conclusion that mankind has grown so
commonplace, dull, and lacking in individuality that playwrights have no material with which to work:

Say from what modern spark would Congreve please
To copy sprightly sense or graceful ease?
Does Mirabel yet grace the polish'd throng?
Or to what club does Valentine belong?
Should Farquhar now his playful pen resume,
Where would he find an Archer or a Plume?
From a tame *brute* not Vanbrugh could extract
An ounce of humour to eke out an act!
In vain we emulate their daring rules,
Whose fools were wits, when all our wits are fools.

The writer further attributes the decline of comedy to
the vogue of German sentimental drama, and he insists
that true comedy is a mirror in which men can see their
faults and amend them.

To the unities the prologuisers could bring little of the
consistency and assurance which they gave to the classical
theory of comedy; rather they express a divergence of opinion and even those who declared themselves convinced
often hedged in respect to the decision of the audience.
Addison's epilogue to Granville's *The British Enchanters*
(1706) is an odd and amusing example of the author's conviction that the rules run counter to the interest of the
audience and that they restrict drama to the point of dullness, but that nevertheless they must be obeyed. Addison
explains that the author while not violating the unity of

place has escaped from its limitations by the rapid varying of settings through the means of numerous stage devices:

> *But as our Two Magicians try their Skill,*
> *The Vision varies, tho' the Place stand still,*
> *While the same Spot its gaudy Form renews,*
> *Shifting the Prospect to a Thousand Views.*
> *Thus (without Unity of Place transgrest)*
> *Th' Enchanter turns the Critick to a Jest.*

The prologues contain constant admission that the rules
alone are insufficient for the creation of great drama.
Hildebrand Jacob discusses the decline of drama in the
prologue and epilogue to his tragedy, *The Fatal Constancy*
(1723). These two pieces are unusually well-written and,
without any deviation from the point, insist that great
drama springs from genius and emotional depth, not from
fidelity to classical models. Jacob indirectly describes what
the audience expected from the theatre, to which he opposes what they ought to expect. Instead of ghosts, machines, and pageantry, he presents an unadorned, simple
plot, abiding by the unities of time, place, and action. To
the ancient dramatists the rules were but a medium for
expressing the most vital emotions. If he could share their
inspiration,[8]

> *Then might our Author too demand Applause*
> *And boldly trust in* Aristotle's *Laws.*

Not the rules but the dramatists were at fault. In 1787
Thomas Holcroft came to a similar conclusion in the

---

8. Jacob's prologue contains an excellent example of the prologuisers'
common practice of introducing into their lines garbled scraps of
Shakespeare:

> *But, O, for such a Muse, and such a Fire*
> *As did of old the* Grecian *Bards Inspire!*

prologue to his comedy, *Seduction*. He offers as a commendation to his play his observance of the unities:

> Tho' rules, alone, would yield a barren fame,
> Such praise as rules can merit he may claim.
> Each unity's preserv'd, nor knows the play
> A lapse of time beyond the close of day;
> No change of scene denotes a chang'd abode,
> Nor has he dar'd indulge one episode.

But he knows that strict adherence to the rules cannot supply the lack of inspiration.

The dramatists' dilemma is sometimes presented in an imaginary conversation in which the author insists that the audience be assured that he has obeyed the unities, and the speaker, wiser than he, considers the audience little interested in dramatic theory. The prologue to *The School for Lovers* (1762), as it was spoken, is a combination of lines by Whitehead and Garrick. The play was printed with the revised prologue and the original piece by Whitehead, "As it was intended to have been SPOKEN." Whitehead planned to inform the audience that his play would please the most rigorous critics:

> *Form'd on the classic scale his structures rise,*
> *He shifts no scenes to dazzle and surprize.*
> *In one poor garden's solitary grove,*
> *Like the primaeval pair, his lovers rove.*
> *And in due time will each transaction pass,*
> *—Unless some hasty critic shakes the glass.*

These lines were entirely omitted by Garrick, who retained for purposes of argument Whitehead's opinion that only great dramatists can safely *"step o'er space and time."* Garrick, speaking the prologue, here interrupts Whitehead's cautious observations by declaring that as actor and manager his rule is to please the audience. Waldron's epilogue

to *The Maid of Kent* (1773) represents the author as
anxious for the audience to know that

> . . . *the piece conforms to critic laws*
> *In scene, time, action* . . . .

Miss Younge, the speaker, replies pertly that he can
"preach" for himself; she is interested in entertaining the
audience with a comic epilogue.

Much more frequently the authors themselves directly
criticize the classical rules as hampering their inspiration,
and they occasionally defy them in deference to the judgment of the house. Prologues written to teach the audience
to appreciate the unities might please the critics but they
did not safeguard the play. Farquhar was following a convention in beginning his prologue to *Sir Harry Wildair*
(1701) by referring to authors who

> *Made great Harrangues to teach you what was fit*
> *To pass for Humour, and go down for Wit.*
> Athenian *Rules must form an* English *Piece,*
> *And* Drury-Lane *comply with ancient* Greece.
> Exactness *only, such as* Terence *writ,*
> *Must please our masqu'd Lucretias in the Pit.*

And he is also conventional in his defiance:

> *Our youthful Author swears he cares not a-Pin*
> *For* Vossius, Scaliger, Hedelin, *or* Rapin:
> *He leaves to learned Pens such labour'd Lays,*
> *You are the Rules by which he writes his Plays.*

The prologue to Charles Johnson's *The Female Fortune-
Teller* (1726) informs the audience that the author is well
aware that they cannot be entertained by comedy written
to accord with the rules:

> *He does not from old* Aristotle's *School*
> *Insist on Learning, to be dull by Rule.*

> *Nor shall Dramatick Regulations teize you;*
> *He sacrifices Time and Place to please you.*

Reasons for abandoning the rules are set forth in the prologue to Bodens's *The Modish Couple* (1732); the play
was written to please a holiday audience and aims only at
entertainment. Critics must not expect scenes *"Correctly
flat, and most profoundly dull."* The author is *"artless"*
and obeys the *"Laws of Nature";* therefore what he offers
is designed to cheer the heart.[9]

Cibber's prologues are frequently concerned with the
theory of drama. His criticism is never conclusive, but it
deserves attention because of his success as playwright and
manager. In the epilogue to *The Non-Juror* (1717) he
represents himself as defying not only the Jacobites but
the critics, whom he has never taken pains to please by
following the unities *"In Time, Place, Action, Rules by
which Old Wits/ Made Plays."* He held, as Garrick later
held, that plot is more important than style, or, as he
declared in the prologue to *Perolla and Izadora* (1705),
"Fable is the Soul," and that if the plot is convincing even
a badly written play will win the audience. He believed
that the unities were a curb on the inspiration of the
author, but that the audience, long accustomed to the
rules, were suspicious of any departure from them. He
knew from experience that the rules alone did not insure
the success of a play, and he was aware of the lack of inspiration in contemporary drama. He contrasts in the
prologue to *Zara* (1736) the rigid adherence of the French
to the rules with the ungoverned genius of the English:

> *'Tis strange, that* Nature *never should inspire*
> *A* Racine's *Judgment, with a* Shakespeare's *Fire!*

9. The prologue, like many of Garrick's, is "culinary" and promises to
suit the taste of all levels of the house.

He then traces the history of *Zara*, showing how *Othello*, a tragedy untrammeled by rules, inspired Voltaire to write *Zaïre*, and how the English play thus transformed won the French audience.

The prologues frequently pointed out that the classical insistence on having no violence or bloodshed presented on the stage ran counter to English practice and ignored the demands of the audience from pit to gallery. Walpole's prologue to *The Mysterious Mother* (published 1768) is a protest against the laws of formal drama and a justification of Elizabethan practice. Walpole explains that the aim of his tragedy is to raise the "domestic woes" with which it deals to the height of ancient tragedy and thus without the bondage of formalism meet Aristotle's law of pity and terror. He boasts that his Muse has no French original.

> She dips her pen in terror. Will ye shrink?
> Shall foreign critics teach you how to think?
> Had Shakespeare's magic dignified the stage,
> If timid laws had school'd th' insipid age?

Instead of arousing terror, the French dramatist, when necessity demands it, produces a "tedious confident" by way of a messenger:

> Chill'd with the drowsy tale, his audience fret,
> While the starv'd piece concludes like a gazette.[1]

Walpole states emphatically that he has drawn his tragedy of incest and parricide from real life and that his sole purpose is to appeal directly to the feelings of the audience. He makes the usual and quite uncritical demand that British dramatists submit to no rule other than that of nature and invention.

John St. John concluded his pseudo-classical tragedy,

1. *The Works of Horatio Walpole* (1798), IV, 396–397. *The Mysterious Mother* was never performed.

Mary, Queen of Scots (1789), with a serious epilogue spoken by Mrs. Siddons that justifies his departure from the unities by contrasting common sense with the strictures of Voltaire. How, demands the actress, can it be right to represent morning, noon, and night in the course of one evening;

> To hail Aurora, swear the sun-beam glows,
> While these vile lamps still flare beneath my nose.

St. John supports his arguments by citing Johnson's *Preface to Shakespeare*, somewhat perverting the text but at least illustrating the tenacious influence of the pseudo-classical rules:

> And as to place—deception's all in vain—
> We've known all night, that this is Drury Lane.
> Thus English Johnson's sterling wit and sense
> Treats this French rule, as a poor, weak pretence
> To cloak their narrow genius.—

He reiterates that the heart alone is the judge of the worth of a play and the decision of pedants is vain in the presence of that touchstone.

Writers of prologues more and more frequently dismissed the rules as foreign impositions and offered as substitutes the uninstructed and unrestricted emotions by which drama, especially tragedy, must stand or fall. Colman wrote an exceptionally interesting prologue for Lillo's *Fatal Curiosity*, revived in 1782, in which he proudly informed the audience that the play had originally been performed at the Haymarket and had never strayed to "prouder" theatres devoted to the rules imposed by French critics:

> Each Tragedy laid out, like garden grounds,
> One circling gravel marks its narrow bounds.

Lillo's plantations were of forest growth—
Shakespeare's the same—Great Nature's hand in both!

He imagines the shade of Lillo rising to prevent the modern dramatist from revising his play in conformity with the French concept of tragedy. A British audience should have the manliness to endure the force of the tragedy unrelieved.[2] John Home's epilogue to *The Siege of Aquileia* (1760) is an exposition of the romantic theory of composition and an argument for the complete abandonment of the unities. He explains that he has not observed the rules of time and place, for poetry is not an art subject to restraint but simply the spontaneous impulses of the heart.

The perplexity and division of opinion regarding the unities, as well as the cleavage between practice and theory, supplied a constant topic for prologues to revisions of plays. In the beginning of the century prologues commend the revisers for their efforts to "regularize" the originals; for example, Dennis's prologue to *The Patriot* (1703) informs the audience that the play is basically Lee's tragedy, *Lucius Junius Brutus,* rewritten and methodized. The revision seeks to keep whatever "*well-proportion'd Raptures*" are in Lee's tragedy but to delete his "*wild and frantick Starts.*" Similarly James Ralph in the prologue to *The Fall of the Earl of Essex* (1731) expresses his admiration for Banks's *The Unhappy Favourite,* upon which he patterned his tragedy. He praises Banks, one of the "*Bards of Old,*" for depth and truth of emotion, but he has attempted to reduce the play to regularity because

A Mass of random Colours rudely laid,
Almost deform'd the noble Sketch he made.

The tone of superiority assumed by the reviser and the purpose of revision are both illustrated at some length in

2. *Lloyd's Evening Post,* June 28–July 1, 1782.

Philip Frowde's prologue to Theobald's *The Fatal Secret*
(1733), an effort to reduce *The Duchess of Malfi* to order
and unity. Frowde acknowledges Theobald's debt to
Webster, but with reservations. The older play was an
uncultivated waste so overrun by weeds that the flowers
were almost hidden.

> *These was the Modern's Labour to display*
> *In comely Order, open'd to the Day:*
> *With decent Grace arrang'd before your Eyes,*
> *He bids them in their genuine Lustre rise.*
> *The rude, old Bard, if Crittck Laws he knew,*
> *From a too warm Imagination drew;*
> *And scorning Rule should his free Soul confine,*
> *Nor Time, nor Place, observ'd in his Design.*

Thus the prologuisers tempered enthusiasm for the Elizabethans with the stricture of their being untamed; nor was
the criticism confined to the first years of the century. In
1785 the prologue to Kemble's revision of Massinger's *The
Maid of Honour* compares the original play to a tree in
need of pruning and applauds Kemble for cutting away
the "wild exub'rance." [3]

The most frequent of defensive prologues are those in
which the revisers of Shakespeare seek to justify their
depredations. An egregious example of critical smugness is
Higgons's prologue to Granville's *The Jew of Venice*
(1701). Granville abridged the text of *The Merchant of
Venice,* transposed speeches, rewrote lines, added other
lines of his own, inserted the monstrous masque of *Peleus
and Thetis,* and in general mutilated Shakespeare in any
way he fancied. The prologue is a panegyric of Granville,
in which the Ghost of Shakespeare, describing the adaptation as *"faultless,"* remarks,

3. *Ibid.,* February 4–7, 1785.

These Scenes in their rough Native Dress were mine;
But now improv'd with nobler Lustre shine.

He further declares that *"all the shining Master-stroaks
are new."* Dennis makes less pretense in the prologue to
*The Comical Gallant: or The Amours of Sir John Fal-
staffe* (1702). He has kept the speeches of *The Merry Wives
of Windsor* but he has regularized the plot, offering in defense of his high-handed liberty the tradition that Shakespeare wrote the play in fourteen days. His alterations are
necessary to reduce Shakespeare to a *"just and uniform
design."* Theobald also expresses the usual attitude toward
Shakespeare in the prologue to *The Tragedy of Richard
the II* (1719):

> *Immortal* Shakespear *on this Tale began,*
> *And wrote it in a rude, Historick Plan,*
> *On his rich Fund our Author builds his Play,*
> *Keeps all his Gold, and throws his Dross away.*

In like manner, Charles Johnson explains in his prologue
to *Love in a Forest* (1723)—a drastic revision of *As You
Like It,* with "Pyramus and Thisbe" appearing as an entertainment in the last act—that he has presumed *"to weed
the beautiful Parterre."* The play ends with an epilogue to
prove the pleasures of the town superior to those of the
country, where the squire and his wife "Vegetate away."
Lillo's prologue to *Marina: A Play of Three Acts . . .
Taken from Pericles Prince of Tyre* (1738) begins with an
encomium based upon practical considerations:

> *Blest Parent of our Scene! whose matchless wit,*
> *Tho' yearly reap'd, is our best harvest yet,*

but contains some sound criticism of *Pericles,* if not of the
revision, and sets forth the usual eclectic methods of revisers:

To glean and clear from chaff his least remains,
Is just to him, and richly worth our pains.
We dare not charge the whole unequal play
Of Pericles *on him; yet let us say,*
As gold though mix'd with baser matter shines,
So do his bright inimitable lines
Throughout those rude wild scenes distinguish'd stand,
And show he touch'd them with no sparing hand.

Nothing is said of the unities, but Lillo informs the audience that he has reduced the play to a single plot.[4]

Usually the prologuisers considered Shakespeare a case apart, a dramatist not to be emulated in genius or imitated in the violation of the rules, those necessary props of lesser men. Steele's prologue to *The Distrest Mother* (1712) gives complete expression to both points of view:

SINCE *Fancy of it self is loose and vain,*
The wise by Rules, that airy Power restrain;
They think those Writers mad, who at their Ease
Convey this House and Audience where they please;
Who Nature's stated Distances confound,
And make this Spot all Soils the Sun goes round:
'Tis nothing, when a fancy'd Scene's in view,
To skip from Covent-Garden *to* Peru.
But Shakespear's *self transgressed; and shall each Elf,*
Each Pigmy Genius, quote Great Shakespear's *self!*
What Critick dares prescribe what's just and fit,
Or mark out Limits for such boundless Wit!
Shakespear *could travel thro' Earth, Sea and Air,*
And paint out all the Powers and Wonders there.
In barren Desarts he makes Nature smile,
And gives us Feasts in his Enchanted Isle.

4. Lillo's revision begins with the machinations of the Queen to have Marina killed and with her capture by the pirates. What the play gains in unity it loses in poetry and interest.

Our Author does his feeble Force confess,
Nor dares pretend such Merit to transgress;
Does not such shining Gifts of Genius share,
And therefore makes Propriety his Care.
Your Treat with study'd Decency he serves;
Not only Rules of Time and Place preserves,
But strives to keep his Characters intire
With French *Correctness and with* British *Fire.*

As has been noticed in the preceding chapter, in this and in similar prologues introducing adaptations from the French, the writers had reasons other than critical for insisting on the superiority of the English, but at any event the dramatist was counseled that he should follow the rules to which Racine conformed rather than the splendid aberrations of Shakespeare. In 1779 Jephson in the prologue to *The Law of Lombardy* pictures the older dramatists wandering at large in the field of history and literature, culling wherever they chose. They had no knowledge or respect for the unities. Plays beginning in Mexico ended in Greece; comedy and tragedy were mingled.

> Rules which the rigid Stagyrite devis'd,
> Our fathers knew not, or, if known, despis'd.

But modern dramatists write for a "frowning pit," demanding obedience to the rules, nor can they claim exemption as followers of Shakespeare;

> Though comets move with wild eccentric force,
> Yet humbler planets keep their stated course.

At the same time other prologuisers were giving contrary advice, urging dramatists to venture boldly in discarding the unities and copying nature as Shakespeare had done. Colman in the prologue to Dr. Thomas Francklin's *The Earl of Warwick* (1766) attributed the dearth of great drama to the restrictions imposed by the critics and complained that every man on the street or in a coffee-house set up to be a Longinus or a Quintilian. The superiority of the Elizabethans arose from the unhampered play of the imagination which allowed them to

Bring Rome's or England's story on the stage,
And run, in three short hours, thro' half an age.

Colman criticizes Francklin adversely for observing the rules and thus impeding himself when he might with more courage trust to inspiration alone. Frowde's prologue to *Double Falshood* (1727), a play attributed by Theobald to Shakespeare,[5] also censures modern dramatists for their servility to the rules and deplores their emphasis on correctness of form, their lack of inspiration, and their neglect of nature. Rowe in the prologue to *The Tragedy of Jane Shore* (1714) boldly declared that he was following Shakespeare rather than the rules. He pictures the Elizabethans as a simple people whose only critical law was the heart.

Johnson began his prologue for the opening of Drury Lane in 1747 with a panegyric of Shakespeare's immediate power in presenting truth and passion so forcefully as to defy and surpass the unities of action, space, and time. Using the pattern of the historical prologue, Johnson contrasts drama springing from genius to imitative drama written in conformity to the rules, and he emphasizes the general apathy resulting from mere adherence to the unities. The prologue is final in its pronouncements:

WHEN Learning's Triumph o'er her barb'rous Foes
First rear'd the Stage, immortal SHAKESPEAR rose;
Each Change of many-colour'd Life he drew,
Exhausted Worlds, and then imagin'd new:

5. Theobald's Preface to *Double Falshood* gives the history of the play.

Existence saw him spurn her bounded Reign,
And panting Time toil'd after him in vain:
His pow'rful Strokes presiding Truth impress'd,
And unresisted Passion storm'd the Breast.
    Then JOHNSON came, instructed from the School,
To please in Method, and invent by Rule;
His studious Patience, and laborious Art,
By regular Approach essay'd the Heart;
Cold Approbation gave the ling'ring Bays,
For those who durst not censure, scarce cou'd praise.

The lines following these are a stern denunciation of Restoration comedy, and, not to the point here, they will be considered in a subsequent chapter.

    Then crush'd by Rules, and weaken'd as refin'd,
For Years the Pow'r of Tragedy declin'd;
From Bard, to Bard, the frigid Caution crept,
Till Declamation roar'd, while Passion slept.

Colman in 1763 adapted these lines in the prologue to his revision of *Philaster* in which he opposes modern tragedy, spinning itself out by exact rule, to the bold, rough English wit of the authors—

Beaumont *and* Fletcher! *those Twin Stars, that run
Their glorious Course round* Shakespeare's *golden Sun.*

Continuing the history of the drama, he pictures fashion and refinement as driving virtue from the court and nature from the stage. The nonsense of heroic tragedy, in which *"Kings rav'd in Couplets, and Maids sigh'd in Rhime,"* was superseded by pseudo-classical tragedy, devoid of all feeling. Colman demands of contemporary playwrights who are devoted to formula,

*Say, where's the Poet, train'd in pedant Schools,
Equal to* SHAKESPEARE, *who o'erleapt the Rules?*

The contrast between Jonson and Shakespeare reappears
in H. S. Woodfall's prologue to a revision of *A King and
No King* (1788). The author presents the Genius of Drama
making a long, prophetic apostrophe to the infant Shakespeare, bestowing on him the mastery of the human heart.
He describes Jonson striving in vain to equal Shakespeare
by building plays in exact agreement with the critics' rules.
He places Beaumont and Fletcher midway between Shakespeare and Jonson, as having the imaginative power of the
one and the art of the other.[6]

Mention of other standard dramatists is common in the
prologues, with Shakespeare alone being paid the tribute
of panegyric extending throughout an entire piece. The
Prologue on Shakespeare and His Writings by Thomas
Cooke, spoken by Garrick at Drury Lane on January 21,
1743,[7] is typical of this ecstatic praise. Cooke also describes
Shakespeare as the sun around which revolve the planets
and the stars of lesser magnitude:

> They, who approach him nearest, are as far
> From him as from the Sun the next bright Star.

This metaphor appears not infrequently, and was used by
John Taylor in the prologue to *Disinterested Love* (1798),[8]
an adaptation by Thomas Hull of Massinger's *The Bashful Lover,* and shows with what veneration the closing
years of the eighteenth century regarded the Elizabethans,
"A giant-race, whom Nature breeds no more." Taylor asks,
"Who knows not MASSINGER?" and adds,

6. The *European Magazine,* February 1788, p. 105.
7. Genest, IV, 33. The piece was printed with the epilogue and an
epistle extolling the Countess of Shaftesbury as the patroness of Hanmer,
the title-page of the pamphlet reading, *An Epistle to the Right Honour-
able The Countess of Shaftesbury, with a Prologue and Epilogue on Shakespeare and His Writings. By Mr. Cooke. . . . 1743.* (Price Six-pence.)
8. John Taylor, *Poems on Various Subjects,* I, 60–61, where the title of
the play is incorrectly given as *The Disinterested Lover.*

And though remote from SHAKSPEARE's matchless height,
He knew the track, and kept the orb in sight.

Other Elizabethan dramatists, for example, Fletcher,[9]
were often mentioned in the prologues, but Jonson alone
was held to equal Shakespeare. Colman's prologue for the
opening of the Old Theatre at Richmond (1767), parodying the prologue to *Henry V*, comments on the physical
appearance of the building, which boasts no Doric pillars,
no elaborate scenery, no "Gingerbread Round O, a Cock-
pit Gilt," and offers the audience as "common fare"
Othello, Henry IV, and *Every Man in His Humour*.[1] Garrick in the prologue to Reed's *Dido* (1767) refers to Shakespeare and Jonson as "our Dramatick Lords," and in the
prologues Jonson remained the great master of comedy.
At the opening of the Crow-street Theatre, Dublin, 1758,
Barry promised that Shakespeare would be the chief dramatist of the repertory and summoned him to "inflame the
soul,"

While ev'ry passion hov'ring o'er the scene,
Waits, from his plastic word, its attitude & mien—

an image developed by Garrick in his "Ode" for the
Jubilee in 1769. Barry added that for comedy he would
draw on Jonson, Congreve, and Vanbrugh.[2] Jonson appears in 1787 with Shakespeare, Otway, Rowe, and Southerne in a list of the dramatists whom John Palmer, the
manager of the short-lived Royalty Theatre, considered
monopolized by the patentees of the licensed theatres.[3]

9. For tributes to Fletcher, see Baker's epilogue to a revival of *The
Pilgrim* (1706); Sir Robert Henley's prologue to *The Triumphs of Love
and Honour* (1731); and Colman's epilogue to *The Capricious Lady* (1783).
1. Colman, *Prose on Several Occasions* &c., III, 176–177.
2. *The Gentleman's Magazine*, December 1758, p. 596.
3. See Arthur Murphy's *Tale from Baker's Chronicle* (Oulton, *The
History of the Theatres of London* [1796], I, 185–186), an occasional pro-

As to the writers of tragedy, Otway and "plaintive Rowe" [4] were linked with Shakespeare until the end of the century. Southerne and Thomson were sometimes included for their fidelity to nature and their power "To pierce the deep recesses of the heart." [5] In 1745 in the prologue to *Tancred and Sigismunda* Thomson flattered the audience by the pretense that they based their judgment on reason and emotion rather than on delight in machines and tawdry scenery, and he asked:

> *What shall we then? to please you how devise?*
> *Whose Judgment sits not in your Ears and Eyes.*
> *Thrice happy! could we catch great* SHAKESPEAR's *Art,*
> *To trace the deep Recesses of the Heart;*
> *His simple plain Sublime, to which is given*
> *To strike the Soul with darted Flame from Heaven:*
> *Could we awake soft* OTWAY's *tender Woe,*
> *The Pomp of Verse and golden Lines of* ROWE.

Foote, announcing in the prologue to *All in the Wrong* (1761) that the summer season at Drury Lane would be devoted to comedy, describes the usual repertory of the winter theatres:

> *We scorn, like our brethren, our fortunes to owe*
> *To* Shakespeare, *and* Southern, *to* Otway, *and* Rowe.

---

logue written for Palmer in answer to Linley, Harris, and Colman, the patentees who threatened to prosecute him for opening a playhouse without a licence.

4. Thomas Hull's prologue to *Henry the Second; or, The Fall of Rosamond* (1772):

> *Had I the slightest Touch of plaintive Rowe,*
> *Whose Numbers oft have bade your Sorrows flow,*
> *Your Plaudit undismay'd I might implore,*
> *And* Rosamond *might plead, like hapless* Shore.

5. Prologue for the Opening of the Theatre Royal in Edinburgh, *Lloyd's Evening Post,* November 29–December 2, 1771.

The prologue for the opening of Covent Garden for the season of 1762–1763 promises in addition to comedy, satire, coronations, and processions,

> . . . Shakespeare's rapid fire, or Otway's woe,
> Or the smooth music of harmonious Rowe.[6]

To a list of standard dramatists—Shakespeare, Dryden, Wycherley, Congreve, Otway, and Rowe—the prologue for the opening of the English Theatre in Ostend in 1781 adds Sheridan, this being one of the few instances in which a prologue includes a contemporary playwright.[7] In the same year the prologue for the opening of the Theatre-Royal in Dublin, spoken by the actor, Crawford, apostrophizes the Irish stage,

> Where Shakespeare, Otway, Rowe, have fir'd the mind—
> Where press'd by ev'ry impulse of despair,
> We wept with Jaffier, and grew mad with Lear! [8]

W. T. Fitzgerald's prologue to a performance at Mrs. Crespigny's private theatre in Camberwell in April, 1790, extols three writers of tragedy—Shakespeare, Otway, and Rowe.[9] Holcroft exclaims in the epilogue to *Love's Frailties* (1794), after deploring the lack of great living playwrights:

> Oh Congreve! Otway! Shakespear! mighty shades!
> Whose genius every realm of thought pervades,
> Gifts such as yours, alas! where shall we find?

Otway and Shakespeare are repeatedly mentioned together as dramatists of equal merit though of different genius. References to what Harriet Lee in the prologue to

6. The *London Magazine,* October 1762, p. 562.
7. *Lloyd's Evening Post,* September 17–19, 1781.
8. *Ibid.,* October 8–10, 1781.
9. The *European Magazine,* April 1790, pp. 309–310.

Almeyda; Queen of Granada (1796) calls "OTWAY's *sweet-ness*, SHAKESPEAR's *fire*" appear constantly throughout the century. Colman begins his inappropriate but sprightly epilogue to Hugh Kelly's dreary tragedy, *Clementina* (1771) with the observation:

> FROM Otway's *and immortal* Shakespeare's *page*
> Venice *is grown familiar to our stage.*

The enduring popularity of Otway and the high esteem in which he was held are evident from tributes such as that in the prologue by Fitzgerald to a performance of *Venice Preserved* (1785):

> FEW *Bards,* like Otway, understand the art
> To touch the strings that vibrate through the heart!
> Most he excell'd in love's pathetic lays;
> And, next to Shakspere, claims unrival'd bays.[1]

Pathos, tenderness, and plaintiveness are not the qualities in Otway which appeal to the modern reader or critic, as much as we may do justice to his skill in relating the emotional intensity of the single episode to the entire plot. The prologues urged the audience to abandon the intellect and to weep at the pathetic without any weighing of plot, characters, or motivation. Nonetheless, the prologues were right in emphasizing Otway's greatness in the creation of true sorrow springing from true suffering, and in contrasting *The Orphan* and *Venice Preserved* with tragedies that had no merit beyond adherence to the rules. This perception of life as the basis of art also accounts for the prologuisers' admiration for Jonson with his hard-headed probing into vice and absurdity. They continued to pay

---

1. *Ibid.,* October 1788, p. 306. *Cf. Childe Harold's Pilgrimage,* IV, iv:

> Ours is a trophy which will not decay
> With the Rialto; Shylock and the Moor,
> And Pierre, can not be swept or worn away.

homage to Otway and Jonson at the same time that they were admonishing audiences to respond to artificiality and sentiment. If the prologue succeeded in saving the play of the evening, they were little worried about being inconsistent.

CHAPTER 8

DEFENSE AND CRITICISM
OF SENTIMENTAL DRAMA

In general, the prologuisers of the eighteenth century were more anxious to please the audience
than to guide it, and didactic though many of their pieces
may seem, they are usually reflections of popular trends.
Prompted by self-preservation, playwrights and actors denounced in many a prologue and epilogue such aggres-
sive rivals as opera and pantomime, but when it came to
matters of literary taste they were willing to agree with
the audience. With what promptness the prologuisers complied with the tendencies of the century is illustrated by
their attitude toward sentimental drama. That their criticism was contradictory and hesitant reveals the uncertainty
of the drama itself.[1]

As it has been observed in the preceding chapter, the
attack on the classical rules was based partly on the as-

1. See Ernest Bernbaum, *The Drama of Sensibility. A Sketch of the
History of English Sentimental Comedy and Domestic Tragedy, 1690–1780*
(Boston, Ginn and Co., 1915); Nicoll, *A History of Late Eighteenth Century
Drama*, pp. 124 ff.; and Arthur Sherbo, *English Sentimental Drama* (Michi-
gan State University Press, 1957) for the importance of the sentimental
drama and discussion of individual plays. Sherbo establishes criteria for
defining "sentimentalism."

sumption that the emotions are superior to the intellect.
Not infrequently the prologues to pseudo-classical tragedies admonished the audience to judge the play not by
their heads but by their hearts, just as they bade them to applaud Otway and Rowe; for example, Thomson ended his
prologue to *Tancred and Sigismunda*, from which I have
already quoted, with a declaration of the validity of the
heart as critic:

> *We to your Hearts apply: let them attend;*
> *Before their silent candid Bar we bend.*
> *If warm'd they listen, 'tis our noblest Praise;*
> *If cold, they wither all the Muse's Bays.*

Thomson had previously in the prologue to Mallet's
Mustapha (1739) described the Tragic Muse as "*Queen of*
soft sorrows, and of useful fears," and he contrasted her
power and directness to the faint lessons of "*reason'd*
rules." One of Garrick's earliest prologues, that to James
Dance's *Pamela* (1741)—a stilted comedy, lacking all genuine emotion—compares the author to a knight "*roman-*
tically" fighting for "*low-born Virtue,*" "*honest Pride,*"
and "*artless Innocence*":

> *A Sense proceeding but from Nature's Light,*
> *(For little Knowledge serves us to be right.)*

The play is directed toward the heartless reprobates in the
audience who deal in guilt, deceit, and seduction:

> *On Minds like these his Morals may prevail,*
> *And who escap'd a Sermon, feel this Tale.*

Garrick's prologue, far from being equivocal banter de-
riding the plot and characters, is an earnest commendation
of the author's motives.[2] Garrick frequently pronounced

2. See Nicoll, *Early Eighteenth Century Drama*, p. 183, for the comic
epilogue to this play in his discussion of comedies of sensibility, pp. 179 ff.

sentimental dicta,[3] as when he declared in the epilogue to
Delap's pseudo-classical tragedy, *Hecuba* (1761): *"Learning! a little feeling's worth it all!"*

During the last two decades of the century, prologues
were increasingly insistent that the audience judge plays by
their feelings alone. Even comedies were introduced by
lengthy declarations of the superiority of the emotions to
reason, and a host of trivial and mediocre plays were fortified by prologues and epilogues dwelling on the merit of
sensibility. The epilogue to the comedy, *The Lawyer*
(1783), written by one Williamson, a minor actor, is typical
of these brazen appeals for the suppression of the intellect.
He invokes sentimental drama:

> Hail sacred science, whose true-painted woe,
> Bids the pure streams of *genuine feeling* flow,
> Whose *hallowed imposition* (heav'nly art!)
> Softens, expands, improves the *human heart:*—
> To this the *drama* took its earliest bent,
> Gave *life* to *fable, tongue* to *sentiment;*
> To *pathos action,* and to *passion force,*
> Presenting *nature* in her various course.

The prologuiser at last reaches the point of all his discourse; as to the author:

> If from his *best intent* he is misled,
> Applaud the *heart*—tho' you condemn the *head.*[4]

Colman in the prologue for the opening of the Haymarket
for the summer of 1786 is explicit about the distrust of the
intellect and the dependence on the emotions:

3. For an appraisal of the critical comments in Garrick's prologues, see
Dougald MacMillan, "David Garrick as Critic," *Studies in Philology,* XXXI
(1934), 69–83. Showing the inconsistency between Garrick's theory and
practice, MacMillan concludes, "Finally, I think it is apparent that with
all his excellence as an actor and practical theatre man Garrick was hardly
a critic."

4. Epilogue to *The Laywer, Lloyd's Evening Post,* September 1–3, 1783.

By Reason's twilight we may go astray,
But honest Nature sheds a purer ray;
While, more by Feeling than cold Caution led,
The heart corrects the errors of the head.[5]

The prologue to Bertie Greatheed's *The Regent* (1788) informs the audience that the only *"simple, plain, and true"* law by which to judge drama is written in *"Nature's ancient code—chapter, The Heart"*:

> *Trust your own hearts; to their free pulse appeal;*
> *Claim liberty in sense, and dare to feel.*

Many of the prologues by Cumberland stress the criterion by which he wished to be judged:

> For you have hearts, and we make no appeal
> But to the test of what those hearts shall feel.[6]

From the beginning of the century prologuisers had fostered a self-conscious attitude toward the humanizing effects of tragedy. Steele in the epilogue to *The Lying Lover* (1703) expounded the theory that pity aroused by the playwright is meritorious and a tribute to the human heart. It was therefore Steele's purpose to call forth pity rather than ridicule, and he denounced laughter as a *"distorted Passion."* The epilogue to *The Lying Lover* established a pattern, although few of Steele's followers attained to his dignity or spoke with his conviction.

In the prologue to Addison's *Cato* (1713) Pope declared that the end of tragedy is to arouse admiration for the hero and to *"mend the Heart."* Tears shed in pity of thwarted love or defeated ambition—the usual subjects of tragedy—are a sign of weakness, but

5. Prologue for the Opening of the Haymarket Theatre, *Town and Country Magazine*, July 1786, p. 383.
6. Cumberland's prologue to *First Love* (1795).

> *Here Tears shall flow from a more gen'rous Cause,*
> *Such Tears as Patriots shed for dying Laws.*

Pope's prologue deserves the praise accorded it by Joseph Warton, who called it "more lofty than any thing in the tragedy itself," [7] but nonetheless it follows a common pattern in bidding a British audience not to be ashamed of tears shed in the theatre.

Only artificial sentiment could be roused by artificial tragedy, but the hopeful prologuiser urged the audience to recognize the inherent moral value of tears. Charles Johnson's prologue to his pseudo-classical tragedy, *The Victim* (1714), makes the appeal incessantly repeated throughout the entire century:

> *Indulge the rising Sorrows in your Breast;*
> *'Tis great to Grieve for Innocence distrest.*

A second prologue to Rowe's *Lady Jane Gray* (1715) admonishes the ladies in the boxes to respond to a sister's woes and flatters them that they look loveliest when weeping. Edward Young in emphasizing the moral purpose of *Busiris, King of Egypt* (1719)—one of the fustian tragedies ridiculed in *Tom Thumb*—assures the audience that all the pomp and splendor of the play serve only to impart "*soft Pity*":

> *Let not the generous Impulse be withstood,*
> *Strive not with Nature, blush not to be Good.*

The "pity" awakened by pseudo-classical tragedies and expressed by tears had implications far beyond the illusion of the stage. Richard West's prologue to *Hecuba* (1726) sets forth the sentimental theory entire in its self-conscious virtue:

7. [Joseph Warton], *An Essay on the Writings and Genius of Pope* (1756), pp. 257–258.

If You let fall a sympathizing Tear,
Blush not that your Humanity you wear:
Pity's the generous Feeling of the Soul,
And ought less gentle Passions to controul.
That Eye which melts at well-dissembled Woe,
Shews what the Heart in real Grief would do.

In the prologue to *The Virgin Queen* (1728) Richard
Barford, instructing the audience how to respond to the
play, declares that *"kind Compassion soften'd and refin'd"*
in tears bespeaks a noble mind, but that the "pity" evoked
must not be that of Aristotle's *Poetics,* a crude emotion
proper to *"savage Natures"* and to *"Climes that bear more
barb'rous Hearts."* For an eighteenth-century English audience there must be *"A softer Anguish! and a gentler
Flame!"* The emotion and tears were a proof not of the
power of tragedy but of the morality and good taste of
the audience, or as Thomas Walker explains it in the prologue to *The Fate of Villainy* (1730):

By just Concern for Innocence *distrest,*
Let your Humanity *be well express'd,*
And shew your Virtues *proof by* Vices *you detest.*

How far remote the pseudo-classical plays were from the
pity and terror of their originals is well-illustrated in the
prologue to Charles Johnson's *The Tragedy of Medea*
(1730):

The Drops, which thus for injur'd Virtue flow,
Must fall from virtuous Eyes, and Hearts that know
The pleasing Pains of sympathetick Woe.
Such soft descending Rain, such social Dews
Support and dignify the tragick Muse.

To create a "pleasing Pain" is the object of all sentimental
prologuisers:

Sweet is that Grief which feels another's Woe,
Which sheds a tear when Pity bids it flow.[8]

By the middle of the century it had become the fashion
for even the epilogues of pseudo-classical plays to bid the
audience to weep. William Whitehead in the epilogue to
The Roman Father (1750) emphasized the moral value of
sentiment expressed through tears. He thanked the ladies
of the audience for the *"indulgent tears"* which they had
shed and informed them that only by such sympathy could
they reflect their intelligence and beauty:

O who could bear the loveliest Form of Art,
A Cherub's Face, without a feeling Heart!

Thus Whitehead dismisses the Millamants and welcomes
self-conscious virtue and sentiment. It is true that he analyzes the character of his hero but in a manner very different from Mrs. Oldfield's comments in 1712 about
Hector in the epilogue to *The Distrest Mother.* When
Thomson's tragedy, *Edward and Eleonora,* altered by the
actor, Thomas Hull, was performed in 1775, the lines
bidding the audience to weep were retained from the
original prologue. The epilogue published with the play
in 1739 had also appealed for tears:

Perhaps too, there may be some gentle Soul,
Who rather likes to weep—than win a Vole.

The "she-tragedies" of Nicholas Rowe, from *The Ambitious Step-Mother* in 1700 to *The Tragedy of Lady Jane
Gray* in 1715, were introduced by didactic prologues asserting that tears are a proof of virtue and discernment.
The ladies who long had made *"the poor Monimia's Grief
their own,"* were flattered for their sensibility and were
now urged to weep for Rowe's injured heroines:

8. Prologue to Anthony Brown's *The Fatal Retirement* (1739).

> *Those Tears, their art, not weakness has confest,*
> *Their Grief approv'd the niceness of their taste,*
> *And they wept most because they judg'd the best.*[9]

Written in general to prove that "Woman's first title is a faithful wife," [1] the "she-tragedies" were inseparable from the domestic tragedies that "o'er-ran the Nation." Rowe introduced *The Fair Penitent* (1703) with an excellent prologue discussing the merits of domestic tragedy. The fate of kings and empires, long the only subject of tragedy, is so far removed from ordinary life that it excites no pity, but the *"melancholy Tale of private Woes"* elicits the sympathy of the entire audience; therefore, abandoning Aristotle, the authors of domestic tragedy strove to present characters who resembled ordinary men and women. If the audience was not yet willing to relinquish heroic tragedy, playwrights compromised by giving their characters heroic names and by inventing or borrowing outlandish settings to present *"a sad true Tale, a Modern Scene of Woe."* [2] The prologuisers emphasized the authors' purpose and demanded sympathy for the persecuted heroine. Theobald, for example, declares in the prologue to *The Perfidious Brother* (1716) that if his play has any claim to success it lies in his effort to "improve the Soul"; and this he thinks he may accomplish,

> *Since, stripp'd of Regal Pomp, and glaring Show,*
> *His Muse reports a Tale of Private Woe.*
> *Works up Distress from Common Scenes in Life,*
> *A Treach'rous Brother, and an Injur'd Wife.*[3]

9. Rowe's prologue to *The Ambitious Step-Mother* (1700), spoken by Betterton.

1. Epilogue to Paul Hiffernan's *The Heroine of the Cave* (1774).

2. Prologue to Charles Johnson's *The Sultaness* (1717); cf. Nicoll, *A History of Early Eighteenth Century Drama*, p. 117.

3. Cf. prologue to Charles Johnson's *The Wife's Relief* (1711):

> *To Night he aims to draw Domestick Life,*
> *A Vicious Husband, and a Virtuous Wife.*

In the prologue to *The Fatal Extravagance* (1721), Aaron Hill asserts that sentimental tragedy with a moral purpose is the *"most natural business of the Stage."* The play is a domestic tragedy in one act, presenting the death of the gamester, Bellmour, and the wretchedness to which his "fatal extravagance" has reduced his family. Compared with such private sorrow, the *"rants of ruin'd Kings"* are lifeless and dull:

> *To ills, remote from our domestic fears,*
> *We lend our wonder, but with-hold our tears.*

Lillo's prologue to *The London Merchant* (1731) begins with the usual dismissal of heroic tragedy, which he admits at least serves to teach kings and heroes that they are governed by common human emotions and are subject to human destiny. But domestic tragedy, adorned by the precious jewels of tears, is of general significance, for it pictures distress raising humble life to greatness. Fielding wrote the prologue to Lillo's *Fatal Curiosity* (1736), instructing the audience to respond to domestic woes:

> *No fustian Hero rages here to Night;*
> *No Armies fall, to fix a Tyrant's Right:*
> *From lower Life we draw our Scene's Distress:*
> *—Let not your Equals move your Pity less!*

Decade after decade prologuisers follow an unvarying pattern: heroic tragedy has too long held possession of the stage; domestic tragedy has the superior merit of presenting to the audience problems and sorrows like their own. On this model Sheridan wrote the prologue to the revision of *Sir Thomas Overbury* (1777); Hannah More the prologue to *The Fatal Falsehood* (1779); Henry Mackenzie the prologue to *The Shipwreck* (1784); Edmond Malone the prologue to Jephson's *Julia* (1787)—the last extolling the play as a "she-tragedy" in which

. . . the false friend, and blameless, suffering wife,
Reflect the image of domestick life.

To the recommendation of the virtuous and humble,
the prologues added, rather surprisingly, the defense of
characters whom the eighteenth century called "low." In
1703 Rowe thought it necessary to defend the "frail, vicious" characters in *The Fair Penitent* by appealing to
nature:

Who writes shou'd still let Nature be his Care,
Mix Shades with Lights, and not paint all Things fair,
But shew you Men and Women as they are.

To Theobald, introducing Christopher Bullock's *Woman's
Revenge* (1715), "low" life was an acceptable source of
comedy. In 1732 the prologue to Charles Johnson's *Caelia*
repeated Rowe's comparison of playwright to painter and
added that the author had tried to make all his characters
speak directly from the heart and talk common sense.
William Whitehead, who was to write one of the most
successful sentimental comedies of the century, felt constrained in his prologue to Garrick's revision of *Every Man
in His Humour* (1751) to warn the audience that the play
presented lifelike characters:

Yet let not Prejudice infect your Mind,
Nor slight the Gold, because not quite refin'd;
With no false Niceness this Performance view,
Nor damn for Low, whate'er is just and true.

Goldsmith expressed the same opinion in the Preface to
The Good Natur'd Man (1768), maintaining that "genteel"
comedy so restricted the playwright that he could not copy
nature. Less well-known than the Preface is an epilogue
for *She Stoops to Conquer,* discarded by Colman, in which
Goldsmith voiced his resentment of the popularity of sentimental comedy:

Of all the tribe here wanting an adviser,
Our Author's the least likely to grow wiser;
Has he not seen how you your favour place,
On sentimental queens and lords in lace?
Without a star, a coronet, or garter,
How can the piece expect or hope or quarter?
No high-life scenes, no sentiment:—the creature
Still stoops among the low to copy nature.[4]

The "low" was acceptable if it was transmuted by sentiment; for example, in the latter years of the century the
soldiers and sailors of the prologues were no longer "low"
as they had been at the time of Farquhar, but were men
of feeling, and brothers all to Uncle Toby. Garrick's epilogue to *Alfred* (1778) pictures the "brave, rough soldier"
at once swearing and weeping at the death of the lovers:

> *Tho' from his eyes the drop of pity falls,*
> *He fights like Caesar, when his country calls:*
> *In spite of critic laws, our bard takes part,*
> *And joins in concert with the soldier's heart.*

Tributes to dauntless but soft-hearted sailors were sure to
win the applause of the upper gallery. Mrs. Esten, the
actress, wrote an epilogue for O'Keeffe's *The World in a
Village* (1793), denouncing the selfishness and irresponsibility of the upper classes and praising the generosity and
sympathy of British sailors. In James Boaden's prologue to
The Rage (1794) and epilogue to *The Secret Tribunal*
(1795), tenderness of heart is called their characteristic
virtue. As a final appeal to the audience to accept his
comedy, *The Birth-Day* (1799), adapted from Kotzebue,
Thomas Dibdin apostrophized the "British mind," ruled
by soft emotions, the ideals of domestic virtue, and anxiety
for the ease of others:

4. Goldsmith, *Miscellaneous Works*, ed. Prior (1837), IV, 137–138.

> Her gallant son, the bold and hardy tar,
> Brave and impetuous in the storm of war,
> Lull'd by the gentle gales of peace to rest,
> Feels all the milder virtues warm his breast;
> He praises heav'n for vict'ry o'er his foe,
> And gives a tear to ev'ry child of woe.

Opposed to such appeals to sentimental response was the comic epilogue, one of the chief obstacles to sentimentalism. The very reluctant abandonment of the indecent epilogue in deference to the demands of a reformed stage will be considered below, but during the third decade of the century writers protested against the conflict of emotions caused by the comic epilogue at the conclusion of tragedy.[5] In the epilogue to *Douglas* (1757) Home denounced the comic epilogue as an enemy to *"celestial melancholy."* Arthur Murphy, suggesting that the audience show their appreciation of his tragedy, *Alzuma* (1773), by thereafter demanding sentimental rather than comic epilogues, makes the usual plea for the ennobling effect of weeping:

> Say, do you wish, ye bright, ye virtuous train,
> That ev'ry tear that fell, should fall in vain?

The epilogue to Henry MacKenzie's *The Prince of Tunis* (1773) is an imaginary conversation between the author and the speaker, in which the speaker hopes that, the tragedy being fairly over, he can at last turn to *"Epilogue and Jest."* The author denounces the comic epilogue as "Feeling's worst offence":

> *Where Pity's soft luxurious tear should flow,*
> *Shou'd Passion warm, shou'd conscious Virtue glow;*
> *This child, of Folly and of Fashion born,*
> *Laughs ev'ry nobler sentiment to scorn.*

5. Nicoll, *Early Eighteenth Century Drama*, pp. 64–66.

The audience is represented as agreeing with the speaker in favoring the *"smart facetious Epilogue."*

Early in the century the sentimental prologue had excited ridicule. In 1728 John Mottley introduced his mock-heroic ballad opera, *Penelope,* with a burlesque prologue making the usual request for tears from manly but soft-hearted Britons:

> *IF Eyes which from a pious Sorrow flow,*
> *If Virtue struggling thro' a Length of Woe,*
> *Are objects to demand a generous Tear,*
> *Who,* Britons, *shall deny the Tribute here?*

After rehearsing the adventures of Ulysses, the prologue addresses itself especially to the ladies and bids them when they presently behold Penelope, *"All beauteous in her Negligence of Dress":*

> *Let a soft Tear adown your Roses steal,*
> *To shew Us what, by Sympathy, you feel.*

Aaron Hill's prologue to *Merope* (1749), spoken by Garrick, for whom the piece was no less an acting part than was the character that he assumed in the play, is proof of the gay derision with which some members of the audience received the admonition to weep. Hill defends the ladies who show the nobility of their nature by the number of their tears:

> *Nobly weep out,—nor let* Shame's *erring Blush*
> Hold back *the struggling* Tear, *that longs to gush;*

and he reprimands the beaux, the scoffers who turn tears to jest. But a feeling mind will console itself by a sense of moral superiority to the "Laughers heard behind."

In 1776 Sheridan brought the sentimental prologue into momentary jeopardy by outdoing all writers of the genre and by daring to criticize Garrick's comic epilogues. In the epilogue written for George Ayscough's pseudo-classical tragedy, *Semiramis,* he addressed the *"beauteous mourners,"*

> *Whose gentle bosoms, Pity's altars—bear*
> *The chrystal incense of each falling tear!—*
> *—There lives the Poet's praise!—no critic art*
> *Can match the comment of a feeling heart!*

How different are the beauteous mourners from the rude spirits in the galleries, who *"love th' accustom'd jest!"*

> *Scarce have they smiles to honour Grace or Wit,*
> *Tho' Roscius spoke the verse himself had Writ!*

Sheridan continued with a ludicrous comparison—the coarse forest trees early shake off the morning dew, but the *"gentle Rose"* is bathed in *"Nature's tears"* till noon:

> *—Thou child of Sympathy—whoe'er thou art,*
> *Who with Assyria's Queen hast wept thy part—*
> *Go search, where keener woes demand relief,*
> *Go—while thy heart yet beats with fancy'd grief;*
> *Thy lip still conscious of the recent sigh,*
> *The graceful tear still ling'ring in thy eye—.*

A comic epilogue would have been a much more fitting conclusion for the trumped up emotions of *Semiramis,* but the writers of epilogues seldom considered problems in aesthetics.

That Sheridan was not in earnest or at least did not practice his theory is proved by the clever comic epilogue that he wrote for Hannah More's tragedy, *The Fatal Falsehood* (1779). Among the admirers of the epilogue to *Semiramis* was Miss Anna Seward, who in her prologue to *The Fair Circassian* (1781) by Samuel Jackson Pratt lamented Sheridan's apostasy to comedy. She added a footnote in praise of the epilogue and expressed the hope that

Melpomene might recapture the "rover." She had no way
of knowing that Sheridan had supplied the quite unsentimental epilogue to Pratt's tragedy.[6]

Garrick (Roscius) replied to Sheridan's criticism in the
epilogue to Murphy's *Know Your Own Mind* (1777), asserting the rights of the audience to laughter, "*From the
screw'd simper, to the* broad-fac'd grin," and his own right

> *To jog you with a joke in Tragic doze,*
> *And shake the dew-drops from the weeping rose.*

Colman also in the epilogue to *The School for Scandal*
(1777) scoffed at Sheridan's defense of sentiment:

> . . . our virtuous Bard!—the pye-ball'd Bayes
> Of crying Epilogues and laughing Plays.[7]

But "crying" epilogues remained, and the "sweet luxury of
virtuous grief"[8] flowed unstemmed.

The problem to be solved by the eighteenth-century
manager is revealed in Garrick's prologues and epilogues,
which present discrepancy and confusion in wavering between commending popular sentimental comedy and opposing it. He himself was the least sentimental of men.
The parts that he most enjoyed acting were those of "laughing" comedy, such as Benedick in *Much Ado about
Nothing;* or of comedy of intrigue, such as Don Felix in
Mrs. Centlivre's *The Wonder: A Woman Keeps a Secret;*
or of Jonsonian comedy, such as Abel Drugger in *The
Alchemist.* These plays he produced along with sentimental comedies. He was the shrewd manager of Drury
Lane Theatre, and his prologue to *False Delicacy* (1768)
proves that he was certain the audience would give a

6. For the epilogue to *The Fair Circassian,* see above, Chapter 3, p.
115, n. 5.

7. *Lloyd's Evening Post,* June 20–23, 1777.

8. Epilogue to *Mary Queen of Scots* (1789) by John St. John.

favorable reception to the play which he describes as
"*quite a* Sermon—*only preach'd in* Acts." In an imaginary
conversation he presents Kelly, the author, as denouncing
the immorality of Restoration drama and exulting that in
"these more moral days" the stage is devoted to virtue. The
answer apparently gives Garrick's own position:

> . . . *O Lud! O Lud!*
> *No muse the Critic Beadle's lash escapes,*
> *Though virtuous, if a dowdy, and a trapes.*

Such pronouncements complicate the question of Garrick's refusal to produce *She Stoops to Conquer*. After
delays and hesitation which exhausted Goldsmith, the
comedy was at last performed at Covent Garden under
Colman's management on March 15, 1773, the prologue
by Garrick spoken by Woodward "Dressed in Black, and
holding a Handkerchief to his Eyes":

> *Pray wou'd you know the reason why I'm crying?*
> *The Comic Muse, long sick, is now a dying!*
> *And if she goes, my tears will never stop;*
> *For as a play'r, I can't squeeze out one drop:*
> *I am undone, that's all—shall lose my bread—*
> *I'd rather, but that's nothing—lose my head.*
> *When the sweet maid is laid upon the bier,*
> Shuter *and* I *shall be chief mourners here.*
> *To* her *a mawkish drab of spurious breed,*
> *Who deals in* sentimentals *will succeed!*
> *Poor* Ned *and* I *are dead to all intents,*
> *We can as soon speak* Greek *as sentiments!*

Then follows a series of platitudes, spoken

> *With a sententious look, that nothing means,*
> *(Faces are blocks, in sentimental scenes).*

The prologue ends with a compliment to the "doctor" who
will revive the dying Comic Muse.

Both Garrick and Colman by temperament and observation agreed with Goldsmith's insistence on truth to character, though as managers they could not, or did not take so determined a stand. In the prologue to Colman's *The Spleen* (1776) Garrick commended the comedy because its characters were drawn from low or middle life, Colman thus following Shakespeare, Jonson, and Molière. The upper classes had become too "refined" to be natural. The following year he urged the audience to favor Isaac Jackman's farce, *All the World's a Stage,* for *"low are our personae dramatis."* Colman in 1778 dared to begin his prologue to O'Keeffe's *Tony Lumpkin in Town* with the defiance:

> IF *there's a Critick here, who hates what's* LOW,
> *We humbly beg the gentleman would go.*

Following *She Stoops to Conquer* Garrick had heartily supported "laughing" comedy in his revision of the Jacobean play, *Albumazar,* in October 1773, in the prologue referring to the popularity of Tony Lumpkin and in general acknowledging Goldsmith's triumph. He began by promising that since the audience had abandoned *"tragi-comic-sentimental matter,"* he would *"furnish stuff to make them laugh forever."* He felt sufficiently sure of public taste at the moment to assert:

> *Each sister muse a* sep'rate *shop should keep,*
> Comedy *to laugh,* Tragedy *to weep,*
> *And* sentimental laudanum *to make you sleep.*

The quarrel between Thalia and Melpomene was a never-failing theme for prologuisers. Sentimental comedy was applauded or condemned as a compromise in which each Muse surrendered all her characteristics to please the audience. Garrick's epilogue to Murphy's *Zenobia* (1768) jestingly describes the effect of the compromise, but it should be noticed that the lines contain no adverse criticism:

What says our COMIC GODDESS?—with reproaches,
She vows her SISTER TRAGEDY encroaches!
And spite of all her virtue, and ambition,
Is known to have an am'rous disposition:
For in FALSE DELICACY—wond'rous sly, ⎤
Join'd with a certain IRISHMAN—o fye! ⎬
She made you, when you ought to laugh, to cry.— ⎦
Her sister's smiles with tears she try'd to smother, ⎤
Rais'd such a tragi-comic kind of pother, ⎬
You laugh'd with one eye, while you cry'd with th' other. ⎦

This was the season when Garrick was producing *False
Delicacy* in opposition to *The Good Natur'd Man;* nevertheless he suggested that each goddess should thereafter
keep her proper place. In the prologue spoken on the
tenth performance of *The Rivals* (1775) [9] Sheridan made
the quarrel of the Muses the basis for a lively and sustained discussion of the respective functions of tragedy
and comedy. Parodying *Hamlet,* he bade the audience
consider the statues of Tragedy and Comedy, which, according to Genest,[1] stood at that time on either side of the
Covent Garden stage. Pointing to Comedy, Mrs. Bulkley,
the speaker, demanded:

—Look on her well—does she seem form'd to teach?
Shou'd you *expect* to hear this lady—preach?
Is grey experience suited to her youth?
Do solemn sentiments become that mouth?

As to Tragedy:

Fair Virtue scorns our feeble aid to ask;
And moral truth disdains the trickster's mask.

9. *The Plays & Poems of Richard Brinsley Sheridan,* ed. Rhodes, I, 27.
1. Genest, V, 459.

Arthur Murphy, who was no advocate of sentiment, began the prologue to Jephson's *Braganza* (1775) with a lament for comedy, which he thought entirely lost to the English stage. Sentiment shoots no arrows at folly, "But if you are distress'd, she's sure to cry." Tragedy in trying to be all sentiment and grace had lost its native power. The author of the prologue to the anonymous farce, *Jehu* (1779), describes comedy as "always crying, or saying her pray'rs":

Why she whines thus of late many things have been said;
Some pretend 'tis because Wit and Humour are dead.[2]

The prologue to *The Critic* (1779) by Richard Fitzpatrick attributes the dearth of great contemporary drama to the defects of the Restoration theatre; heroic rant stifled tragedy, and indecency drove comedy from the stage:

But some complain that, former faults to shun,
The reformation to extremes has run.
The frantick hero's wild delirium past,
Now insipidity succeeds bombast;
So slow Melpomene's cold numbers creep,   ⎫
Here dullness seems her drowsy court to keep, ⎬
And we, are scarce awake, whilst you are fast asleep. ⎭
Thalia, once so ill behav'd and rude,
Reform'd, is now become an arrant prude,
Retailing nightly to the yawning pit,
The purest morals, undefil'd by wit.

Until the end of the century and long after it had become apparent that neither Muse was to win the battle for the English stage, prologues continued to suggest that Thalia stop crying and Melpomene resume her dagger and poison.[3]

2. *Lloyd's Evening Post*, February 24–26, 1779.
3. See, for example, Topham's prologue to Andrews's *Dissipation* (1781); Fitzgerald's prologue to Reynolds's *How to Grow Rich* (1793); Litchfield's

Prologues that exhorted the audience to weep and that dwelt on the moral value of tears are a part of the social history of the eighteenth century. They made no distinction between "moral" and "sentimental"; tears shed for bravery, virtue in distress, honesty, and kind-hearted stupidity were equally efficacious. In an age of common sense that existed vigorously beside sentimentalism such pieces naturally met ridicule in answering prologues and in comic epilogues.

---

prologue to Boaden's *The Secret Tribunal* (1795); and Reynolds's prologue to *Speculation* (1795), ending: "Morals from Seneca have gain'd the day." See James J. Lynch, *Box, Pit and Gallery*, Chapter XIV, for the response of the audience to "morals and sentiment."

CHAPTER 9

THE METAMORPHOSIS OF
THE COMIC EPILOGUE

The prologues and epilogues of the early eighteenth century are in many respects—theme, attitude toward society, turn of humor—a continuation of those which entertained the court of Charles II. There are fewer gibes at Puritans; fewer excursions into politics; a less vigorous lashing of the absurd and dull. Playwrights still thought of the prologue and epilogue as having the same function as the play itself in holding the mirror up to a nature restricted to the ridiculous and vicious, but it must be granted that these early pieces are distinguished by a vitality, a critical vigor, and a directness of observation usually lacking after the second decade of the century. Fairly early in the century, satire began to make way for sentiment; the upper classes were no longer predominant in the audience; prologues and epilogues were addressed to honest "cits" and their families. Scourers, roaring boys, and vizard masks were finally replaced by Colman's Madame Fussock and Garrick's Peter Puff.

The lashing prologues of the first two decades passed no moral judgment on the knaves and gulls who were accepted as a constant, ineradicable, certainly entertaining

part of society, and essential to comedy. If satire had succeeded in correcting

> . . . *young Prentices, and Cits,*
> *Rakes, Whores, Town-Bullies, Sharpers, Fools, and Wits,*[1]

playwrights and prologuisers would have found their oc-
cupation gone. The life reflected in the early prologues
and epilogues is that of *Jonathan Wild* or *Gin Lane.* The
epilogue to William Walker's *Marry, or Do Worse* (1703)
is an excellent example of hundreds of pieces recording
the bustling daily life of the city, with its immorality,
hypocrisy, dishonesty, and, above all else, its excitement.
It is early November, the vacation over; the theatres re-
opened; the troops, sent home to winter quarters, parading
in their new scarlet coats, the prostitutes rejoicing at their
return; gay young blades on the watch to cuckold grave
aldermen; unscrupulous lawyers squeezing now wax, now
clients. Farquhar's similar and equally vivacious prologue
to Manning's *All for the Better,* also 1703, with its indecent innuendoes, warns the ladies in the boxes that *"The
Conquering* Venlo-*Sparks are coming home"* to begin their
winter siege against beauty. The braggarts will now make
their conquests:

> *Rejoyce ye Sparks that walk about and huff*
> *From* Will's *to* Tom's *and so take Towns—and Snuff.*

The early prologues often viewed mankind with cynical
objectivity, submitting it to unsentimental analysis; for
example, the prologue printed with the revisions of both
The Scornful Lady and *Wit without Money* [2] reminds
the audience that in Fletcher's "just" characters they can
see themselves:

---

1. Prologue by Charles Johnson to Corey's *The Metamorphosis* (1704).
2. No date is given with either, but see Genest, II, 388, 400.

How Vice does lord it, Modest Vertue starves,
Ignorance rules, and patient Merit serves:
How Miss endeavours to undo her Cully,
And then's both stript and ruin'd by her Bully:
How tricking Sharpers do the Town surround,
Bubbles their Fathers ill-got Gold confound.
Parsons ne'er Practise what they daily Preach;
Not by Example, but by Precept teach:
No Pangs of Conscience does the Lawyer dread,
But for his Fee will for both Parties plead.

There is no indication that from all these the observant prologuiser would be gone. The epilogue to Charles Knipe's *A City Ramble: or, The Humours of the Compter,* spoken by Bullock in the character of the turnkey, which he played in the comedy, is a direct, vivid picture of street life in 1715:

Experience, I dare say, has Taught some here,
To know me in this rough-drawn Character;
If any doubt, let them for once get Drunk,
Insult the Watch, or Pick up Stroling Punk;
'Tis Odds then but the Original they view,
And find the Humors *of the* Compter *true.*

For once the epilogue is moral—much more moral than the play itself. The author had first-hand information about the setting, for the apparently biographical prologue sadly observes in asking the audience to be merciful: *"The* Bird *that hatch'd it, sings but in a* Cage.*"* Both pieces are far removed from the humanitarian zeal of the later prologues and epilogues dealing with prison conditions.[3]

3. See, for example, Cumberland's epilogue presented after a performance of *The Jealous Wife,* December 23, 1773, for the relief and discharge of persons imprisoned for small debts. The piece is provided with complete stage directions and settings: "The curtain rises, and discovers a prison; at some distance a woman poorly habited, and in a disconsolate attitude; after standing for some time motionless, in a posture of fixed attention, she speaks." The *Universal Magazine,* 53 (1773), 373–374.

The characteristic acceptance of grossness and brutality appears by way of illustration in Rowe's prologue to Mrs. Centlivre's *The Gamester* (1705), spoken by Betterton when he was vainly struggling to succeed in Lincoln's Inn Fields. Many years since, the public, a "cursed, dogged Husband," married the new theatre, "a humble wife," but growing at length tired of her, he turned her out to starve, in spite of the comely children she had borne him. As for the babe to be presented that evening, the writer declares that it resembles its father, the audience:

> *For us, if you think fitting to forsake it,*
> *We mean to run away, and let the Parish take it.*

Rowe developed the metaphor throughout the prologue to reprimand the audience for deserting Betterton's theatre. Infidelity is one of the commonplaces of the early prologues and epilogues, but in general they merely describe rather than condemn or even comment. Cibber continued Rowe's comparison in his epilogue to Mrs. Centlivre's *The Man's Bewitch'd* (1709) in which the faithless public prefers the mistress, Drury Lane, to the wife, the theatre in the Haymarket. Here the profligate reels home after a night of dissipation—

> *Then Power'd for th' ensuing Day's Delights,*
> *Bows thro' his Croud of Duns, and drives to* White's.

Epilogues like Farquhar's to Oldmixon's opera, *The Grove, or, Love's Paradise* (1700) make no discrimination between the ladies in the boxes and the vizard masks in the middle gallery.

To Charles Johnson belongs the credit of writing one of the few decent early epilogues describing the daily life of the city. The piece was spoken by Mrs. Bradshaw, who in the play—*The Generous Husband: or, The Coffee House Politician* (1711)—acted the heroine, Fictitia, "Elopt from her Father in Pursuit of her Lover, in Boy's Cloaths." She has rambled over the town to acquire a rakish air and manly grace:

> *First then, two Fellows box me up, and walk*
> *To* Will's, *I long'd to hear the Poets talk;*
> *I hop'd to find the Rooms all fill'd with Bards,*
> *I saw no Wits, but Beaus; no Books, but Cards.*
> *I ask'd Friend* Morris *where his Authors met,*
> *He smil'd, and shew'd me which was* Dryden's *Seat.*
> *Thence I gave secret Orders to my Chair,*
> *To trot to a learn'd House near* Temple-Bar,
> *Where sober Atheists sipping simple Tea,*
> *Correct Religion, and the Ministry.*

By the end of the day, she has learned two lessons: the age is devoid of poets, and all mankind are hypocrites masquerading in borrowed dress.

During the first three decades of the century the indecent epilogue continued to be the rule and was spoken in every theatre in London. Plays introduced by prologues asserting the moral value of drama ended with ribaldry. The licentiousness of these pieces can be illustrated by a third epilogue spoken after a performance of Mrs. Centlivre's *The Platonick Lady* (1706).[4] The comedian, Henry Norris, in the character of a drawer from the Rose Tavern—an extension of his part in the play—comes forward and directs his remarks to the pit, pretending that he is a paid procurer from a near-by brothel:

> *We Drawers are Men of Parts in our Vocation,*⎫
> *And countenance the crying Sins o' th' Nation,*⎬
> *That is, since Vice first grew a Recreation.*⎭
> *We imitate the hungry Lawyers too,*⎫
> *Take Fees on both Sides, and both Justice do,*⎬
> *I mean, if we think proper to do so;*⎭

4. The third epilogue to *The Platonick Lady* was not printed with the play but is given in *The Works of the Celebrated Mrs. Centlivre* (1761), II,

> *Nay, we're in Fee with them, and on occasion,*
> *Are sent to witness some damned Obligation.*
> *Thus all the World by different Ways wou'd thrive.*

Epilogues such as this are most convincing evidence of
wide-spread corruption and show that Collier's attack and
the work of the reformers had not been entirely effectual.
Norris ends his remarks with a Restoration lashing of the
poverty-stricken playwrights:

> *And foolish Poets think by Plays to live,*
> *They're the worst Customers that we receive;*
> *They score, and score, and brag of a third Day,*
> *And then they'll certainly—hum—never pay.*
> *Much more I have to say, but never stir—*   [Bell rings
> *O lack, I'm wanted at the Bar—Coming up, Sir.*
>   [Runs off.⁵

---

[189]. Norris had previously spoken the epilogue at the conclusion of *Vice
Reclaim'd* (1703) by Richard Wilkinson.

5. Compare with the epilogue to *The Platonick Lady* Garrick's prologue
to *The Jubilee*, using the same stage device. The piece was spoken by
Thomas King in the character of a waiter, and begins:

> FROM London, your Honours, to Stratford I'm come;
> I'm a Waiter, your Honours—you know bustling *Tom?*

He compares Drury Lane and Covent Garden to two taverns in friendly
rivalry, serving the best Jubilee punch:

> We've all Sorts and Sizes, a quick Trade to drive;
> We've one Shilling, two Shillings, three Shillings—*Five;*
> From this Town of Stratford you'll have each Ingredient,
> Besides a kind Welcome—from me, your Obedient.
> I'll now squeeze my Fruit, put the Sugar and Rum in,
> And be back in a Moment—[*Bell rings*] I'm coming, Sir—Coming!
>   [*Exit, running.*

This was the kind of piece in which Garrick best succeeded. It was suited
to King's vivaciousness and is full of references to the theatre and to
Colman and Garrick himself as successful managers. This, incidentally,
is a great contrast to the many woeful allusions in the earlier pieces to the
destitution of the playwrights and the struggles of the managers to sur-
vive. For the text of the prologue, see *Lloyd's Evening Post*, October 30–
November 1, 1769, p. 420.

As we have seen in the preceding chapter, the comic epilogue at the conclusion of tragedies was denounced as destructive to the sentimental response called forth by the play. The critics were on firmer ground when they attacked the monotony of pieces limited to marital infidelity; the ludicrousness of the deceived husband— "Your Don Cornuted," as he is called in the epilogue to Mrs. Centlivre's *Mar-Plot* (1710); the "modesty" of the prostitutes with their vizards; the prevalence of syphilis. Such are the subjects of epilogues by Farquhar, Ambrose Philips, Pope, Fenton, Aaron Hill, and a multitude of minor scribblers. Genest, writing in the early nineteenth century, thought that Theobald's epilogue to *The Persian Princess* (1708) was "good" but that it must not be quoted. It is difficult to see why he selected this piece for special comment as it is not different from the usual indecent epilogue. Although Fielding frequently denounced epilogues in general, yet, using the established form during his theatrical career, he wrote bantering and ribald epilogues, picturing and sometimes criticizing viciousness. The defiance of prudery which he achieved in the epilogue to *The Covent-Garden Tragedy* perhaps contributed to the damning of the play.[6] Even the vivacity of Miss Raftor (Mrs. Clive), the speaker, could not make acceptable his cynical appraisal of the difference between *"a virtuous Lady, and a Miss confest."* In epilogues such as those to *The Coffee-House Politician* (1730) and to *Caelia* (1732) —also spoken by Miss Raftor to prove that

> *[For] as each Man is brave, till put to rout,*
> *So is each Woman virtuous, till found out—*

Fielding denounced the immorality and the hypocrisy of the upper classes.

The change of taste which occurred by the middle years

6. Wilbur L. Cross, *The History of Henry Fielding*, I, 130.

of the century is clearly illustrated by Mallet's disastrous
epilogue to Dr. Young's tragedy, *The Brothers,* performed
at Drury Lane in 1753. Young himself had written a serious
but dull epilogue which was discarded by Garrick, who to
secure applause substituted a comic but by no means un-
sympathetic epilogue by Mallet. Young intended to give
the proceeds of the play to the Society for the Propagation
of Christian Knowledge and to this proposed charity
Mallet referred in terms which brought him general dis-
approval:

> A scheme, forsooth! to benefit the nation!
> Some queer, odd whim of pious *propagation!*
> Lord! talk so *here*—the man must be a widgeon:—
> *Drury* may *propagate*—but not *Religion.*[7]

The piece was spoken by Mrs. Clive with all her characteristic stir and noise, and ended with a somewhat im-
pertinent compliment to Young, commending his charity:

> Well, shall the *novelty* then recommend it?
> If not from liking, from caprice befriend it.
> For *Drums* and *Routs,* make *him* a while your *passion.*
> A *little while* let *virtue* be the fashion:
> And, spite of real or imagin'd blunders,
> E'en let him *live, nine* days, like other *wonders.*

A comparison of these lines with the epilogues spoken by
Mrs. Clive to John Kelly's *Timon in Love* (1733), to
Fatal Falshood (1734), and to *The Connoisseur* (1736)
will immediately prove the difference in point of view and
purpose. Young's early pseudo-classical tragedy, *The Revenge* (1721), was concluded by an indecent and un-
censured epilogue "By a Friend." The severe, highly
prejudiced criticism of Mallet's epilogue in *Biographia
Dramatica* is a further indication of the disappearance of

7. *The Works of David Mallet* (1759), I, 42.

the indecent epilogue. Quoting Mallet's unseemly quatrain, the editor commented:

> This pleasantry might have set the whole clan of the Macgregors on a roar, but excited contempt only in an English audience; their ears till then having escaped the insult of such vile ribaldry. Dr. Young was much offended by it, nor would suffer it to be printed at the end of his piece. He was scarcely less angry with Mr. Garrick, at whose instigation it was written, as well as delivered to Mrs. Clive, who spoke it in her broadest manner.[8]

Arthur Murphy thought that Mallet's purpose was "to turn the reverend author's plan to a jest." He describes Young's indignation and surprise on hearing the epilogue:

> Dr. Young went once to Garrick's box, which was at the top of the house opposite to the king's side, to hear his play; he had not seen the Epilogue, but when the above lines came from the mouth of Mrs. Clive, he was highly offended at such coarse obscenity. Instead of publishing it at the end of his play, he added from his own pen an *Historical Epilogue,* which . . . sets forth the fate of *Perseus.* . . .[9]

Murphy was so deeply impressed with the fine patriotism of Young's lines that he felt the play should be revived if "only for the sake of introducing the Epilogue." [1]

Attack, denunciation, and protest were almost entirely levelled against one particular form of epilogue which, undergoing various transformations—finally becoming quite moral—held the stage from the Restoration until the nineteenth century. At the end of a tragedy an actress,

8. *Biographia Dramatica,* II, 70–71.
9. Arthur Murphy, *The Life of David Garrick* (1801), I, 227–228.
1. *Ibid.,* I, 231.

often the heroine of the play, "came forward" and informed the audience that as she had at last escaped all her difficulties, she was free to turn plot and characters to ridicule by suggesting that unheroic conduct and a little common sense would have prevented the disaster. This device, which destroyed the artistic unity of the play, had been a favorite with Nell Gwyn and achieved a new popularity during the first three decades of the eighteenth century in exactly suiting the genius of Mrs. Oldfield. The opening lines of Vanbrugh's epilogue to *The False Friend* (1702) illustrate both the method and substance of this most persistent of all forms of epilogue. The lines question whether the heroine's virtue and suffering were not after all a little silly and perhaps hypocritical and are followed by the indecent observations inseparable from the epilogues written for Mrs. Oldfield, all seeking to show that if the lady had behaved naturally, she would have encouraged her lover and tricked her husband. There are extant more than thirty such epilogues assigned to Mrs. Oldfield, the last being to Benjamin Martyn's *Timoleon*,[2] spoken in 1730, the year of her death. Mrs. Oldfield attained her greatest triumph in the epilogue to *The Distrest Mother* (1712), which, as Johnson noticed, was closely patterned after Prior's epilogue to Edmund Smith's *Phaedra and Hippolitus* (1707).[3] Writing in 1780, Johnson described the piece as "the most successful Epilogue that was ever yet spoken on the English theatre," and attributed it to Addison, who had given it to the "wretched Budgel," under whose name it appeared. Mrs. Oldfield, who as Andromache has just bewailed the death of Pyrrhus and given orders for his "Funeral Pomps," comes forward

2. For the epilogue to *Timoleon*, see above, pp. 67–68.
3. Samuel Johnson, *The Lives of the English Poets* (ed. Hill), III, 315–316. For the popularity of the epilogue to *The Distrest Mother*, see above, pp. 22–23. For Augustan epilogues, see Malcolm Goldstein, *Pope and the Augustan Stage* (Stanford University Press, 1958), p. 16.

and thus addresses the audience whom Steele in the prologue to the play has admonished to "applaud with Tears":

> I H*ope you'll own that with becoming Art*
> *I've play'd my Game, and topp'd the Widow's Part;*
> *My Spouse, poor Man! could not live out the Play,*
> *But dy'd commodiously on Wedding-Day,*
> *While I his Relict made at one bold Fling*
> *My self a Princess, and young* Sty *a King.*

The presentation of the epilogue and its popularity
with the audience are discussed by Richardson in the detailed account of *The Distrest Mother* given by Pamela to
Lady Davers. Pamela has criticized the play somewhat
severely for she considers the ending weak and unsatis-
factory although not entirely lacking in moral purpose.

> BUT judge, my dear Lady, what, after the Play was
> over, I must think of the Epilogue, and indeed of that
> Part of the Audience, which called for it.
>
> AN Epilogue spoken by Mrs. *Oldfield* in the Char-
> acter of *Andromache,* that was more shocking to me,
> than the most terrible Parts of the Play; as by lewd,
> and even senseless *Double Entendre,* it could be cal-
> culated only to efface all the tender, all the virtuous
> Sentiments, which the Tragedy was design'd to raise.
>
> THE Pleasure this was receiv'd with by the Men,
> was equally barbarous and insulting; every one turn-
> ing himself to the Boxes, Pit, and Galleries, where
> Ladies were, to see how they look'd, and how they
> stood an emphatical and too well pronounc'd Ridi-
> cule, not only upon the Play in general, but upon the
> Part of *Andromache* in particular, which had been so
> well sustain'd by an excellent Actress; and I was ex-
> tremely mortify'd to see my favourite (and the only
> perfect) Character, debas'd and despoil'd, and the
> Widow of *Hector,* Prince of *Troy,* talking Nastiness

to an Audience, and setting it out with all the wicked Graces of Action, and affected Archness of Looks, Attitude, and Emphasis.[4]

Spectator No. 341 maintains that there should be no confusion between the emotions excited by the epilogue and those excited by the play, for "every one knows that on the British stage they are distinct performances by themselves, pieces entirely detached from the play, and no way essential to it." Like the epilogue, the paper is ascribed to Budgell, who cites Dryden's epilogues as precedents and observes that "the new epilogue is written conformable to the practice of our best poets."

The claim was just, and the success of the epilogue gave new life to the vicious practice. Until the middle years of the century writers used the epilogue to *The Distrest Mother* as a model, imitating not only its manner but its obscenities. The dignity of the prologues to plays such as Brooke's *Gustavus Vasa* (1739) and Johnson's *Irene* (1749) is in startling contrast to the frivolity of the epilogues. Discussing Pope's epilogue to *Jane Shore* (1714), unspoken but "designed" for Mrs. Oldfield—another of the many pieces which follow the pattern established by the epilogue to *The Distrest Mother*—Warton commented:

> It is written with the air of gallantry and raillery, which, by a strange perversion of taste, the audience expects in all epilogues to the most serious and pathetic pieces. To recommend cuckoldom and palliate adultery, is their usual intent. I wonder Mrs. Oldfield was not suffered to speak it; for it is superiour to that which was used on the occasion. In this taste Garrick has written some, that abound in spirit and drollery.[5]

4. Samuel Richardson, *Pamela* (Third Edition, 1742), IV, 85–86.
5. Joseph Warton, *An Essay on the Writings and Genius of Pope*, p. 272.

Warton's last statement should not go without comment. Garrick's prologues and epilogues frequently reverted to the stock innuendoes; for example, his reference
to the "china" scene of *The Country Wife* in his prologue
to Foote's comedy, *Taste* (1752). He wrote Oldfieldian epilogues to Havard's *Regulus* (1744); to Crisp's *Virginia*
(1754); to Brown's *Athelstan* (1756); to Murphy's *The
Orphan of China* (1759); to Mallet's *Elvira* (1763); and to
Dow's *Zingis* (1768). He began the epilogue to Moore's
The Foundling (1748) by making Mrs. Cibber, the speaker,
declare:

> I *Know, You all expect, from seeing Me,*
> *An* Epilogue, *of strictest Purity—*

a sufficient indication of the kind of epilogue that she
usually spoke, but the mock condemnation of the characters, following the opening lines, emphasizes the moral
of the play. Miss Bride in the epilogue to Delap's *Hecuba*
(1761) addresses the audience just as Nell Gwyn and Mrs.
Oldfield had done:

> *STRIPP'D of my tragic weeds, and rais'd from death;*
> *In freedom's land, again I draw my breath:*
> *Tho' late a Trojan ghost, in Charon's ferry;*
> *I'm now an English girl, alive, and merry!*
> *Hey!—Presto!—I'm in Greece a maiden slain.—*
> *Now!—stranger still!—a maid in Drury-lane!*

The remaining lines are not indecent but silly, and the
epilogue concludes by urging the audience to support
Garrick's pageant, "The Coronation." Some of his pieces,
such as the epilogue to *Alonzo* (1773), ridicule the deceived husband, but the banter, admittedly commonplace
and coarse, is less offensive to morality than to taste.
Writers could no longer bid the audience as Congreve had
done in the prologue to *The Way of the World:*

have no Commiseration
For Dulness on mature Deliberation.

Garrick at his best substituted for the innuendo, leer, and
obscenity of the Oldfieldian epilogue a kind of sprightly
banter in ingenious acting pieces; at his worst he wrote
dull raillery purporting to be social criticism. With the
indecent epilogue, as with sentimental comedy, he
wavered between the old mode and the new, and compromised.

No single influence brought about the metamorphosis
of the comic epilogue. The change was due in part to such
external checks as the explicit and insistent policy of
Garrick who, in spite of his retention of the Oldfieldian
epilogue after tragedy, insisted as manager on general
decency in the theatre. It may be attributed also to the
rise of sensibility; the growing demand that the stage
inculcate morality; and the gradual alteration in the character of the audience. Woodfall in the prologue to a
revival of *A King and No King* in 1788 describes the indecent epilogue as no longer condoned, for modern audiences

At ev'ry grossness feel a gen'rous rage,
And hoot the graceless ribald from the stage.[6]

The prologuisers themselves rebelled against the monotony of the indecent epilogue and the paucity of its
comment. Fielding, whatever his practice, denounced these
"Ragouts of Smut and Ribaldry," in which, as he said in
the epilogue to *The Miser* (1733), *"There's scarce one dou-*
ble Entendre left that's new." Writing the epilogue to
Orestes (1731),[7] he singled out the epilogue to *The Dis-*

6. The *European Magazine*, February 1788, p. 105.

7. Charles B. Woods discusses the epilogue to *Orestes* in the *Philological Quarterly*, xxvIII (July 1949), 418–424, bringing this forgotten piece to light.

trest Mother as the model of all the kind, the omission of
the title proving its continuing popularity:

> *Virtue by Theory taught in five dull Acts is,*
> *The Epilogue reduces Vice to Practice.*
> *Tho', in his Play, the* Greek *or* Roman *Dame*
> *Shuns the least Hint of an indecent Flame;*
> *Tho', rather than submit to naughty Wooing,*
> *She laughs at Danger, and encounters Ruin;*
> *Wait till the* Epilogue, *she stands confest*
> *E'en* One of Us,—*her Virtue all a Jest.*

The anonymous epilogue to James Miller's *Mahomet the
Impostor* (1744) begins with an earnest denunciation of the
Oldfieldian epilogue:

> *Long has the shameless Licence of the Age,*
> *With senseless Ribaldry disgrac'd the Stage;*
> *So much Indecencies have been in vogue,*
> *They pleaded Custom in an Epilogue.*

This epilogue, which was spoken by Garrick, is an excellent example of the change taking place in the audience
in the 1740's. In 1738 the audience at Drury Lane refused
to listen to an indecent epilogue to Thomson's *Agamemnon,* spoken by Mrs. Cibber. The piece was with-
drawn, and on the second night Thomson substituted lines
commending the audience on their discernment and owned
himself in the wrong:

> *Charm'd by your Frown, by your Displeasure grac'd,*
> *He hails the rising Virtue of your Taste.*
> *Wide will it's Influence spread, as soon as known:*
> *Truth, to be lov'd, needs only to be shown.*
> *Confirm it, once, the Fashion to be good:*
> *(Since Fashion leads the Fool, and awes the Rude)*
> *No Petulance shall wound the Publick Ear;*

No Hand applaud what Honour shuns to hear:
No painful Blush the Modest Cheek shall stain;
The worthy Breast shall heave with no disdain.
Chastis'd to Decency, the British Stage
Shall oft invite the Fair, invite the Sage.

Thomas Odell's epilogue to his comedy *The Prodigal* (1744) condemns

The Jest obscene, ill-couch'd, and rudely strong
And doubly shameful, from a female Tongue.

In the 1730's serious declarations of the moral purpose of drama were not infrequent in prologues to comedies. The prologue to John Mottley's *The Widow Bewitch'd* (1730) describes the writer of comedies as the nation's foremost patriot in fighting for right. Matthew Draper's *The Spend-Thrift* (1731) is introduced by a dialogue setting forth the author's determination to have his play unsullied by obscenity. Miller ended his prologue to *The Mother-in-Law* (1734) by declaring the play *"Fit for the modest Ear, and manly Mind."* Johnson in the prologue for the opening of Drury Lane in 1747 denounced Restoration comedy as obscene and vicious and therefore justly forgotten: "Virtue call'd Oblivion to her Aid." The epilogue to *The Foundling*, which I have already quoted, is a compromise between tradition and the growing insistence on decency, but Garrick was certain that Mrs. Cibber would meet approval when she exclaimed:

Happy that Bard!—Blest with uncommon Art,
Whose Wit can chear, and not corrupt the Heart!
Happy that Play'r, whose Skill can chase the Spleen,
And leave no worse Inhabitant within—

a sentiment entirely foreign to the early epilogues. In Mrs. Pritchard's *Farewell Address* (1768), Garrick made the

actress add to her most fervent hopes that the stage would
"Grow ev'ry day more moral, more refin'd." By 1760 even
farces had a moral which was often emphasized in the epilogue. *"No Breach of Modesty herein is shewn,"* declares
the epilogue to *L'Amour A-la-Mode* (published 1760), a
farce attributed to Hugh Kelly, and the writer makes the
further boast:

> *Critics must own a useful Moral reigns*
> *Thro' the whole Tenour of our Comic Scenes.*

An anonymous epilogue spoken at Drury Lane on May 20,
1761, ends by stating the aim of current drama:

> All *Vice* to banish be the *Player's* part,
> All Virtue to restore, and mend the heart.[8]

Cumberland used his epilogues to point the moral of his
plays:

> He writes, and ever to some moral end,
> Because the world is not too good to mend.[9]

How far the "lashing" epilogue had moved from its
Restoration predecessors can be judged from the serious
and didactic lines with which Cumberland stressed the
lesson of his tragedy, *The Mysterious Husband* (1783). He
has placed two opposite characters before the audience—
one a lady unlike her modern sisters in that she is gentle,
truthful, and modest; the other a man very like his modern
brothers:

> *. . . Cards, harlots, horses, dice*
> *Croud the back-ground with attributes of vice:*
> *This, this is something like; these colours give*
> *Some semblance of a man:* 'Tis so we live,
> 'Tis so we look, *you cry—behold once more!*

8. *Lloyd's Evening Post,* May 18–20, 1761.
9. Epilogue to *False Impressions* (1797).

The suicide is welt'ring in his gore.
Hah! does it strike you? say, do you still cry,
'Tis so we live?—so live, and so you'll die.

When Mrs. Centlivre held the mirror up to her audience, she saw rogues, dunces, fops, who through knavery, stupidity, or conceit fell into amusing and deserved embarrassments; when Cumberland held up the mirror, he saw sinners capable of repentance. John Hawkesworth, revising *Amphitryon: or, The Two Sosias* for the mid-eighteenth century stage, partly exculpated, partly condemned Dryden, acknowledging that he lived in an age "When wit and decency were constant foes." Hawkesworth found that uniting the two qualities was attended with difficulties: "To make *Wit Honest* is no easy task." [1]

During the first three decades of the century, marriage had been the chief jest of the epilogues; the vizard masks and the Mr. Horners were subjects of banter but not of the contempt excited by the dull, unsuspicious husband. Addison in the epilogue to *The Drummer* (1716) had denounced this *"ill-bred Raillery"* and was no less earnest than Steele in his insistence on the dignity of marriage. Protests against matrimonial infidelity are not uncommon in the prologues and epilogues of the 1730's. The serious epilogue stressing domestic virtues with which Henry Carey concluded his ballad farce, *The Honest Yorkshire-Man* (1735), is a far cry from the Oldfieldian epilogues for which the audience was still calling. In Miller's epilogue to *The Universal Passion* Mrs. Clive pretends that she refuses to *"cant,"*

And whine, and preach, and tell you that you an't
As good as you should be . . . ,

in order to emphasize the author's moral *"that Love and Wedlock truly are the same."* Garrick's epilogues were no

1. The *Gentleman's Magazine*, December 1756, p. 585.

less serious in their praise of marital fidelity. His epilogue
to Havard's *Regulus* (1744) follows the traditional pattern
and contains some indecent banter, but far from setting
forth adultery as at least expedient if not meritorious, it
is written to commend the heroine's loyalty. With Henry
Brooke's prologue to *The Foundling*, the Mr. Horners
were dismissed from the English stage:

> *And hence the Libertine, who builds a Name*
> *On the base Ruins of a Woman's fame,*
> *Shall own, the best of human Blessings lie*
> *In the chaste Honours of the nuptial Tie;*
> *There lives the home-felt Sweet, the near Delight,*
> *There Peace reposes, and there Joys unite;*
> *And female Virtue was by Heav'n design'd*
> *To charm, to polish, and to bless Mankind.*

How ingenious writers adapted the traditional banter to
the reformed stage is illustrated by Sheridan's epilogue
to Hull's revision of Thomson's *Edward and Eleonora*
(1775). Like another Mrs. Oldfield, the speaker, Mrs.
Mattocks, comes forward and poses the general question:

> *May not we boast that many a Modern Wife,*
> *Would lose her own to save a Husband's Life?*

Pit, boxes, and galleries receive the proposition with contempt. The modern lady is grieved at the death of her
husband because she must forego the rout and coterie
and cancel orders for lace and brocade. The modern husband is so disturbed at the death of his wife that he even
interrupts his game to lament it:

> *His Valet enters—Shakes his meagre Head,*
> *"*CHAPEAU*—what News?—Ah! Sir, me Lady dead."*
> *'The deuce!—'tis sudden, faith—but four Days sick!—*
> *'Well, Seven's the Main—(poor Kate)—Eleven's a Nick.*

But the epilogue ends seriously. In spite of his raillery, Sheridan is certain that English husbands and wives are devoted to each other, and he could name among the audience

> *Domestic Heroines—who with fondest Care*
> *Outsmile a Husband's Griefs—or claim a Share;*
> *Search where the rankling Evils most abound,*
> *And heal with Cherub-Lip the poison'd Wound.*

Nothing could be further from the usual epilogue of the first two decades of the century. More and more frequently writers pictured contentment in marriage as the aim of life. They became at last so conscious of the moral responsibility of the stage that John Taylor in the prologue to O'Keeffe's comedy, *Wild Oats* (1791), boasts that the "scenic band" can offer as fair patterns of domestic bliss as those represented in the play.[2] The prologue to Macready's *The Bank Note, or, Lessons for Ladies* (1795) turns with loathing from wives who involve their families in debt through gaming to those

> Who think that life can sweeter joys afford
> In friendly converse at the social board,
> Than in the dull monotony of play
> Shuffling for ever cards and life away.

From the beginning of the century writers had denounced gaming. Such epilogues as that to Mrs. Centlivre's *The Gamester* (1705), addressed to *"You Roaring Boys,"* are entirely unsentimental but vivid pictures of the anxiety and final ruin of the gamester. Garrick, presenting his

2. Other serious and hortatory epilogues emphasizing the domestic virtues conclude Mrs. Cowley's *The Belle's Stratagem* (1780) and *The Town before You* (1794); Jackman's farce, *The Divorce* (1781); Jephson's *Julia* (1787); Harriet Lee's *The New Peerage* (1787); Cumberland's *The Fashionable Lover* (1772), *The Carmelite* (1784), *The Country Attorney* (1787), and *The Jew* (1794).

prologue to Moore's *The Gamester* (1753) to an audience quite different from Mrs. Centlivre's, in good earnest admonished *"Ye Slaves of Passion"* to *"Shake off the Shackles of this Tyrant Vice."* He compared Moore to a modern knight riding forth to conquer the monster, gaming;

> *Cou'd our romantic Muse this Work atchieve,*
> *Wou'd there one honest Heart in* Britain *grieve?*

He continued the attack in the prologue and epilogue to the revivals of Shirley's *The Gamesters* in 1757 and in 1772. He ended the epilogue to Burgoyne's *The Maid of the Oaks* (1775) with a denunciation of the "fatal madness of the age," [3] and in the epilogue to Colman's *The Suicide* (1778) he urged the ladies of the audience to "Drive out that demon gaming, by the angel love." [4] Shenstone wrote a serious epilogue to Dodsley's *Cleone* (1758) in which he accused women of corrupting society by spending their time in gaming rather than in attending to their families. "Pray, is there such a thing as Gaming now?" asks Arthur Murphy in the epilogue to *What We Must All Come To* (1764):

> Do Peers make laws against that giant Vice,
> And then at *Arthur's* break them in a trice?

Colman in the cleverly constructed epilogue to *The Oxonian in Town* (1767) has the speaker, Mrs. Mattocks, "enter with a pack of cards" to predict how gaming will ruin various persons in the audience. The attorney's clerk who sets up for *"Gambler 'Prentice"* will prove himself a knave,

> *And thence his broken Fortunes to repair,*
> *At Hounslow first, then Tyburn, takes the Air.*

3. The new epilogue to *The Maid of the Oaks* is printed in the *Public Advertiser*, December 11, 1775.

4. The *London Magazine*, July 1778, p. 331.

The young man who has just come into his estate to the sorrow of his dependants and servants—*The sympathizing Trees and Acres quake*—ends quite as tragically. With these is the *"beauteous Gamester"* who would *"pawn her Virtue to preserve her* Honour." In 1785 in the epilogue to Mrs. Inchbald's *I'll Tell You What*—a comedy which has no reference to gaming—Colman describes *The Lady's Last Stake,* the lines making it clear that he is referring to Hogarth's picture rather than to Cibber's play:

At Hazard, suppose, an unfortunate Cast,
Has swept her last Guinea, nay, more than her last.
Her Diamonds all mortgag'd, her Equipage sold,
Her Husband undone, genteel Friends looking cold;
At her Feet his sweet Person, Lord Foppington throws,
The most handsome of Nobles, the richest of Beaux.[5]

Holcroft's epilogue to *The School for Arrogance* (1791)—and here again with no applicability to the play—presents with much greater seriousness a ghastly picture of a woman ruined by gaming. From Mrs. Centlivre to Holcroft epilogues denouncing gaming constitute in a series of vivid portraits a record of an important phase of social history. In spite of the insistence that the stage should be an exemplar and no longer a mirror, epilogues remained in one vital respect what they had always been—a lively, amusing commentary on life.

The later epilogues often assume the nature of the Theophrastan character. A pert, ill-bred girl is one who behaves like the intractable daughter, devoted to the cir-

5. Two years before Cibber's play, *The Lady's Last Stake,* Mrs. Centlivre in the epilogue to *The Gamester,* from which I have quoted, describes ladies "drawn in" by "fatal play":

A Thousand Guineas for Basset *prevails,*
A Bait when Cash runs low, that seldom fails;
And when the Fair One can't the Debt defray,
In Sterling Coin, does Sterling Beauty pay.

culating library, in Garrick's epilogue to Colman's *Polly Honeycombe*, and an amorous old beau is one who makes speeches like Garrick's *Sir Anthony Branville's Address to the Ladies*. Sheridan in the epilogue to Hannah More's *The Fatal Falsehood* (1779) paints with the liveliest detail a picture of a bluestocking, half authoress, half housewife:

> *What motley cares* Corilla's *mind perplex,*
> *While maids and metaphors conspire to vex!*
> *In studious deshabille behold her sit,*
> *A letter'd gossip, and a housewife wit;*
> *At once invoking, though for different views,*
> *Her gods, her cook, her milliner, and muse,*
> *Round her strew'd room, a frippery chaos lies,*
> *A chequer'd wreck of* notable *and* wise;
> *Bills, Books, Caps, Couplets, Combs, a vary'd mass,*
> *Oppress the toilet, and obscure the glass;*
> *Unfinish'd here an Epigram is laid,*
> *And there, a mantua-maker's Bill unpaid;*
> *Here new-born Plays fore taste the town's applause,*
> *There, dormant Patterns pine for future gauze;*
> *A moral Essay now is all her care,*
> *A Satire next, and then a Bill of Fare:*
> *A Scene she now projects, and now a Dish,*
> *Here's Act the First—and here—remove with Fish.*
> *Now while this Eye in a fine phrenzy rolls,*
> *That, soberly casts up a Bill for Coals;*
> *Black Pins and Daggers in one leaf she sticks,*
> *And Tears and Thread, and Bowls and Thimbles mix.*

The epilogue to *Ways and Means* (1788) by George Colman, the younger, is an excellent character of a newspaper critic, giving the "puff direct" in return for free admission to the playhouse and "knocking down Reputations by one inch of candle!"

At the end of the century when the theatre was given

over to farce, comic opera, and miscellaneous entertainment, both prologues and epilogues were entirely severed
from their plays, frequently making no reference to actors,
plot, theme, or performance. The prologues spoken by
Bannister, jun. and the epilogues spoken by Mrs. Mattocks and Mrs. Jordan afforded as much amusement as the
plays themselves. They ridiculed the gentleman whose
shoes are concealed by his buckles and the lady whose
towering headdress is caught in the chandelier. "With
feathers six feet high behold her come," exclaims Holcroft in the epilogue to *The Man of Ten Thousand*
(1796). They are full of news of elections and of the most
recent ascent of the balloon; they consider the relative
merits of hyson and bohea; they recount the delights of
setting out for Margate in the hoy:

> The Margate Hoy! well freighted—what a scene
> For Hogarth's pencil, in a laughing vein! [6]

In the 1790's a group of young writers—among them
Colman, the younger, W. T. Fitzgerald, John Taylor,
Miles Peter Andrews—supplied the stage with clever prologues and epilogues in which the audience was reflected
with liveliness and perspicacity. The epilogue to Frederic Reynolds's *Notoriety* describes a young man "by some
unlucky tailor trusted" who appears at the theatre, wear-
ing his new coat and greeting his friends in the upper gallery where he "sports a language which is quite his own":

> "Hey, Tom, how do?—Oh, is that you, Dick Docket!
> "You've stole my stick—No, damme, it's in my pocket."

He is the companion of the equally engaging young man
in Colman's epilogue to *The Box-Lobby Challenge*, who
defiantly introduces himself as "Mr. Plumb, the Banker's,

---

6. Prologue to Frederick Pilon's revision of *All's Well That Ends Well*
(1785), *Lloyd's Evening Post*, July 27–29, 1785.

fifteenth clerk." Miles Peter Andrews, who had a Dickensian zest for commonplace and ridiculous people, developed character epilogues as acting pieces for Mrs. Mattocks, depicting rising tradesmen and their families and friends. In these the reader at once recognizes the familiar world of *Sketches by Boz*. The kind of epilogue in which Andrews excelled is illustrated by the "Address" spoken by Lewis in the character of Goldfinch after a performance of *The Road to Ruin*, March 23, 1793:

> Young Jemmy Whirlagig, drives four in hand,
> All down the Haymarket, and up the Strand,
>
> .   .   .   .
>
> Safe, as he thinks, from artful Bailiff's dodging,

to the home of the young lady with whom he plans to elope. He has her finally in the carriage, but

> A skulking Knave unseen by each beholder,
> Just as he mounts, taps Jemmy on the shoulder;
> The luckless Fair One sees her wishes crost,
> Groom, Horses, Phaeton, Jemmy, all are lost!
> He, in sad durance, o'er his gill of Port,
> Sobs thro' the iron casement—"Here's your sort!" [7]

Fitzgerald's prologue to Thomas Morton's *The Way to Get Married* (1796) describes the more practical activities of the enterprising young man:

> The modern buck,—how diff'rent from the beau
> In bags and ruffles, sixty years ago!
> The city coxcomb then was seldom seen,
> (Confin'd to Bunhill-row, or Bethnal-green:)
> West of Cheapside you then could scarcely meet
> The gay Lothario—of Threadneedle-street!

7. Unidentified newspaper clipping in the Yale Library, Folio Pamphlets, No. 10, p. 157.

His folly rarely met the public eye,
Or, like a shadow, pass'd unheeded by:
Tradesman and rake were then remov'd as far
As gay St. James's is from Temple-bar.
And now the cit must breathe a purer air,
The 'Change he *visits*—lives in Bedford-square—
Insures a fleet—then Bootle's club attends,
Proud to be notic'd by his titled friends;
And tries to join, by Dissipation's aid,
The man of fashion with the man of trade.

With the disappearance of tragedy from the stage, prologues, in keeping with the trivial entertainment they
introduced, became indistinguishable from epilogues; the
banter of the epilogue, so long attacked as destroying the
effect of tragedy, was entirely appropriate to comedy. Reformed and chastened, often blurring sensibility and morality, the epilogue was still an accurate reflection of contemporary manners and of the audience, without whom
it could not exist. Like all drama, it was protean, but no
metamorphosis could alter its basic quality—the stir and
excitement of life itself.

CONCLUSION

In this book I have sought to prove that prologues and epilogues are important in studying the eighteenth-century theatre and that they have a value of their own in being alive and amusing. Some of them belong to literary history. An edition of prologues and epilogues by Addison, Steele, Pope, Fielding, Johnson, Goldsmith, and Sheridan would show how a conventional pattern could be used for personal expression. Hundreds of pieces, forgotten as soon as they were printed in the *London Chronicle* or *Public Advertiser,* and from which I have quoted so frequently, help to bring into focus others of unquestioned merit, such as Addison's prologue to *The Tender Husband,* Pope's prologue to *Cato,* or Johnson's prologue for the opening of Drury Lane under the management of David Garrick. They also explain why a tragedy like Johnson's *Irene,* introduced by a prologue designed, as Boswell said, to "awe" rather than "soothe" the audience, should be concluded by a flippant epilogue.

The prologuisers earnestly considered the various problems and trends of the drama—the decline of tragedy; the usurpation of the stage by opera, pantomime, and other kinds of spectacle; the uncertain course of the comedy of sensibility. Even when their comments have little critical acumen, they deserve attention as first-hand pronouncements. Many of them, such as Fielding's prologue to *The Universal Gallant* and Garrick's prologue for the opening of Drury Lane in 1750, are of double significance as the writers were also theatre managers and dramatists.

Written to be acted, and designed in general for specific speakers, the prologues and epilogues help to restore to us some of the greatest English actors and actresses. They supply a reality often lacking in contemporary biographies. To choose only two examples, the epilogue to *Zara,* spoken by Mrs. Clive, and the prologue to *Bon Ton,* spoken by King, refute Garrick's dictum:

> Nor Pen nor Pencil can the Actor save,
> The Art, and Artist, share one common Grave.

A prevalent and most important characteristic of the prologues and epilogues is their power of conjuring up the theatre itself, the stage, and the speaker addressing the audience. The epilogue to Mrs. Centlivre's *The Basset-Table,* Goldsmith's prologue to *Zobeide,* Colman's prologue to the revisal of *Eastward Hoe* are representative rather than unusual in creating an impression of liveliness. Pieces of no intrinsic merit, like Garrick's prologue to *Britannia* or Miles Peter Andrews's epilogue to *The Dramatist,* serve as well as their betters for the imaginative reconstruction of the theatre.

In tone and subject matter the prologues and epilogues responded to social trends and to changes in public taste. As the century progressed, they showed an awareness of some of the problems confronting society. But as reflections of the audience their real distinction lies elsewhere. Like so much of the literature of the eighteenth century, the prologues and epilogues picture daily life—its dress, its turns of speech, interests, diversions, and follies. In this their success depended on the promptness with which they seized on the ephemeral and on the timeliness of their observations. Making no claim to the force of the Restoration prologue with its arraignment of the public, these pieces have a lighter touch, recording their own times with ingenuity and humor.

INDEXES

General Index
Index of Writers of Prologues and Epilogues
Index of Speakers
Index of Plays by Author

GENERAL INDEX

Abington, Frances, actress: offends
Woodward, 64; her roles, 77;
speaker of epilogues, 36, 43, 50,
77–80; success as "fine lady," 77;
vexation to Garrick, 77
Actors, at mercy of audience, 116,
152, 153
Actors' Fund. *See* Drury Lane The-
atre
Addison, Joseph: *The Spectator*,
245, 297; sponsors Edmund Smith,
190; as writer of prologues, 8, 67,
312
Adolphus, John, *Memoirs of John
Bannister, Comedian*, 66
Ambivius, Lucius, Roman actor-
manager, 182
Andrews, Miles Peter, 31, 309, 310
Anne, Queen, tributes to her in prologues, 174, 206
Annual Register, 6
Arblay, Madame D'. *See* Burney,
Frances
Aristotle, 80, 109, 251, 273; *Poetics*,
271
Audience, 127, 128; apprentices, 138,
139, 161; beaux, 136, 138, 161,
165–72, 175, 176, 215, 241, 278;
"cits," 138, 286; critics: 84, 118,
128, 135, 139–54, 159, 175, 176,
their brutality, 143–6, "butchers,"
143, "curs" and "dogs," 142,
"dragons," 150, "hangmen," 129,
"jury," 108–12, 143, jealous rival
authors, 143–4, "vultures," 142;
denounced for lack of critical
standards, 146, for lack of taste,
180, 181, 184, 201–4; of early
eighteenth century, 286; factions
in, 153–7; footmen, 139, 160–1,

163; inattention of, 135, 136, 137,
142; ladies in the boxes, 109, 114–
5, 135, 136, 174–6, 289, urged to
weep, 270, 272, 278; packing the
house, 114, 143, 154, 157, 159; pit,
102, 115, 116, 149–54, 163, 201;
sailors and soldiers in, 163, 165,
177, 276; on stage and behind
scenes, 170–2; on benefit nights,
173; upper gallery, 43, 55, 102,
115, 136, 139, 160–5, 187, 196, 205,
215, 227, pay shilling for admission, 162; vizard masks, 115, 135,
138, 286, 289
Austen, Jane, *Mansfield Park*, 94
Author: asks mercy of audience,
145; baited by audience, 141; on
stage behind curtain or scenes,
82, 84, 139, 150; in terror of critics,
115, 151, 154; youth reason for
mercy, 140–1
Authors' nights, 124

Ballad opera, 30 n. 1
Banister, Mr., musician, 179
Banks, John, his drama reduced to
the rules, 253
Bannister, Charles, actor, 65
Bannister, John, actor: acclaimed as
speaker of prologues, 65–6, 81,
309; as Dick in *The Apprentice*,
66; as Sheva in *The Jew*, 100
Barry, Ann, actress: as speaker of
epilogues, 50, 75; her roles, 75
Barry, Elizabeth, actress, 38
Barry, Spranger, actor, manager:
with Woodward of Crow Street
Theatre, Dublin, 19; in prologue
to *Constantine*, 34–5; in role of
Essex, 9

317

Estcourt, Richard, actor, 5 n. 1, 36
Eugene, Prince of Savoy, 155, 179
"An Eulogium on Mr. Garrick's leaving the stage," 17
European Magazine, 6, 80 n. 9, 90 n. 6
Evans, Mr., acrobat, 179

Farquhar, George: his death, 3 n. 6; protests against prologues, 23–4; as writer of prologues and epilogues, 8, 34, 292
Farren, Elizabeth, actress, 50, 81; extolled by Burgoyne, 80; Fanny Burney describes her speaking epilogue, 80 n. 9; Conway dedicates play to her, 13; popularity of her epilogues, 36, 80–1
Fawcett, John, actor: as Dr. Pangloss, 93; as Mist, 97–8
Fenton, Elijah, his epilogues, 292
Fielding, Henry: attacks pantomimes, 200; attacks prologues in *Tom Jones*, 28–9; denounces foreign singers, 191–2, indecent epilogues, 299–300, miscellaneous entertainment, 182–3; manager of theatre, 13 n. 9, 312; parodies prologue to *Sophonisba*, 228; ridicules fustian tragedies, 270, patriotic prologues, 209–10, 228, vogue of prologues and epilogues, 25–8, 146; his theory of comedy, 235–6, 239–40; *Tom Jones*, 28–9, 125 n. 6; *The True Patriot*, 104 n. 2; *The Universal Gallant*, Advertisement to, 146; as writer of prologues and epilogues, 8, 13 n. 9, 29, 292, 312; writes epilogues for Mrs. Clive, 68–70. *See also* Clive, Catherine
Fitzgerald, W. T., writer of prologues and epilogues, 309
Fleetwood, Charles, manager of Drury Lane, 160 n. 4
Fletcher, John, mentioned in prologues, 261. *See also* Beaumont, Francis and Fletcher, John
Folger Shakespeare Library, 81 n. 1, 126 n. 2, 199 n. 5, 216 n. 2
Foote, Samuel: as Dr. Squintum,

37; his method of satire, 237–8; manager of the Haymarket Theatre, 13 n. 9, 121 n. 2; ridicules Italian singers, 192–3; as speaker of prologues, 19 n. 4, 43, 49–50, 57–8, 62, 89; in *The Trip to Paris*, 45 n. 3; as writer of prologues, 2, 13 n. 9, 237
Footmen. *See* Audience
Foreign entertainers, 115, 186–93. *See also* French dancers; Italian singers
Forster, John, *The Life and Times of Oliver Goldsmith*, 12 n. 4
Foster, Elizabeth, Milton's granddaughter, Johnson writes prologue for benefit of, 4
France, tributes to her arts and graces, 212
French dancers, 186–9, 205; excessive salaries paid them, 188–9; hatred of, 187. *See also* Vestris, Gaëtan, and Sheridan, Richard Brinsley
French, disdained in the prologues, 212–6, 227. *See also* Prologues, patriotic
French plays, adaptations of: 213, 214, 222–31; acknowledged, 218, 221, 229, 232; denounced, 222–3, 230; disclaimed or palliated, 213, 224–5, 251; disliked by audience, 221; disguised, 228–9. *See also* Native sources
French, prejudice against fostered in prologues and epilogues, 205, 222, 231. *See also* Prologues, patriotic
French Revolution: fall of Bastille hailed with joy, 218; "Liberty is Law!", 219–21; principles of freedom supported by prologues, 217, 218–9
Fryer, Mrs., actress, 182

Gallery, 201, 203. *See also* Upper Gallery *under* Audience
Gaming, denounced in prologues and epilogues, 305–7
Gardner, William Bradford, *The Prologues and Epilogues of John Dryden*, 1 n. 1, 141 n. 9

2, 66; to school drama, 6–7; separate publication of, 4; spoken in character, 42, 66, 88, 90, 92–107, 151, 157, 159, 161, 162, 165, 166, 167, 168, 179, 197, 206, 208, 231, 310, in dialogue, 78, 93; as imaginary conversations, 47, 60, 78, 139, 196; stage business in, 88–92, 105–8, 175; sung, 74, 91–2, 127, 190, 190 n. 8; titles of plays basis of, 127–31; trends of drama reflected in, 266, 312; uncertain about sentimental drama, 266, 280–5; "Whiggish," 155, 206–7
Prologues, occasional: On his Majesty's Birth-day, a Prologue, spoken at Goodman's-Fields Theatre . . . , 219; for the opening of Covent Garden for the season of 1750–1, 196; for the opening of Covent Garden for the season of 1762–3, 263; for the opening of Covent Garden Theatre in 1774, 89; for the opening of Covent Garden Theatre, Sept. 1777, 236; for the opening of the new Drury Lane Theatre, 1794, 220; for the opening of the English Theatre in Ostend, 1781, 263; for the opening of the Theatre-Royal in Dublin, 1781, 263; for opening the Theatre Royal in Edinburgh, 1771, 195 n. 6, 262 n. 5; A Prologue sent to Mr. Row . . . , 112 n. 4; prologue spoken before performance of The Bath, 5
Protestant Succession, the, 207
Public Advertiser, 6, 53, 65 n. 5, 215 n. 1, 312

Quick, John, actor, 88, 89–90, 120; his roles, 90
Quin, James, 38, 158; as Falstaff, 122 n. 4; Garrick's tribute to, 122–3
Quintilian, 258

Racine, 257; adaptations of, 229
Raftor, Miss, see Clive, Catherine

Ralph, character in The Knight of the Burning Pestle, 138
Rebellion of 1715, subject of prologues, 156, 207
Rebellion of 1745, 208
Reed, Isaac. See Biographia Dramatica
Reformers, the, 24, 233, 242
Restoration, The, vi, vii, 24, 208
Rhodes, R. Crompton, editor of Sheridan, 110; Harlequin Sheridan, 203 n. 8
Rich, Christopher, manager of Drury Lane Theatre, 160
Rich, John, manager of Covent Garden Theatre, 63, 127; his death, 201; revives Perseus and Andromeda, 200; as Harlequin, 63, 64, 196, 198–201, extolled by Davies, Jackson, and Walpole, 198; his Lilliputian Troupe, 63; his pantomimes, 198–201; his processions, 195 n. 6; proposals for share-holders of Covent Garden Theatre, 171; Shirley dedicates The Parricide to, 158
Richardson, Samuel, denounces epilogue to The Distrest Mother, 296–7
Robinson, Miss, actress, leader of a Lilliputian company, 104
Romeo and Juliet, rival productions of, 63
Rosciad, The, satire by Charles Churchill, 76
Rosenfeld, Sybil Marion, Prologues and Epilogues of the Restoration Period, 1660–1700, 1 n. 1
Ross, David, manager of the New Theatre Royal in Edinburgh, 193
Rowe, Nicholas, 184, 267; asks Pope for prologue, 12; enduring popularity of, 261–3; protests against prologues, 24; his "she-tragedies," 186, 234, 272–3; Tamerlane performed annually, 208; as writer of prologues and epilogues, 8, 67
Ruel, Du, dancer, 179
Rules, psuedo-classical, 252, 257, 266, 267. See also Unities, classical

Ryan, James, patentee with Garrick of Drury Lane Theatre, 54 n. 4, 172

St. James's Chronicle, 6, 126 n. 1
Santlow, Hester (Mrs. Barton Booth), actress, 103, 105
Satire, the purpose of comedy. See Comedy
"Savoyard Travellers," ballet at Drury Lane Theatre, 194
Sawyer, Paul, "John Rich; a Biographical Sketch," 198 n. 2
Scots Magazine, 6
School of Roscius, The, 37
Sensibility, drama of, 233, 312; growth of, 244; its merit, 268. See also Drama, sentimental
Sentimentalism, growth of, 164
Seward, Anna, 3, 279–80
Shakespeare, William, 184, 197, 229, 233, 237, 242; Ghost of, 107, 186, 254; parodied: 50, Hamlet, 283, Henry V, 247 n. 8, 261, Othello, 172, Tempest, 98; revisions of: All's Well That Ends Well, 309 n. 6, As You Like It, 255, Measure for Measure, 107, 181, The Merchant of Venice, 107, 254, Merry Wives of Windsor, 255, A Midsummer Night's Dream, 89, Much Ado about Nothing, 71, 255, Pericles, 255, Richard II, 255, The Taming of the Shrew, 122 n. 5, 226, The Tempest, 123, The Winter's Tale, 122; superior to the rules, 256–60
Shakespeare Jubilee, The, 99
"She-tragedies." See Rowe, Nicholas
Sherbo, Arthur, English Sentimental Drama, 266 n. 1
Sheridan, Richard Brinsley, 64, 204; denounces comic epilogues, 278–9; engages French dancers, 189; first speech in Parliament, 114; manager of Drury Lane Theatre, 13 n. 9; named as standard dramatist, 263; Pizarro ridiculed in mock prologue, 203; The Plays & Poems of Richard Brinsley Sheridan, ed. Rhodes, 110 n. 3, 115 n.

5; his prologues and epilogues, 8, 13 n. 9, 76, 312; The Rivals, original prologue to lost, 110
Shirley, William, his Parricide a rioted play, 158
Shuter, Edward, actor, 45, 66
Sichel, Walter, Sheridan, 110 n. 3
Siddons, Henry, 150 n. 3
Siddons, Sarah, actress, 23, 75, 153; roles: Andromache, 48, Sigismunda, 49; unsuccessful in comic epilogues, 49
Smith, Charlotte, ridicules stage spectacle (1799), 202–3
Smith, Horace and James, Rejected Addresses, 32 n. 4
Social contract, emphasis on in prologues, 219
Southerne, Thomas, 184, 261–2; Oroonoko, performance of, 179
"Spiletta," character in Gli Amanti gelosi, 192 n. 9
Spouting Clubs, 73
Stage machinery: commended, 174; denounced, 181, 202–3; means of evading unity of place, 246–7; superior to the unities, 196
Steele, Sir Richard: "Bickerstaff," 239; epilogue to The Lying Lover sets pattern for appeal to sentiment, 269; Guardian, No. 82, quoted, 35; packs house, 157; as writer of prologues, 8, 312
Summers, Montague, The Restoration Theatre, 83 n. 2
Supplement to Bell's British Theatre, 54 n. 4
Swift, Jonathan, A Tale of a Tub, 124

Taylor, Isaac, engraving of Garrick, 37–8, 102 n. 6
Taylor, John: Poems on Various Subjects, 7 n. 5, 130 n. 7, 260 n. 8; Records of My Life, 90 n. 5; as writer of prologues and epilogues, 7, 130, 309
Tears: audience urged to indulge in, 269–74, 277–80; inherent merit of, 267, 270

INDEX OF WRITERS OF
PROLOGUES AND EPILOGUES

The Index includes only the writers whose names are given in the text. For those not included the reader should consult the early editions of the plays and the prologues and epilogues as they appear in the newspapers and magazines. The two volumes comprising Part 2 of *The London Stage* (Southern Illinois University Press, 1960), edited by Emmett L. Avery, were published while this work was being printed. Mr. Avery records the prologues and epilogues presented between 1700 and 1729, gives the names of the speakers, and lists in his Indexes the titles of the occasional pieces. The reader should also consult his Introduction, pp. cxliv–cxlvii, for a discussion of prologues and epilogues of the first decades of the century.

INDEX OF SPEAKERS

INDEX OF PLAYS BY AUTHOR

343

YALE STUDIES IN ENGLISH

This volume is the one hundred and forty-ninth of the Yale Studies in English, founded by Albert Stanburrough Cook in 1898 and edited by him until his death in 1927. Tucker Brooke succeeded him as editor, and served until 1941, when Benjamin C. Nangle succeeded him.

The following volumes are still in print. Orders should be addressed to YALE UNIVERSITY PRESS, New Haven, Connecticut.